The African Christian Diaspora

Also available from Bloomsbury

Christianity as a World Religion, Sebastian Kim and Kirsteen Kim
Christianity in Africa and the African Diaspora,
edited by Afe Adogame, Roswith Gerloff and Klaus Hock
World Christianity in Local Context, edited by Stephen R. Goodwin

The African Christian Diaspora

New Currents and Emerging Trends in World Christianity

Afe Adogame

BLOOMSBURY
LONDON • NEW DELHI • NEW YORK • SYDNEY

Bloomsbury Academic
An imprint of Bloomsbury Publishing Plc

50 Bedford Square
London
WC1B 3DP
UK

175 Fifth Avenue
New York
NY 10010
USA

www.bloomsbury.com

First published 2013

© Afe Adogame, 2013

All rights reserved. No part of this publication may be reproduced or transmitted in any form or by any means, electronic or mechanical, including photocopying, recording, or any information storage or retrieval system, without prior permission in writing from the publishers.

Afe Adogame has asserted his right under the Copyright, Designs and Patents Act, 1988, to be identified as Author of this work. No responsibility for loss caused to any individual or organization acting on or refraining from action as a result of the material in this publication can be accepted by Bloomsbury Academic or the author.

British Library Cataloguing-in-Publication Data
A catalogue record for this book is available from the British Library.

ISBN: HB: 9781441188588
PB: 9781441136671
PDF: 9781441112729
ePub: 9781441196989

Library of Congress Cataloging-in-Publication Data
Adogame, Afeosemime U. (Afeosemime Unuose), 1964–
The African Christian diaspora: new currents and emerging trends in world Christianity / Afe Adogame.
pages ; cm
Includes bibliographical references and index.
ISBN 978-1-4411-8858-8 (HB) – ISBN 978-1-4411-3667-1 (PB) –
ISBN 978-1-4411-1272-9 (pdf) – ISBN 978-1-4411-9698-9 (ePub)
1. Christianity – Africa. 2. African diaspora. 3. Africa – Emigration and immigration – Religious aspects – Christianity. 4. United States – Emigration and immigration – Religious aspects – Christianity. 5. Europe – Emigration and immigration – Religious aspects – Christianity. 6. Globalization – Religious aspects. I. Title.
BR1360.A39 2013
270.8'308996–dc23
2012033251

Typeset by Newgen Imaging Systems Pvt Ltd, Chennai, India
Printed and bound in Great Britain

*This book is dedicated to my dear mother,
Madam Caroline Ajibola Adogame (1942–2011)
who passed on while I was putting finishing touches
to the book. You are the best mother in the world.
You lit a candle in my life and I shall strive to ensure
that it is not extinguished.*

Contents

Preface viii

1 Trajectories of African migration 1
2 Narratives of African migration 15
3 Situating the local scene(s) 37
4 Historiography of new African Christianities in diaspora 59
5 A phenomenology of African Christian communities in diaspora 79
6 African Christianities as social, cultural and spiritual capital 101
7 Negotiating identity, citizenship and power 123
8 Globalization, media and transnationalism 145
9 Reverse mission 169
10 The politics of networking 191

Notes 213
Select bibliography 227
Index 243

Preface

An unprecedented upsurge, especially in the last few decades, in the number of African immigrants into Europe, North America and elsewhere heralds a new phase in the history of African diaspora. The concept of 'diaspora' is an enduring one in the context of globalization. I have utilized it here in a sociological rather than a theological sense. The idea of an *old* and *new African Christian Diaspora* depicts continuity in variation, a description of past and contemporary global economic and political processes that pitched Africans on the receiving end and present them with access to alternative interpretations of fluid power relations. Many Africans who undergo complex forms of immigration processes have largely carried traits of their religious and cultural identities with them. As a matter of fact, their sojourn in new geo-cultural contexts has enlivened these immigrants to identify, organize, and reconstruct their religion both for themselves and their host societies. The last three decades have witnessed a rapid proliferation of African Christian communities, particularly in Europe and North American diaspora, thus resulting in the remapping of old religious landscapes. This migratory trend and development bring to the fore the crucial role, functions and the import of religious symbolic systems in new geo-cultural contexts. While religion has remained a constant identity variable in African diaspora communities, the historiography of new African diaspora and migration has often largely neglected this religious ferment. Why has and is religion still so important for the new African immigrants in Europe, North America and other Western societies? How and why do the majority of the new African immigrant Christians in Europe and North America establish their own churches or congregations rather than identify with European-led and American-led churches? What links and networks do they establish and maintain with European/American churches? What transnational links do they forge and keep with Africa and other host contexts? What is their social relevance/public role within the European and American local contexts?

When I first commenced religious ethnography on African-led churches in Europe and North America in the mid-1990s, the library research yielded very modest results in terms of available scholarly literature on new African immigrants and their religious dimension in Europe and North America. The quest for extant literature on the phenomenon took me to major university libraries, particularly those of the Universities of Bayreuth and Hamburg, the School of Oriental and African Studies in London, Rhodes Library at Oxford University, Harold Turner Collections in Selly Oak and the University of Birmingham library, the CMS Archives in Birmingham, and the Andrew Walls library within the Centre for the Study of Christianity in the non-Western world (now Centre for the Study of World Christianity at the University of Edinburgh), Harvard University library to mention a few.

A robust scholarly conversation and media attention, particularly in Europe and North America, on the proliferation and activities of new forms of African Christianity are evident from the mid-1990s. Therefore, in contrast to when I commenced my research, research history of recent years has evinced a burgeoning of publication, a process that has gradually launched these religious initiatives into global academic and public discourses. There are recent and current Europe- and US-based research projects and several graduate/undergraduate theses and dissertations tackling different aspects of this phenomenon. Although there are now a few monographs focused on specific religious groups, journal articles and book chapters that explore aspects of this religious development, there is hardly a textbook that captures the complexity and dynamism of this growing religious phenomenon in Europe and North America and their relation to Africa. The book, *African Christian Diaspora* seeks to fill this lacuna in information, interpretation and systematic analysis of African Christian communities in Europe and North America and their impact on the wider local-global religious scene.

African Christian Diaspora is based on in-depth field research undertaken among African Christian communities in Europe (United Kingdom, Germany), United States and Africa (Nigeria and Ghana) since 1995. Drawing from this wide knowledge and broad experience of the field, I map, describe and analyse the incipience and consolidation of new brands of African Christianities in diaspora by locating it within different historical epochs. I managed to piece together the rather disparate knowledge, available in sometimes fairly obscure contexts in continental Europe, and contrasted with developments elsewhere in Europe and the United States. Relevant literature on Anglophone and non-Anglophone African Christians, including German-, French- and Portuguese-speaking African Christians has been included in this book. The religious trends in these varied contexts are necessary for presenting a historiography of new African Christianities in Europe and the United States in particular. Thus, the importance of the book lies in its attempt to offer a comprehensive discussion of one of the most important religious trends in contemporary Christian history, the rise of African Christian communities outside Africa, in Europe and the United States, which has largely come about as an unexpected by-product of international migration.

PREFACE

The book is interdisciplinary in outlook, taking up theoretical and methodological issues. It balances theory with case studies in demonstrating how and to what extent religious, social, cultural, political and economic realities of specific host contexts impact and shape their *raison d'tre*, *modus operandi* and worldviews. The book is structured to follow a certain logic and chronology, moving from *description* to *analysis*, thus providing a meaningful analytical lens for viewing one of the most significant trends in contemporary Christian history. The chapters follow this line in a particular order, starting with trajectories and narratives of African migration (Chapters 1 and 2), followed by situating the local scenes in Africa, Europe and North America; and a concise historiography of new African Christianities in diaspora (Chapters 3 and 4). Chapter 5 provides a phenomenology of African Christian communities that involves thick description of their demography, organizational structures, worldviews and ritual patterns. The rest of the book focuses on analytical discussion of particular themes: African Christianities as social capital (Chapter 6); Identity, Citizenship and Power (Chapter 7); Globalization, Media and Transnationalism (Chapter 8); Reverse Mission (Chapter 9); and the final chapter, Politics of Networking (Chapter 10) offers a conclusion, pointing to emerging trends and prospects. The analytical themes discussed in this book emanated from the rich data I collected over the years, and have been based primarily on *emic* perspectives and cautiously balanced with *etic* sources. Through the author's own crucial attention to reflexivity, priority is given in this book to the practitioners' world of ideas, their stories, expressions, life experiences and realities in the face of local-global conditions. While some of the concepts discussed in this book may appear to have become overused in modern academia, to the extent of almost losing their analytical value, abundant data and case examples were used to substantiate these concepts in order to endow them with concrete meaning and relevance.

African Christian communities have helped in the reconfiguration of Christianity in Europe and the United States, and have contributed to the increasing religious diversification of host Western societies. The salience of Christianity has been assisted by African-led churches in Western societies, particularly Europe, where secularizing trends within Christianity are prevalent. The book demonstrates how African Christian communities through their developmental processes, have become more and more variegated in their social composition, membership structures, as well as in their modes of operation. The host sociocultural, economic and political milieu largely impacts on and shapes the nature, course, and scope of African Christianities in diaspora. Thus, within the locus of changing, more complex migration trends and policies, these collective religious representations will continue to assume immense meaning and relevance particularly for African immigrants as the churches serve both as loci for identity, security, as well as avenues for adapting into the host social, cultural and religious milieu. The book demonstrates how African Christianities are negotiating and assimilating notions of the global, while maintaining their local identities.

African Christian communities demonstrate their determination to build local-global links and make non-Africans as primary targets in their membership drives. However, the majority of these churches may lack a cross-cultural appeal, thus leaving their membership predominantly African. However, these churches serve as an important source of 'social', 'cultural' and 'spiritual' capital. The relevance of African Christian communities is not only located in the unique expression of African Christianity they exhibit, they also constitute international ministries and groups that have implications on a global scale. The importance of local and global networks among these churches in Africa and in diaspora cannot be overemphasized. The impact and import of the 'exportation' of African-led churches, driven by a vision of winning converts, is that it offers a unique opportunity to analyse its impact at local levels. African Christian communities in Europe and the United States are no longer just 'African', they are also – and increasingly so – European and American churches, especially in view of the new religious networks that are being formed that are relatively independent from the continent of origin, Africa. This begs the question of the significance of these new churches for the host contexts, both in a religious as well as in a secular sense. African Christian communities in diaspora should not simply be considered as outposts of Africa in an alien continent, but as institutions that are also part of European and American life.

The transnational linkages between African Christian communities in the countries of origin (Africa) and the 'host' societies, such as Europe and the United States are assuming increasing importance for African immigrants. The links and networks that are established and maintained between these contexts are of immense religious, cultural, economic, political and social importance. This suggests how African Christianities can be understood within processes of religious transnationalism. The conscious appropriation of new media technologies by these new brands of African Christianity and the growing reverse-mission dynamics are analysed as new, evolving dimension of the transnational process. Significant initiatives and development are also taking place within the mainline churches (Roman Catholic Church, Anglican, Methodist, Presbyterian churches) in Europe and the United States, where African (and other non-Western) priests are recruited to respond to the crisis in priestly vocations. This development is a remarkable change in the religious relations between Africa, Europe and North America.

The style and general approach is deliberately chosen to enhance the book's readability and to attract a wide readership. It is hoped that it will appeal to and assist scholars, graduate and undergraduate students, religious practitioners, media, policymakers and interested readers to understand

and further investigate the texture, stature and impact of African Christian communities in specific local and multiple contexts. Due to its interdisciplinary nature, the book seeks to make an important contribution to a number of disciplines/subject areas including Religious Studies, World Christianity, Diaspora and Migration Studies, African Studies, Sociology of Religion and History of Contemporary Christianity. It is also hoped that the book will appeal to audiences in the United Kingdom, Europe and North America, as there is growing scholarship and interest on this topic.

The first decade of this research was part of the Humanities Collaborative Research Group (SFB 560/FK1) research project 'Local Actions in Africa in the Context of Global Influences' (2000–2005) and the Special Research Project (SFB 214) 'Identity in Africa' (1995–1997) at the University of Bayreuth, Germany. As a senior research fellow and principal investigator within these major projects, my extensive library research and field trips in Nigeria, Ghana, Germany, Great Britain and the United States would probably have been unimaginable but for the generous funding from the *Deutsche Forschung Gemeinschaft* (DFG)/German Research Foundation. I am profoundly grateful to the German Research Foundation. My deepest gratitude goes to Prof. Dr Berner and Prof Dr Christoph Bochinger who anchored the sub-group projects during this research period; and to all dear colleagues with whom I shared a largely congenial atmosphere of interdisciplinarity and collegiality. I am immensely thankful to Prof Ogbu Kalu (of blessed memory), Prof Jacob Olupona and Prof Gerrie ter Haar for their useful inputs to this book.

I am indebted to numerous church leaders, organizations, congregants, individuals who literally opened their doors to me and provided tremendous assistance during my data collection. Space does not permit to mention all their names here but I whole heartedly acknowledge their support. Please permit me to single out only a few. I appreciate the generous help and hospitality received from Pastor (Dr) Ajibike Akinyoye and Cornelius Oyelami (RCCGNA Headquarters, Dallas, TX, USA); Pastor (Dr) Samuel Shorimade (RCCG, Boston); Pastor Bosun Ajayi (RCCG, Bonn); Pastor Samuel Jegede (RCCG, Hamburg); Pastor Brown Oyitso (RCCG Festac Town, Lagos); Bishop (Dr) Abraham Bediako (CCOMI, Hamburg); Pastor Kingsley Nimo (CCOM, Berlin); Pastor Onyina-Waye (COMI, Accra); Pastor Festus Olatunde (MFM, Edinburgh); Dr Rufus Ositelu (CLA, Ogere) to mention but a few. My thanks to all those individuals, church leaders, church workers, church members and informants we spoke to and those who volunteered information, resources and time that have helped bring this book to fruition. My profound gratitude goes to Margaret Acton who generously provided a rigorous copy-editing of this book. My dear wife, Esther, and lovely kids, Faith, Blessing and Midafe, provided the much needed emotional support and endured my several travels and staying away from home. You were all exceptionally helpful. Thank you!

1

Trajectories of African migration

Introduction

The historiography of the new African Christian diaspora is located within recent trajectories of international migration, a dynamic process in which Africans are largely implicated as both actors and benefactors. They are not just passive recipients but active participants. The increasing volume, dynamism, trends and complex patterns of international migration have continued to generate wide-ranging interests within both the academic arena as well as the public sphere.

Earlier simple perceptions about migration and diaspora in terms of a single individual action or mass movement of people in their quest for greener pastures, better-life chances from their home of origin (sending) and settlement in host (receiving) societies have become rather tenuous. Migration is usually now thought of as multidirectional and not as unidirectional. It is not simply a process that is characterized by movement from poor, less-developed, war-stricken, crisis-prone, overpopulated contexts to affluent, developed ones. It does not only comprise undocumented, asylum seekers, refugees and economic migrants, but is also now shaped by highly and less-skilled migrants, students, diplomats, businesspersons, missionaries, tourists, but also temporary, long-term or circular migrants.

The new texture of migration is one in which it is not just men who migrate, accompanied by their wives and children as dependants; women are also migrating in their own right, in search of the golden fleece. Through that process they are becoming highly mobile socially and economically, and emerging as the breadwinners of their families, where men (their husbands) join them as dependants and even serve as babysitters. It is also often speculated that immigrants simply 'live and survive' at the behest and or mercy of their host societies. In this case they are seen to totally depend, receive and sometimes exploit the scarce social benefits, hardly contributing in any meaningful ways to the economic wealth and social well-being of these 'receiving' contexts. Migrants and their communities can no longer be perceived as simply receptors of social benefits and consumers of 'welfare goodies' provided by their host societies. They are also to be understood in terms of their public, civic roles and social relevance to their new permanent or temporary homes.

More so, there has been the assumption that migrants settle, adapt or quickly assimilate into their new homes, and no sooner do they do this than they sever ties or links with their original homelands as a consequence. There is now an increasing tendency to think of the long *duree* of the migration process, migration and (non-) settlement as a transient, lifelong process encapsulating crucial life stages and sometimes transcending death. While Castles and Miller (1993: 21) aptly describes migration as 'a collective action, arising out of social change and affecting the whole society in both sending and receiving areas', even this idea of 'sending' and 'receiving' has now shifted from a two-way, bi-polar node to multiple, fluid nodes of 'home' or 'contexts'. Thus, the conceptual 'goalpost' of migration is increasingly becoming elastic and mutable, experiencing constant shifts just as the theoretical grid-making of migration is in flux. This necessitates a revisiting of existing paradigms to see how adequately they explain the enigmatic nature of the migratory process in the global era that we now live in.

Revisiting theories of migration

Classical theories of migration are, in many respects, becoming moribund as explanation paradigms of migratory processes, thus paving the way for new ones or at least being subsumed by them. The discourse of international migration has attracted huge interdisciplinary interests, from the social sciences to the humanities, with each discipline constructing a matrix for framing its own objectives and goals, specific research questions, concepts and methodologies, appropriating dominant theories and hypotheses, and generating its respective frameworks of analysis and conclusions. Rather than a shared paradigm, the study of migration benefits from a variety of competing theoretical viewpoints fragmented across disciplines, regions and ideologies (Brettell and Hollifield 2000: 2). Although driven by differences in theories and methods, disciplinary orientations, interpretations, biases and pretensions, these varied explanations are not, in themselves, mutually exclusive.

Bretell and Hollifield's *Migration Theory: Talking across Disciplines* provides an illuminating cross-disciplinary conversation about the epistemological, paradigmatic and explanatory aspects of writing about and theorizing migration in history, law and the social sciences. This scholarly gaze and talk on international migration across disciplines has tended to ebb and flow with differing waves and trends of emigration and immigration. Massey et al. (1993)

have provided a detailed survey and appraisal of theories of international migration.

However, a cursory purview of the theorizing of migration in historical perspectives is expedient at the outset of this book, especially against the backdrop of deciphering how, and to what extent, old and new patterns of African emigration and immigration fit, contest, contradict or challenge extant paradigms of causal explanation and interpretation. Broadly speaking, the theorizing of migration has evolved around at least four distinctive, though not mutually exclusive, trajectories with each historical phase contributing its own quota to the dynamic process of theory building and analysis of the migration phenomenon.

The neoclassical economic perspective

The earliest systematic theory of migration, the neoclassical economic perspective, is linked to the nineteenth-century geographer Ernest Ravenstein, who formulated the statistical laws of migration in the 1880s, employing census data from England and Wales to develop his 'Laws of Migration' (Ravenstein 1885). He concluded that migration was governed by a 'push-pull' process; that is, unfavourable conditions in one place (oppressive laws, heavy taxation, etc.) 'push' people out, and favourable conditions in an external location 'pull' them in. This genre conceptualized migration as 'individual' relocation of human beings across space, within or between countries, and strove to achieve an elegant formal model that would account for such movements (Zolberg 1989: 403). These general theories often expressed as 'push-pull theories' emphasize tendencies of people to move from densely to sparsely populated areas, or from low- to high-income areas, or link migrations to fluctuations in the business cycle.

This theoretical paradigm which originated in neoclassical economics has influenced and continues to shape discourses in the social sciences to a large degree. The economic variable predominates in most theories that seek to explain why the decision to migrate is made in the first place. Migration has often been predicted using variations of this model, operating at different levels of analysis. While the neoclassical economic theories of migration are far from being redundant, they are invaluable in grasping the complexities of international migration, such a genre has been largely critiqued as being too individualistic and ahistorical. As Castles and Miller (1993: 22) note, its central concept is 'human capital': people decide to invest in migration, in the same way that they might invest in education or vocational training, because it raises their human capital and brings potential future gains in earnings. Empirical studies based on contemporary international migration would overturn the assumptions of this theory. As we indicated earlier, those who migrate are not usually the poorest of the poor, nor is it simply a movement from the poor, least developed countries to richer ones.

The breadth of contemporary migration suggests a multidirectionality of movements across different contexts: from so-called poor, less-developed contexts to rich, more-developed contexts and vice versa. More interestingly, there is a huge movement also from one poor to another poor, developing country, and from one rich to another rich, more-developed country. In fact, most of those who engage in frequent movements are the upwardly mobile and people of intermediate social and economic status. For instance, although Africa is mirrored in global terms, albeit surreptitiously, as a 'poor continent', Paul Zeleza (2002: 9) shows that many Africans who migrate go to other African countries. He notes that between 1965 and 1990 Africa's migrant population grew at a faster rate than in any other region in the world. The continent increased its share of international migrants from 10.6 per cent to 13.1 per cent.

The push-pull model is also suspect in predicting unilateral demographic shifts, movements from densely populated to more sparsely peopled contexts. This cannot be denied as a universal human feature, but the direct opposite also occurs in which urban, densely populated cities attract huge drifts from the rural villages and remote contexts. Our global cities are facing huge, pragmatic challenges on whether and how they can manage their teeming populations and human resources in the face of dwindling material resources and failing welfare systems. The push-pull factor can hardly explain why a certain group of migrants choose to go to one country rather than another. For instance, African migration to Europe from the 1960s has tended to follow the historical and linguistic trails of colonialism, so that Britain and France were the preferred destinations of migrants from the former British and French colonies, respectively (Zeleza 2002: 10).

Besides, the neoclassical model tends to treat the role of the state as an aberration which disrupts the 'normal' functioning of the market (Castles and Miller 1993: 24). Zolberg (1989: 405) note in retrospect how strange it was that classical migration theory altogether ignored borders and their effects. Thus, owing to the neglect of historical causes of movements and their undermining of the role of the state, neoclassical theories were generally criticized as simplistic and incapable of explaining actual movements or predicting future ones (Sassen 1988).

The historical-structural approach

In the 1970s, neoclassical economic genre gradually gave way to the historical-structural approach as an alternative explanation of international migration. It had its intellectual thrust in Marxist political economy and in world systems theory, stressing the unequal distribution of economic and political power in the world economy (Castles and Miller 1993: 24). In this regard, migration was generally perceived as a way of mobilizing cheap labour for capital, in this case, mass recruitment of labour by capital. The alternative theories developed to treat international patterns of migration are largely variants of the push-pull variable. The dual labour market theory posits that First World economies are structured so as to require a certain level of immigration (Piore 1979).

World systems theory sees migration as a natural consequence of economic globalization and market penetration across national boundaries (Wallerstein 1974). The world systems theory contends that international migration is a by-product of global capitalism (Sassen 1988). The current world system is structured around a power hierarchy between core and periphery in which so-called powerful and wealthy 'core' societies (advanced or developed societies such as Europe and the United States) dominate and exploit weak and poor 'peripheral' (less-developed societies such as Africa, Latin America) societies. The approach shows that contemporary patterns of international migration tend to be from the periphery (poor nations) to the core (rich nations) because factors associated with industrial development in the First World generated structural economic problems, and thus push factors, in the Third World.

This theory has some merits but can hardly advance our understanding of the complexities of past and contemporary migration on grounds that it downplayed the individual/group motivations in the process, and over-prioritized the interests of capital. Besides, the world systems theory rarely does justice to the huge volume of migrants that move within and across one African country or society to another. For instance, it fails to explain the migration of Nigerians to Ghana and of Ghanaians to Nigeria and Cote d'Ivoire from the 1970s and 1990s; the recent exodus of Zimbabweans to South Africa, Botswana and elsewhere in Africa; the movement of Congolese, Zaireans, Rwandese, Sudanese nationals to other parts of East and Central Africa; nor the movement of Liberians and Sierra Leoneans across the West African subregion.

The theory is not mindful of migratory trends from one rich, advanced context to another, such as the well-known European migrations to the Americas prior to 1914, or even the recent influx of migrants from Eastern Europe to other parts of the European Union; nor does it explain internal migration within a rich country such as the historic movement of African Americans out of the Southern United States to the North, Midwest and West from 1910 to 1930, or the great number of GDR citizens moving from East Germany to West Germany in the 1950s and much later, following the collapse of the Berlin Wall in 1989.

The historicization of migration theory has led to the modification of theoretical concerns and emphases, in light of changing social realities. The classical and neoclassical migration theories were supplanted by new theories. The predominant question in earlier research and theorizing on international migration is why people migrate (intentionality), and less on the dynamics of migration, such as the actual situation of migrants in the migratory states and process, chain migration in migration networks, contextual factors that shape migration policies and trends.

The migration systems theory (MST) and the transnational theory (TNT) have become the preferred new analytic frameworks for understanding and contextualizing international migratory trends and processes. Both theories, encapsulating several levels of analysis, account for the direction, texture of international migration and the complex dynamics. This book is largely based on the theoretical framework of these latter genres.

The migration systems theory

The MST was first articulated by Mabogunje (1970) and extended by Kritz et al. (1992) and other scholars such as Portes and Böröcz (1989) and Levitt (1998). Mabogunje (1970) defined a migration system as a set of places linked by flows and counter flows of people, goods, services, and information, which tend to facilitate further exchange, including migration, between places. While Mabogunje focused on rural-urban migration within the African continent, Kritz et al. (1992) extended this to international migration.

The MST situates international migration as a product of interacting nation-states and congruent sociocultural, geopolitical, and economic factors and policies (Zlotnik 1992). These interdependencies give rise to sustained and sizeable bilateral migration flows such that the determination of a migration system can presumably be made on the basis of these largely exogenous characteristics. The fundamental assumption of MST is that migration alters the social, cultural, economic, and institutional conditions at both the 'sending' and 'receiving' ends – that is, the entire developmental space within which migration processes operate. Castles and Miller (1993: 27) best encapsulates the parameters of MST as they enthuse:

> The migration systems approach is part of a trend towards a more inclusive and interdisciplinary understanding, which is emerging as a new mainstream of migration theory – at least outside the domain of neo-classical orthodoxy. The basic principle is that any migratory movement can be seen as a result of interacting macro- and micro-structures. Macro-structures refer to large-scale institutional factors, while micro-structures embrace the networks, practices and beliefs of the migrants themselves.

These two levels are linked by a number of intermediate mechanisms, which are often referred to as 'meso-structures'.

For Castles and Miller (1993: 27), the macro-structures include the political economy of the world market, interstate relationships, and the laws, structures and practices established by the states of sending and receiving countries to control migration settlement; while macrostructures are the informal social networks developed by the migrants themselves, in order to cope with migration and settlement. The informal networks in the latter structure include personal relationships, family and household patterns, friendship and community ties, and mutual help in economic and social matters.

Such informal networks and links generate social capital, providing vital resources for individuals and groups (Bourdieu and Wacquant 1992: 119); and bind migrants and non-migrants together in a complex web of social roles and interpersonal relationships (Boyd 1989: 639). In this regard, the family and community (religious, social, cultural, ethnic, economic and political) are crucial in migration networks. Family linkages often provide both the financial and the cultural capital which make migration possible, while migration systems also provide the basis for processes of settlement and community formation in the immigration area (Castles and Miller 1993: 28).

The intermediate meso-structures would refer to certain individuals, groups or institutions that take up a mediating role between migrants and political or economic institutions. The 'migration industry', including recruitment organizations, lawyers, agents, smugglers, NGOs, charitable bodies and other intermediaries that emerge can be both helpers and exploiters of migrants. Castles and Miller contend that macro-, meso- and micro-structures are intertwined in the migratory process, and there are no clear dividing lines between them (28).

The transnational theory

A further consideration of a new, emerging migrant population whose networks, activities and life patterns encompass and transcend their home and host societies has produced a new body of theory on 'transnationalism' and 'transnational communities'. Debates on transnationalism were stimulated by the work of Basch et al. (1994), which argued that 'deterritorialized nation-states were emerging, with potentially serious consequences for national identity and international politics'. The TNT in this regard capture migrants, their lives, experiences and consciousness as one that cuts across national boundaries and bring two (or more) societies into a single social field. Basch et al. (1992) defines transnationalism as the processes by which immigrants build social fields that link together their country of origin and their country of settlement.

Transmigrants is the designation used for those immigrants who build such social fields, develop and maintain multiple relations – familial, economic, social, organizational, religious and political – that span borders. Transmigrants take actions, make decisions, and feel concerns, and develop identities within social networks that connect them to two or more societies simultaneously (Glick-Schiller et al. 1992: 203). Thus, the notion of a transnational community puts the emphasis on human agency. 'In the context of globalization, transnationalism can extend previous face-to-face communities based on kinship, neighbourhoods or workplaces into far-flung virtual communities, which communicate at a distance' (Castles and Miller 1993: 29). Portes (1999: 464) defines transnational activities as

> those that take place on a recurrent basis across national borders and that require a regular and significant commitment of time by participants. Such activities may be conducted by relatively powerful actors, such as representatives of national governments and multi-national corporations, or may be initiated by more modest individuals, such as immigrants and their home country kin and relations. These activities are not limited to economic enterprises, but include political, cultural and religious initiatives as well.

Portes et al. (1999) seek to turn the concept of transnationalism into a clearly defined and measurable object of research. They acknowledge that transnationalism involves individuals, their networks of social relations, their communities, and broader institutionalized structures such as local and national governments. For methodological reasons, however, they define the individual and his/her support networks as the proper unit of analysis because they believe that a study that begins with the history and activities of individuals is the most efficient way of learning about the institutional underpinnings of transnationalism and its structural effects. Furthermore, they distinguish between *transnationalism from above*, that is, activities 'conducted by powerful institutional actors, such as multinational corporations and states'; and *transnationalism from below*, that is, activities 'that are the result of grass-roots initiatives by immigrants and their home country counterparts' (1999: 221).

Generally, the MST and TNT should be viewed more as complementary approaches rather than as being mutually exclusive. They both provide the necessary template within which we shall explore the complexity of African migrations in this book, as part of global processes of international migration. Zolberg (1989: 403–4) aptly contrasts these two approaches and I shall quote them generously here. They note that

> despite many differences, attributable to different intellectual traditions and disciplinary backgrounds, the most stimulating newer approaches

share a number of common features: (1) they are generally historical, not in the sense of dealing mostly with a more distant past, but rather in paying appropriate attention to the changing specificities of time and space; (2) they are generally structural rather than individualistic, focusing on the social forces that constrain individual action, with special emphasis on the dynamics of capitalism and of the state; (3) they are generally globalist, in that they see national entities as social formations as interactive units within an encompassing international social field, permeable to determination by transnational and international economic and political processes; and (4) they are generally critical, sharing to some degree a commitment to social science as a process of demystification and rectification, and in particular are concerned with the consequences of international migrations for the countries of origin and destination, as well as the migrants themselves.

The spatial delineation of the transnational social field in terms of country of origin and country of settlement, point of departure and destination, sending and receiving countries, and between home and host societies is too simple, and undercuts its complex breadth and width.

Transnational social fields are not bi-polar but multipolar; they envelop migrants' countries of origin and other host contexts. Diasporas are webs, and webs consist not only of fibres and ropes, but also of nodes that link them together (Haller 2001: 7). Haller's description of diasporas as webs comprising fibres, ropes and nodes is useful in comprehending transnational social fields too. The research on which this book's description and analysis is based captures this multipolarity of the transnational social field having been based on a triangular context of research – Africa, Europe and North America. Thus, the book will explore the triad relationship within the transnational religious field, demonstrating the relevance of micro- and meso-structures, and what I shall describe in chapter eight as 'religious transnationalism from below'.

The feminization of contemporary African migration and diasporas

Female migration is evidently a key constituent of global migration.[1] While a gendered understanding and contextualization of migration and diaspora is quintessential, only recently have efforts been exerted to incorporate gender into theories of international migration and discourses of diaspora. Grieco and Boyd (2003) represent an excellent attempt at developing a gender sensitive approach to the study of international migration. They have employed a three-stage analytical framework in exploring how gender is intricately involved in the entire migration process and to demonstrate how gender relations, roles and hierarchies differently shape the migratory behaviour and experiences of men and women. Elsewhere, few scholars – for example, Boyd (1989), Castles and Miller (1993), Simon and Brettell (1986) have focused on female immigrants and the fact that their migration experience may be largely different from that of men. These relatively few works lend credence to the fact that migration and diaspora theories are increasingly becoming gender-sensitive, thus marking a shift from perception of female immigrants simply as 'dependants', 'wives' and 'children' of male immigrants to incorporating explanations of the unique experiences of women migrants themselves.

There are a few notable historical, sociological and anthropological works such as those by Terborg-Penn and Rushing (1996) that engage women and gender in the historical African diaspora. Griffith and Savage (2006) represent a significant scholarly breakthrough in the field, with its transnational scope, cross-disciplinary focus, and interrogation of interrelated themes and paradigms in rich, diverse ways that suggest emergent models for studying women, religions, and diasporic shifts across space and time. The book illuminates 'some ways in which diverse women of African descent have practiced religion as part of the work of their ordinary and sometimes extraordinary lives' (2006: x).

This phenomenal work throws up a challenge to scholars of African migration and diaspora to begin to focus special attention on the gendering of these processes; the recentering of women; and the complexity of their religious lives in distinct settings. Earlier, Gunning et al. (2003: 398) underscore this urgency as they noted 'the use of gender as a category of analysis remains something of a challenge for African Diaspora Studies'. I would add that this is particularly so with the specific context and lived experiences within the contemporary African diaspora where issues of religion and gender have rarely being interrogated. Scholars should not take for granted the fact that the African diaspora is far from being a homogenous entity. Although the rhetoric bears semblances and shares certain commonalities, the mere fact that the historical African diaspora and the new African diaspora occurred within two different historical epochs and in a multiplicity of contexts is suggestive of the rationale for paying close attention to the contextual factors that shape migratory processes and diasporic formations in each respective geo-cultural context.

Women's religious experiences and expressions in their everyday lives will undoubtedly vary when located in time and space. Griffith and Savage (2006: xiv) best encapsulate this complexity as they assert:

> Diverse places of origin, different experiences of displacement, and disparate living conditions are connected in women's religious lives to equally distinctive modes of spiritual expression and ritual action, dynamics

of adaptation and innovation, and strategies that manoeuvre within and across religious and social settings. Just as Africanness is not a single point of origin and diaspora is not a single geographic or ontological destination, so black womanhood in this transnational context signifies patterns of divergences and convergences.

Against this backdrop therefore, our especial focus in this book was on the dynamics of women, gender and religion within the threshold of recent African immigration and what is now described as the new, second African diaspora.

Gender is a social, spatial construction perceived as 'a matrix of identities, behaviours, and power relationships that are constructed by the culture of a society in accordance with sex' (Boyd 2003). As Castles and Miller (1993: 9) note, 'gender variables have always been significant in global migration history, but awareness of the specificity of women in contemporary migrations has grown'. The anatomy of migration was teased out on certain assumptions of the near invisibility of women as migrants, their presumed passivity in the process, and their traditional place in the home. These assumptions that shape migration discourse as a male-dominated venture are not unconnected with canvassed economic variables as in the perceived negligibility of women's participation in international labour migration and flows. Any theorizing of international migration needs to take cognisance of remote and immediate factors that coalesce to create different gendered experiences along the spectrum. A gendered perspective of migration is fundamental to understanding the motives for migration. The conceptualization and hermeneutics of these varying forces and outcomes will enhance the theoretical grounding of individual experiences of men and women in international migration processes.

The complex dynamism of contemporary migration within and beyond Africa is partly reflected in the growing feminization of migration. Adepoju (2005: 36) vividly captures changing migratory configurations as he notes that 'traditional male-dominated short-to-long distance migratory streams in West Africa are becoming increasingly feminized. Independent female migration has become a major survival strategy in response to deepening poverty in the sub-region.' Generally, current migratory trends within the continent and from Africa to Europe and North America in particular, largely challenge traditionally perceived migration patterns in that they are noticeably becoming feminized. African women, along with men, are now increasingly engaged in migration partly as a family survival strategy or a way of furthering the climb up the socio-economic ladder in their respective societies.

Women have not only accompanied or joined their husbands abroad through family reunification; professional women are sometimes leaving their spouses temporarily to care for their children while they take advantage of greener pastures or fall prey to the brain drain syndrome. The access to a variety of educational and employment opportunities acts as a magnet for women wishing to be economic and social actors in their own right. In such cases, their husbands and children have subsequently reunited with them. Others have plugged into transnational, organized sexual labour and trafficking or what Adepoju aptly described as 'commercial migration' (see Adepoju 2005: 37). The demography of female migrants has been further swelled by refugees, asylum seekers and other local-global circumstances born out of wars, natural disasters, economic collapse, as well as religious and political crises. This geo-mobility is neither constrained by nor confined to rural, urban, national and continental borders.

By 2000, it was estimated that 46.7 per cent of the 16 million international migrants in Africa were female, up from 42 per cent in 1960 when the number of international migrants in the continent stood at 9 million (Zlotnik 2003). In 1960, Africa had the lowest proportion of females among international migrants in comparison to other contexts such as Latin America, the Caribbean and Asia. The phenomenon of females migrating independently, even internationally, enables them to fulfil their economic needs rather than simply joining their husbands; indeed more and more professional women are emigrating from Nigeria, Senegal and Ghana leaving husbands behind to cater for their children (Adepoju 2005: 36). Female nurses and doctors have been recruited from Nigeria to work in Saudi Arabia, while their counterparts in Ghana are taking advantage of the better pay packages in the United Kingdom and the United States to work for a spell of time in order to accumulate savings to survive harsh economic conditions at home. It is estimated that there are currently over 5,000 Ghanaian and Nigerian nurses in the United Kingdom, working in that country's National Health Service, in nursing and private care homes (Adepoju 2005: 36). Therefore, the relatively steady rise in the share of female African migrants, skilled and less skilled, among all international migrants is consistent with an increasing feminization of migration.

In the face of migration-related challenges, women in the African diaspora are appearing less fixed in the gendered roles of dependant, wife and mother. In many cases, men are assuming more responsibilities for domestic duties, cooking meals for the children while the woman is at work; and undertaking childcare as babysitters and 'nannies' in a new social context where working class men are also entitled to 'paternity leave' from their jobs, if they so wish, to stay home with children while the wives take turn at work. Gender relations, roles and hierarchies impact on the migration process and produce differential outcomes for women and men through the distinctive stages of pre-migration, transition across state boundaries, and the particular experiences of migrants in the host context (Grieco and Boyd 2003). New economic roles and new responsibilities affect spousal relationships, in some instances leading to considerable negotiations and resistance to change by both men and women.

Migration represents a challenge in women's economic and familial roles, as well as in their usual pattern of relations with husbands and children. For some women, migration means an increase in social mobility, economic independence and relative autonomy. For others, getting better-paid employment is only a means of improving the family's economic base. The impact of moving from one form of gender stratification system to another can be understood through the interaction between societal and family contexts. All stages of the migration process are important for considering the influence of gender. Migration can have a positive, negative or neutral impact; it could enhance or erode the status of women as the case may be.

As 'breadwinners', female migrants put pressure on gender roles within the traditional African family structure. The division of family labour poses a significant challenge to gender roles in Africa and the African diaspora, just as the feminization of migration represents a means towards socio-economic and religious (spiritual) empowerment. Women are increasingly assuming roles as resource managers, decision-makers and captains of industries. Some have become church founders, leaders and visible religious functionaries on both sides of the Atlantic. In Chapter 7, I shall focus more on the post-migration stage dealing with factors that occur within the host society or diasporic context that shape the adaptation and integration of women and men into the receiving society. I shall explore the increasing feminization of African immigrant religiosity; and demonstrate with specific examples of female leadership dynamics and the appropriation of empowerment rhetoric, how the polity and demography of African diasporic Christian communities are increasingly becoming feminized.

From a cursory exploration of how theories of migration have evolved, and how contemporary African migration and diaspora is increasingly becoming feminized, I now turn in the next chapter to capturing the reality of individual African life stories and institutional narratives that shape migratory processes from the home of origin as a point of departure through the travails of the transit – the journey itself, to the destination(s), new home(s) and then possibly return migration to the point of take-off (original home of origin). Religious repertoires and experiences are implicated in these webs of mobility both in how individual and collective motive(s), decision(s) to migrate are often imbued with religious narratives; and or in whether, how and to what extent the 'journey', 'sojourn', 'return' heightens or rather dwindles religious zeal, enthusiasm, belonging, participation, praxis, expression and experience. The religious variable thus becomes a vital marker in charting the causes, courses and conduits of contemporary African migration.

2

Narratives of African migration

Introduction

Narratives of migration are woven around the different kinds of people who move; the intentionality and stimulus to migrate; the realities of the local context from which they move; the anxieties of the journey to the 'unknown eldorado (land)'; the uncertainties of moving to a new cultural context; the realized or dashed hopes upon arrival at the temporary/permanent destination; contextual factors in the new abode of sojourn and the global factors that shape international migratory processes in different historical epochs. The narratives of one phase or within one space/time are integral to and contingent upon our understanding of the entire migratory story.

Scholarship on immigration is often so focused on the salience of religion among immigrants in the new host society to the extent that it sidesteps the place of religion and spirituality through the long *dureé* of the migration process. Religious attitudes and motivations of immigrants in the context of temporary or permanent sojourn are often a reflection of religious/spiritual experiences and resources employed during the decision-making, preparatory stages of the journey and the liminal trajectories of the journey. Scholars should pay more attention to individual life stories and institutional narratives that shape and mirror migratory processes.

Jacqueline Hagan and Helen Ebaugh (2003) draw upon the migratory and religious history of a transnational Maya community to highlight the important role that religious and spiritual beliefs and practices play in the process of contemporary undocumented migration. They explore how migrants use religion in six stages of the migration process: decision-making; preparing for the trip; the journey; the arrival; the role of the ethnic church in immigrant settlement and the development of transnational linkages. Interesting as this case study is in explicating the migrants' use of religion in the migration process, their focus on only undocumented migrants, at the expense of documented migrants, presents a one-sided picture of a transnational Maya community.

The present book captures both documented and undocumented African immigrants. Migrants' travel can be both difficult and clandestine, through the travails of crossing the desert, sneaking across borders with boats and canoes, or being concealed in trucks/lorries to beat the eagle-eyed surveillance of border police patrols and immigration officials. Other undocumented migrants have travelled by air and sea with other people's travel documents or by using fake travel documents to exploit the ignorance of immigration officials. Documented migrants at the same time employ religious resources and appropriate religious rituals through the different stages of the migration process.

Nwando Achebe (2004) provides a useful glimpse into the role of religious rituals in the lives of prospective migrants in Nigeria. Her ethnography of the lives of Nigerian sex workers 'at home and abroad' describes how the potential traveller undergoes a series of rituals 'designed to break her spirit, instil fear, and ensure total compliance to the decrees of her soon-to-surface pimp' (182). Her example indicates the appropriation of traditional religious rituals by prospective migrants, in this case, commercial sex workers.

Ogbu Kalu (2007) best elucidates the complex dynamics of a diasporic condition, where he identifies four phases of the problem: the home base conditions that compel emigration, the journey, the diasporic condition and the prospects of re-entry. Kalu canvasses two competing models, the 'exile' and 'crossing Jordan', for contextualizing the diasporic condition. He explicates the impacts of emigration on both homelands and destinations of migration by likening these phases of the *Andrew Syndrome* to strands of an *akwete cloth* and weaving them through a composite tapestry located in history. The desire to emigrate or the factors that triggered *the Andrew Syndrome*[1] are partly linked to dearth of incentives, good governance, political culture and policies on capacity development, quest for meaning and self-development (62ff.). Kalu alludes to these dynamics elsewhere, addressing specifically how vital Pentecostal Christian religiosity is in the lives of would-be migrants. He remarks:

> The immigrant condition is riddled with hope, hardship, broken dreams, and measures of success. Immigrant Christianity serves as a balm in the entire process, ranging from why and how the immigrants came to their new countries, to how they cope in the new homeland. The journey begins with prayers in Pentecostal churches and prayer camps for travel visas, to prayers in immigrant churches for everyday survival needs such as working permits, employment, and money for rent mortgage, health insurance, and other bills. There is also the added pressure to accumulate money and goods to transfer home. (Kalu 2008: 282)

Ebenezer Obadare and Wale Adebanwi (2010) also expound on the role that religion plays in transnational migration before actual migration. Drawing on their ethnography in Nigeria, the United Kingdom and the United States, they highlight how would-be migrants turn to and instrumentalize religion in a context in which the entire migration process has become defined by perplexing contradictions.

The complex dynamism of African migration and how religious beliefs, practices and spiritual resources are employed and negotiated within the various stages of the migratory process are central to this book. The narratives of migration take due cognisance of documented/undocumented migrants and voluntary and involuntary migration; some decisions to migrate are spontaneous while others are planned in and through a long time. While narratives emerged from and focused on West Africans, specifically Ghanaians and Nigerians, in the earlier stages of the migration process, the picture widens and becomes more complex in the latter stages of the migration process as the religious communities they forged in diaspora take on a multi-ethnic and multinational outlook. Other African immigrants, but also non-Africans have joined the membership of churches founded by Ghanaian and Nigerians, besides forming their own communities. Below, I shall turn to examine the dynamic stages of migration and the religious and spiritual stamps they may engender in the process. But first, I will provide a short exposition of the context within which migration was nurtured.

In spite of the explanations for why individual people migrate, the decision and preparation for take-off hardly occurs in a socio-historical vacuum. The economic, political, social realities of a specific local context are quintessential for understanding the shape, volume and flow of emigration. It helps to put in proper perspective why there is more emigration from one region or among specific ethnic groups rather than another, or in one decade more than another. For instance, it partly explains the puzzle of why Nigerians from the south/west are more likely to migrate outside Nigeria than those from the north. The demography of Nigerian youth who undertake regular/irregular international migration is suffused with Yoruba, Igbo, and Edo migrants rather than Hausa, Fulani and other ethnic groups in northern Nigeria. Social (education) heritage, access to gainful employment, job opportunities and the structure of the political economy are partly responsible for this lopsidedness. The socio-economic and political context for understanding the migration from Lagos and Accra to New York, London, Amsterdam, Berlin, Dublin and so on, can be periodized under different historical phases.

It would be ambitious to provide a general historical, socio-economic and political background of Africa owing to the complex diversities of context and peoples. To avoid huge generalizations, I shall briefly sketch (in the next chapter) the social history and political economy of Nigeria and Ghana, two anglophone West African countries that represent the most conspicuously described 'home of origin' in my research, and from which context the triad transnational nexus between prospective migrants, migrants and their religious communities in Africa, Europe and North America are better understood. Such a backdrop provides insight for mapping the history of migration in and from Africa (Ghana and Nigeria) and the internal/external dynamics that shape the process in time and space.

The migration configurations and histories of the two member countries[2] of the Economic Community of West African States (ECOWAS) are long standing, extending back to the largely involuntary, historical slave trade of the seventeenth and eighteenth centuries; the intra-West African migration from the precolonial to the post-independence era. In fact, Article 27 of the ECOWAS Treaty recognized the historical record of free labour migration in the subregion; and affirmed a long-term objective to establish a community citizenship that could be acquired automatically by all nationals of the member states (Adepoju 2005: 30). ECOWAS and the Protocol on Free Movement of Persons greatly funnelled intra-West African mobility but also enhanced international migration within, to and from Africa (see Adepoju 2010). This book has its focus on more recent configurations of international immigration that are now generally described as the second or new Africa diaspora.

Home of origin as point of departure

The discourse on home of origin as the first point of departure in the migration process often undermines the rural-urban matrix. Most people who migrate or travel abroad do that from the town/city and rarely from the village/rural context. The urban space is rich with the infrastructure for travel by air, sea and land. This is where the embassies/consulates are located. It is within the city/urban spaces that the networks, contacts with the migration industry, media information about the journey and the prospective abode of sojourn are brokered, circulated and consumed. In a sense, just as the urban centre serves as a magnet for rural migrants, it also represents the springboard for prospective migration across national/intercontinental levels. Thus, home of origin as adumbrated here also mirrors mobility across rural-urban environs within the same country. The volume and rapidity of migration within the African continent far exceeds that from Africa to any context beyond it. Many potential migrants have migrated to other African countries that share national borders with other continents such as Europe, but also to countries with a thriving migrant industry and with abundant opportunities to generate further income to enhance their travel.

The intentionality and motives behind migration are as complex and diverse as the different kinds of people that move. One explanation of migration, as we have shown, that gets constantly refined by social scientists who ground migration at the nexus of pull-push variable (based on a rational choice model of the world); and the demand-supply paradigm. Collinson (1993) identifies four kinds of migrants based on their motives for moving and the circumstances under which they leave their countries of origin. These levels of migration are summarized as: economically motivated migration and voluntary circumstances under which it occurs; migrants with strong political motives who relocate voluntarily; another instance where strong political motives combine with involuntary circumstances resulting in a category of migrants best characterized as refugees; and lastly, economic migrants who leave their countries involuntarily (2). The last level refers to newer types of migrants who move because their economic livelihood is threatened by civil strife, environmental degradation, and other natural disasters in their countries of origin. Comprehensive as this scheme appears, it misses out some other vital aspects in this process, one of which is the religious impulse.

The classical and contemporary theories of migration are hardly concerned with interrogating the complex interconnectedness between religion and migration processes (Cohen 1996; 1997; Kritz et al. 1992). Migration flows are not to be explained only in terms of the oversimplified pull-push, and demand-supply variables. In fact, the new quality of migration in an African context and beyond demands an approach that recognizes both the complex dynamics of international migration and the impact of religion on migrants and the migration process. Thus, the motives for migration therefore include economic, political, cultural, historical, studying abroad, religious, mission as well as reverse mission and other factors.

Next to the intentional expansion of religion (mission), migration is the most important factor determining the spread of religion. Religious network processes and the ways in which religious movements appropriate new media are features which encourage migration by providing valuable information, material and emotional support for potential migrants as well as newcomers. These enter the migration equation and influence the direction and magnitude of the migratory movements. Other features are the phenomenon of chain migration – spouses and families follow after first comers; studying abroad and taking up employment or marriage and then deciding to remain in host country; and lastly the issue of remigration.

The role of family, family linkages and community (cultural capital) are crucial in this early stage of the migratory process. Family members often provide information, material backing, moral support and the cultural capital which make migration possible. While the immediate family may rally round an individual giving him/her the necessary support, there could also be secrecy associated with an individual's intention and preparation to migrate for fear of witches' machinations and manipulation by evil ones. These are believed to have the potential to frustrate such ambitions and plans. Sometimes, even close family and relatives are not to be fully trusted because of envy that might lead to mischievous actions. There is a local African saying that 'the witch that will kill or harm you is within your home and (extended) family'.

During the planning and take-off stage, the prospective migrant is already linked up with different stakeholders within the migration industry such as recruitment organizations, immigration lawyers, immigration officials and manufacturers of fake documents, agents, human smugglers, NGOs, and even charitable bodies. These and other intermediaries provide assistance freely or for a fee, while others exploit or swindle potential migrants to gain their own advantage. The visa and passport business thrives exceedingly and produces a plethora of migration counsellors including immigration lawyers, advisers, agents, pastors, prophets and diviners. Immigration lawyers display expertise in such services as filling in the visa application forms on behalf of their clients (the potential migrant) in order to beat embassy 'tricks' and legalities. In cases where visas are refused, they provide, for a fee, additional services with respect to appeal applications.

The role of religious specialists such as Christian pastors, prophets and prophetesses, indigenous diviners, Muslim clerics – Imams and Alfas – underscore the centrality of prophecy, divination and spiritual armament in the preparatory stages of the journey. Prospective migrants and their families patronize sacred/religious sites, shrines, prayer camps, religious events where they undergo spiritual 'incubation' and 'inoculation' to fortify themselves against the machinations of witches, sorcerers, the evil eye, envious family relatives and friends. Prospective migrants become vulnerable amid their desperation and anxiety to travel. Some fall prey to manufacturers of bogus travel documents, visas, passports, bank statements, invitation letters, letters of employment; but also of birth/death, marriage, health fitness, and police clearance certificates. Many firms are known to thrive on the production and commodification of fake travel documents in a booming visa economy. Even some nationals working as embassy/consulate staff have become visa entrepreneurs – very strategic within the visa/passport industry – from office workers to the security personnel, they have become very powerful in the scheme of things. They are well patronized behind the scenes and often take advantage of the gullibility of prospective migrants to extort money and demand all sort of favours even when, in any real sense, they have little power and influence over the visa decision-making process.

In the face of global security fears, most embassies have increased security in a way that now makes the architectural structure of the embassy very daunting and intimidating, turning them into modern-day gated, high-fenced maximum security prisons and concentration camps. The appearance of these buildings and their vicinity bamboozles, and even intimidates some applicants in the first instance. The huge walls mark a crucial frontier, battle-line between the applicants in long, unending queues under the scorching sun or messy rain; and the embassy staff behind opaque windows in fortified air-conditioned rooms. The typical embassy exterior (entrance) scene from the early morning queues to the activities of vendors and touts, migration agencies and even the underground transactions of embassy employees is akin to street trading in a highbrow commercial precinct.

The passage through the embassy on visa application and the interviewing stage is often a nightmare; an insurmountable hurdle that can be surmounted only by the courageous, bold, aggressive and sometimes canny ones. This explains why many successful applicants would render testimonies in church or mosques afterwards; undergo thanksgiving rituals in churches or mosques and organize parties to celebrate their success in obtaining a visa. Some who are denied visas remain undaunted as they prepare to apply the next time or seek to block the loopholes that led to their refusal. It is again at this refusal stage that many seek further spiritual resources for assistance. Religious specialists are again patronized for advice, guidance and solution towards attaining a visa and, or, to spiritually legitimize the plan to migrate or travel.

Recent changes in visa application procedures in some foreign embassies/consulates in Africa have however contributed to decongesting the traffic of applicants who throng embassies/consulates daily. In the process, it has also made the local economies of embassy staff (even gatemen) less lucrative. The same is true for the activities of vendors, religious or commercial, who earn a living simply by patronizing applicants (prospective migrants). In a way, changes in the visa application procedure has taken 'butter out of the bread' from some embassy workers and given it instead to new courier agencies who now act as visa brokers between the embassies/consulates and applicants in the booming visa economy. For instance, VFS Global is a commercial company, working in partnership with UK Border Agency in Nigeria to provide services to help people apply for a visa to enter the United Kingdom. VFS also manages visa application centres for the UK Border Agency in Nigeria, where applicants submit their visa application, supporting documents and biometric data.[3] They also take charge of forwarding the application packages to the respective embassies for an exorbitant fee. Although they do not play any significant role in the visa decision-making processes, many have taken undue advantage of unsuspecting applicants to charge extra fees or extort money and favour from applicants.

The indiscriminate increase of visa fees by embassies/consulates in Africa, it might be assumed, could reduce the number of applicants or discourage potential applicants in view of the fact that fees are non-refundable upon visa refusal or rejection. Ironically, the uncontested increase in visa fees have economic undertones in that it makes the economic base of the embassies robust, thus ventilating the visa economy. Quite inadvertently, this makes the quest to travel or migrate even more lucrative for some. It makes potential migrants more desperate to get the funds at all cost, through legitimate/illegitimate means.

Most of my informants contend that the approval or denial of a visa is contingent upon a number of factors. It is not only dependent on the veracity or falsity of the reasons adduced for travel and the authenticity and genuineness of the travel and other required documents. It is also largely tied to the ignorance of the visa officials in discerning fake, spurious documentation from original documentation or the narratives of the applicants themselves. Some claim that the mood of the visa official attending to an applicant is important too. In fact, the 'journey' begins here at the embassy, that is, the reality to travel or not to travel. In many respects, prospective immigrants become extremely vulnerable in the face of these actions and decisions. It is sometimes these ordeals that justify their recourse to spiritual insurance and panacea. An informant once told me,

> Since the visa officials have become slaves to paper documentation, we will continue to exploit their ignorance. Even if they request for signatures from God before they approve visa, we will get them. It is only a matter of time and money.

The religious impulse, experiences encountered in the preparation and take-off stage of the potential immigrant has consequences for the journey itself, but also implications for the latter stages of the immigration process, the settlement and return migration. In fact, the religious encounter during this stage has the tendency to generate a transnational backlash. Many would-be immigrants tap into internet prayer sources. The Prayers Online site is replete with requests in connection with visa interviews and international travel. Under the template 'Prayers to Jesus from thousands of believers around the world', one Caleb Ilesanmi petitioned for 'Prayer for God's Grace, favour and courage for success in visa interview'. He asks:

> Pls join me in prayer for God's Grace, Favour and Courage liken to that of Caleb as I go for my fiancee Visa interview at the U.S. embassy in Lagos, Nigeria on the 9th of May, 2007 ... We need to reunite soon to save our marriage. Amen.[4]

Would-be immigrants take their supplications to the virtual public by tapping on these virtual spiritual resources. You are welcome to submit online prayer.[5] A customized prayer for getting a visa is even based upon 'If you ask anything in My Name, I will do it' (Jn 14: 14).[6] Successful applicants also use the internet sites as avenues to display narratives of success, often attributed to God's divine favour and grace. The above examples show how appropriation of internet prayer sources has a transnational dimension. If the visa application is successful, then the would-be migrant prepares for the next phase of the migratory process, the journey itself.

In transit – the journey to eldorado

The transitory journey to eldorado is itself characterized by its own ambivalences of liminality depending on the route that is embarked upon. Transients are betwixt and between, in limbo, having left home but not having arrived at their temporary or permanent destination country. The anxiety and preparations before the trip may make the journey either a smooth voyage or a bumpy ride, immediate or long-drawn-out, and in a successful or truncated journey. As the liminal phase of the migratory process, immediate travel can be contrasted with long, transient movement. The narratives of transients depicted by Sorious Samura's *Exodus from Africa* are far different from travels of regular migrants linked for instance to the US Diversity Lottery Programme, the Canadian Diversity Visa, the UK recruitment of skilled workers – the Highly Skilled Migrant Programme and the recent Tier 1 (General) category which attracts highly skilled people to the United Kingdom for work or self-employment opportunities.

While regular migrants may have a smooth sail/travel through airports and seaports, irregular migrants often undergo harrowing experiences. Truncated journeys are often a common denominator of irregular migration. Such journeys are not always successful; migrants could be redirected and repatriated. Both tracks are unsafe and unpredictable, thus making migrants vulnerable. Irregular migrants in particular are vulnerable to inhuman treatment by both law enforcement agencies as well as by organized criminal networks.

Generally, destination countries criminalize and control migration when cracks begin to be witnessed in their economies. The increasing politicization and criminalization of immigration often blurs the eyes of police/immigration personnel from easily distinguishing the 'documented' from the 'undocumented'. Several African immigrants recount woeful tales and experiences of inhuman treatment, singled-out for unnecessary random checks among multitudes of travellers, often stop-searched by police and security agents, unwarranted delays by immigration/police offices in the guise of a thorough scrutiny of travel documents, and even sometimes rude interrogation, intimidation and manhandling by some immigration personnel and police at international entry points. In this way, regular African migrants/travellers also become vulnerable in the hopeless attempt to impede the mobility of irregular immigrants/travellers. Many travellers dread such unwarranted scenarios. Thus, to avert any potential embarrassment and vicious checks, African migrants embark on prayer rituals and tap into spiritual resources to ensure smooth sailing, problem-free transit/journey to the chosen destination.

As the European Union, through its harmonized immigration policies, cooperates across borders to crack down on people being smuggled, migrants chart new avenues to elude them. Tougher controls mean navigating a tighter gauntlet, often at greater risk to life. Sorious Samura's 45-minute film documentary *Exodus from Africa – an Immigrant's Journey*[7] brought clearly the plight of irregular African migrants in Spain to international attention. Samura follows migrants from sub-Saharan Africa in their attempt to break and breach the walls of 'fortress Europe', and pave the way to the 'promised land'. In a rhetorical tone, Samura queries:

> Have you ever wondered what it would be like to pack up your bags and leave the country you call home? Once you've squirreled away enough money and decided on your destination, there are other, more daunting aspects of moving to deal with. The emotional ordeal of leaving behind your family, your community, your friends – indeed, your whole culture, is huge ... Sometimes, however, with the passage of time, your memories may become blurred. Your focus will switch to the present; to where you have arrived rather than where you have left behind. And once you begin to appreciate the benefits of your new home and your new culture, the ordeal of leaving your friends behind will hopefully start to make sense. This can't be said for everyone who ups and leaves home. People who move not because they choose to but because they have to, because the place they're leaving behind offers them nothing, no future, and no security whatsoever ... These people head for the West with no proper documentation, with the worst means of transportation and are at best aiming for a bizarre and dangerous means of entry into an unknown land ... thinking that once they get here, all their problems will be solved. This journey that keeps claiming thousands of lives of desperate Africans is now on the increase.[8]

I do not in any way suggest that all African migrants to Europe and elsewhere follow this hazardous course. There are, in fact, a remarkable number of skilled/unskilled migrants, students, business people and professionals that have been attracted and drawn to live, settle and work in Europe, the United States and elsewhere legitimately and legally. Any attempt therefore at comprehending the complexity of the African immigrant repertoire must carefully weave together and balance both sides of the trajectory.

Destination(s) and return migration

The final arrival at the destination will depend on the migratory track that is charted by the migrant. Regular migrants may arrive at their destination point in no time, with just a direct flight or a transit through one or more countries. For irregular migrants, a few may beat immigration checks and make it through direct flights to their destination. Quite typically, for others, the travel may take some days to several years to arrive at the final destination. The volume of immigrants who arrive at a particular destination country, and how long they remain there, is contingent upon the prevailing immigration policies at the time, the nature of welcome and reception by the host country, perceived opportunities available, and the real situation faced by the migrants upon arrival.

Return migration is neither a secondary nor ancillary phenomenon, but rather an integral and crucial component of much international migration.[9] Migration does not always and necessarily culminate in return and where it occurs, return may not be permanent. Instead of migration being a one-time journey, migrants and their families often subsequently move to a second or third country of destination. While a migrant has the right to return to his/her own country, return is not necessarily the final stage in the migration process. Many migrants do not envision returning to their country of origin, and a multitude of factors influence their final decision whether or not to return. Thus, the very process of return migration or the hope of a return to the home of origin depends on a number of factors.

First, the decision is often based on whether the policies and regulations of the host country are immigrant friendly and accommodating or harsh, racist and unfriendly particularly towards immigrants. Second, it also depends on whether the immigrant's hopes and plans have been fulfilled and accomplished or dashed and frustrated. In either case, return migration could be voluntary or involuntary. Migrants could be attracted to better job opportunities back home; or may have invested enough at home and wish to go back and manage their own business or investments. In other cases, the plan to return may be spontaneously induced by frustration and hopelessness in the new home, especially where attempts to improve living conditions hang in the balance, or as a result of family considerations. Migrants who fail to regularize their immigration papers commit crimes and thus forcefully removed and repatriated back to their home country or in the case of a Schengen state, to the first country of entry into the Schengen area countries.

In some cases, return could be part of a contractual arrangement, as for example in most temporary and circular labour migration schemes or in intra-corporate transfers. Furthermore, where return takes place, it may be of a permanent or temporary nature, keeping open the possibility of renewed outmigration and family reunion. Recently, innovative options such as 'virtual' return have also emerged, helping migrants to contribute to development projects in their countries of origin while remaining abroad. The IOM programme has put in place incentives such as, the Assisted Voluntary Return and Reintegration strategy[10], to support returning migrants and in enhancing the role of return migration to foster development and change.

The exile metaphor epitomized by the Back-to-Africa Movement or the American Colonization Society resonated very powerfully among African Americans. Kalu (2007: 13) asserts that the two ideologies, 'exile' and 'crossing Jordan', jostle for pre-eminence among immigrant communities. This rhetoric also finds space among new African migrants, although with a slightly different slant. The imagery of 'black exiles' in diaspora returning home to regain control of their homelands was conceptually different in the eyes and minds of new African migrants in Europe and the US. As exile is characterized by the notions of leaving and dreams of returning, many Africans in Europe and the United States clearly indicate their intention to return home at the sunset of their sojourn. Irrespective of the duration of stay in Europe, virtually all my informants express a desire to return home at some point. Although this claim of return may just be wishful thinking and a myth of ambiguity for many migrants, the mere fact of this consciousness rekindles forlorn hopes. Nevertheless, this claim of return is contingent upon a number of factors, such as improving their economic base, fulfilling expected dreams, completion of academic programmes and trainings. Much more interestingly, some reveal their status as perpetual transients claiming they would return home after 'stopping' in one or two places (countries). Figuratively, North America becomes the terminal point of migration for many African migrants in Europe.

This discourse is further strengthened at the altar of religion. It is commonplace through sermons that church leaders reify identity by articulating the biblical conceptions of diaspora and the exigencies of 'leaving' and 'return' as in Ezekiel 37 on 'the Valley of Dry Bones' and in Psalm 68: 31, 'Princes shall come out of Egypt; Ethiopia shall soon stretch out her hands unto God'. The hermeneutics of these oft-quoted narratives gives a religious twist and legitimacy to their sojourn, empowerment and hope to the sojourners. The intention to migrate, remote and immediate circumstances surrounding the actual decision to migrate, the journey itself, arrival at the temporary or final destination of migration, and the diaspora condition itself is located in spiritual locus as designed and predestined by God. Popular rhetorical phrases echoed through sermons are expressed this way:

> Do you think you are here in Germany (Europe) by accident? No, far from it! I am not interested in how and why you came here in the first place. As God's own, He has designed it that you are here at this time. Or do you think He (God) has abandoned you? No! If He has not abandoned you, make sure you do not also abandon Him (God). No matter what hardships, no matter what 'Red Seas' you are crossing or how many you have crossed

already, no matter what humiliation you are experiencing at the moment, no matter what names you are called, no matter how people stare at you as if you have just dropped from the sky, no matter what physical, emotional and psychological torture you are passing through, it is only a phase. God has brought you to Deutschland for a specific purpose. He will definitely see you through this temporary phase (exile) until you are ready to return home or even if you decide to remain here for the rest of your life ... But you owe God something. You must put all your trust in Him (God) for this to come to pass.[11]

The powerful symbol of the biblical covenant becomes a motivating concept for 'exile' and 'crossing Jordan' narratives (Kalu 2007: 12). Migrants are encouraged not to lament about their past, but to use the past to make meaning out of the present for the future. The covenant idea envisions hope and meaning for the rather hopeless and disillusioned migrants. At the same time, it is an act that would attract contractual reciprocation to make it meaningful and rewarding to migrants. A further twist to the exilic metaphor that resonates well with members is the biblical assertion that all humans are 'pilgrims' and 'foreigners' in this mundane world. Two plains of religious interpretation are canvassed. On one level, African Christians in Europe and the United States mirror themselves as 'foreigners' or 'strangers' in both mundane and spiritual terms. They are foreigners or exiles in the physical space of Europe and the United States. The cosmos is a marketplace and they are only temporary sojourners in the journey through life. Heaven is indeed home (Adogame 2000a: 3–29). In this wider theological sense, they would assert that all humans, whether Africans, Europeans or Americans, are foreigners or strangers in this world. This is one way they have attempted to critique the stringent EU immigration policies and the conscious construction of a fortress Europe. In a later chapter I shall demonstrate how the process of return migration could also lead to religious expansion and proliferation, a case in which African immigrants are not simply establishing religious communities in diaspora, but also through a kind of spiritual remittance mechanism, such communities are charting their 'routes' and 'roots' back to Africa.

The unfolding of the African diasporas

The transcultural encounter and exchange between Africa, Europe, the Americas and the Arab world has a long history that predates the fifteenth century and the era of obnoxious human trafficking. Contacts between Europe and Africa in particular were constant throughout Europe's antiquity, Middle Ages and the so-called Modern Age (Debrunner 1997). European presence and interest in Africa through these periods have been largely mixed and split along the contours of commerce, politics and religion. The imperial expansionist agenda generated new situations, circumstances and posed as a catalyst towards diaspora formation. One of the inherent consequences of these exploits was that it later created several situations that brought Africans at varied times to other continental shores including Europe and the New World, thus also resulting in the formation of enclaves and communities.

African diaspora is one theoretical construct to describe this global dispersal of indigenous African populations at different phases of world history. By employing 'Black Atlantic' Gilroy (1993) contextualizes the voluntary and involuntary migration of Africans to Europe, Latin America and North America since the Age of Discovery. The breadth of African diaspora even transcends the popular geographical fixation to Europe and the New World and includes the Mediterranean and Arab worlds as well as the cross-migration within the African shore itself. Zeleza (2002: 9) notes that

> The flow of people at the global level has lagged behind the flows of capital and commodities ... African migrations are as much a part of the complex mosaic of transnational cultural flows as they are of labour and other economic flows ... Between 1965 and 1990 Africa's migrant population grew at a faster rate than any other region in the world. The continent increased its share of international migrants from 10.6 percent to 13.1 percent ... By 1995 African countries were second only to European countries in the numbers of economically active migrants they hosted, excluding refugees and asylum seekers ... Clearly, many Africans who migrate go to other African countries.

The emergence of communities can be linked to different waves of emigration. The earliest strata aggregated young, virile Africans caught up in the offensive web of human trafficking and catapulted them involuntarily into various metropolises in Europe, the Americas, and the Mediterranean and Arab geo-spaces. The survivors of this excruciating ordeal and their descendants in the post nineteenth-century abolition scheme constituted the first African diaspora. During the entire period of the first African diaspora to America, the slave trade is estimated to have transported between 10 and 20 million Africans (Arthur 2000: 1).

Physical contact between Africa and the West increased in frequency in the nineteenth century. Decades-long agitation for overseas colonies as settlement areas, sources of raw materials, and markets for the manufactured goods preceded the colonial politics of the 1880s and the subsequent bisecting of Africa. Thus, a second coterie of African diaspora communities may be located in the wave of migrants that swelled as a consequence of the Berlin-Congo 1884-5 Conference's official partition of the African continent into spheres of artificial geographical zones of European influence, exploitation and expropriation. The colonial enterprise added its overlay of new routes in the Africa diaspora and enlarged the European presence within Africa. The interwar years (1914-1945) and their aftermath also saw a reasonable degree of demographic shift within and beyond Africa. African colonies were not only drawn into the war effort through imposed taxes, food and cash crop production, and conscription; several thousand African troops were deployed, as the colonial African army, lost their lives in the process (Akyeampong 2000: 198-200). 'France made more liberal use of its African subjects during the First World War, sending 450,000 soldiers to the war arena in Europe and a further 135,000 wartime workers to French factories'.[12] An estimated 65,000 men from North and West Africa died on active service in Europe (Akyeampong 2000: 199). And about 100,000 more Africans – most of them carriers – died in East Africa, largely from disease rather than from armaments (Roberts 1990: 16). A similar deployment of African troops was witnessed during the World War II, though this time sub-Saharan Africa was not an arena of war. About 80,000 African troops from French colonies were in France, a quarter of whom lost their lives during the German invasion in May 1940 (Davidson 1989: 63). After the collapse of France, the French army was basically an African army based in Africa and British African troops were used in northern Africa and Burma (Killingray and Rathbone 1986: 1-19).

The deployment of African servicemen in European battlefields was a temporary measure. Following demobilization at the end of the wars, the uprooted but surviving Africans commissioned as pawns in the 'European war game' returned to their homes in Africa. Others remained and charted for themselves new destinies, pathways and family relationships in the now desolate battlefields of Europe.

> Post-war reconstruction in Europe encouraged the immigration of North Africans. Gradually, African communities expanded in Europe as African immigrants gravitated to the colonial or former colonial metropoles. For instance, the number of Africans in France rose from a mere 2,000 in 1953 to 22,000 in 1963. (Akyeampong 2000: 200)

Germany's brief colonial contacts with Africa brought a few Africans to Germany. This number was augmented by black soldiers (majority African Americans) in occupied Germany. Peter Fryer (1984), Shyllon (1992) and Killingray (1994) best capture the early history of black people and Africans in Britain. Few Africans went to the United States following the abolition of slavery in the 1880s. It was estimated that only 350 Africans arrived between 1891 and 1900. From 1900 to 1950, however, during the period of colonial rule in Africa, over 31,000 Africans immigrated to the United States (Gordon 1998: 79–103). African independence translated into an enhanced positive presence of Africans in the international arena (Akyeampong 2000: 203).

An unprecedented upsurge, especially in the last decades, in the number of new African immigrants into Western Europe, North America and elsewhere heralded a new phase in the history of African diaspora (Zeleza 2002: 9–14). Remarkable changes are evident in the composition and direction of international migration, features that makes contemporary migration different from the historical African diaspora in several respects. In 1990 there were estimated to be 30 million voluntary international migrants in sub-Saharan Africa, about 3.5 per cent of the total population (Castles and Miller 2003: 139). Hitherto, African migration to Europe had followed the historical and linguistic trails of colonialism with Great Britain and France as preferred destination of migrants.

Despite Britain's massive export of migrants, its immigrant population has historically been lower than that of France. Foreigners made up 3.2 per cent of its total population between 1986 and 1990, and 3.4 per cent between 1994 and 1996. Immigrants from Western and Eastern Africa increased from 79,000 in 1984 to 127,000 in 1995 of which 69,000 were women. Between 1993 and 1996, 32,400 Africans were granted citizenship in the United Kingdom, out of a total of 173,400 citizenship grants (Zeleza 2002: 11). In the 1990s, more than half of the immigrants into France from non-European Economic Area (EEA) countries came from Africa. Similarly, in 1996, a quarter of the 109,800 foreigners who acquired French citizenship were African nationals and another quarter were Europeans (101–7).

In more recent times, African migration assumed a more diffused dimension with noticeable numbers of immigrants from several African countries flocking to countries with which they had no colonial ties, mainly in Western Europe, North America, Asia and the Arab world. For instance, Sweden, because of its liberal policy towards political refugees, became an attractive place for Eritreans, Ethiopians, Somalians and Ugandans. Persons of Ghanaian origin living in Germany between 1996 and 2003 was estimated at 44, 500, with 24,000 residents and 22,000 undocumented (Manuh 2005). An estimated 109, 382 Ghanaians, comprising 79,382 residents and 30,000 undocumented persons, live in the United Kingdom. The estimated population of Ghanaian immigrants in the United States is put at 115,572, with figures of residents and undocumented totalling 65,572 and 50,000 respectively. The estimated number of persons of Ghanaian origin in Europe and North America shows 298,049 residents and 163,500 undocumented and a total average of 461,549. Out of these estimates, Europe is home to 310,977 immigrants of Ghanaian home origin, while the United States and Canada record 150,572.[13]

African immigration has thus become marked by increasing diversification, in both the number of countries sending and receiving immigrants. The emigrants increasingly include both highly and less-educated labour migrants thus resulting in a loss of scarce manpower in their home countries. Adepoju (2010: 13) notes:

> Twelve of the thirty OECD countries – Australia, Belgium, Canada, France, Germany, Ireland, the Netherlands, Portugal, Spain, the UK and the USA – are all major recipients of Africa's skilled professionals, due largely to the colonial legacy. Between 1960 and 1987, for instance, Africa lost 30 percent of its highly-skilled nationals, mostly to Europe; between 1986 and 1990, an estimated 50 to 60 thousand middle and high-level managers emigrated as local socio-economic and political conditions deteriorated.

The mass migration of skilled workers out of Africa to the developed economies of the world is at a crisis stage. From 1960 to 1989, an estimated 70,000 to 100,000 highly skilled Africans left the continent to settle in Europe and the United States (Gordon 1998: 86). Since then, about 23,000 qualified academic staff have been emigrating each year in search of better working conditions (IOM 2003). Through a generational analysis of African scholars, Kalu made a useful differentiation between three cohorts of scholars. The first were trained overseas under the ideology of questing for the golden fleece, many returned home and trained others. The second coterie mostly undertook undergraduate programmes at home and travelled out in pursuit of graduate studies. These were more likely to stay abroad; a crop of them returned temporarily. As he aptly argued, this tendency 'was driven by limited upward mobility, economic crisis that affected remunerations and widespread political repression that constrain academic freedom' (Kalu 2007: 3). The third generation is less fortunate in the migration scheme. Suffering from stringent limitations in changing immigration policies by Western nations and lack of scholarships, they are more likely to be trained in the national universities under extremely difficult conditions, without the guidance of senior scholars, without adequate books and laboratories.

Of the estimated 4 million sub-Saharan Africans living in rich OECD countries, more than 100,000 (2.5%) are professionals. About 23,000 university graduates and 50,000 executives leave sub-Saharan Africa annually; about 40,000 of them with PhD degrees now live outside Africa. In 2002, 18 per cent of Nigerian doctors worked abroad. Ghana has lost 50 per cent of its doctors to Canada, Britain and the United States

(Adepoju 2010: 4). Three-quarters or more of Zimbabwe's doctors have left the country since the early 1990s and half of its health workers have relocated abroad since 2001. In 2005, more than 16,000 nurses and about 12,500 doctors from the region were registered to work in Britain (UKNMC 2005). Apart from the highly skilled and professionals, most African immigrants in Europe and North America were graduates and postgraduates holding first, second degrees and even PhD degrees. These qualifications do not necessarily guarantee them jobs commensurate with their qualifications in a challenging economic setting that is socially regulated and keenly contested. Against this backdrop, the majority of these graduates have to take on low-paid jobs such as cab drivers, gas station attendants, carers and domestic service operators for survival in the new, hostile economic environment.

This demographic mobility forms an integral part of the global phenomenon of international migration. Africans form a significant part of the international migration of talents. The upsurge in migration is due to rapid processes of economic, demographic, social, political, cultural and environmental change, which arise from decolonization, modernization and uneven development (Castles and Miller 2003: 152). Incessant crises and upheavals in some parts of Africa have exacerbated immigration and exodus, thus generating the economic pool of mostly able-bodied youths particularly to Western Europe and North America.[14] Zeleza (2002: 10) aptly argues that the complex maelstrom of rapidly changing international migration that African migrants, including the intellectual elites (brain drain syndrome) found themselves in has led to what he calls 'the racialization of immigrants' in the North. Immigrants become an alibi for national failings; their presence serves as both threads that tie together and threats that tear asunder the cherished but increasingly troubled marriage between nation and state. The 1990s witnessed a major increase in involuntary or forced migration and, by the middle of the decade, refugees and internally displaced persons in some countries outnumbered voluntary international migrants by a ratio of more than two to one. By 1997, there were almost 17 million forced migrants, inclusive of nearly 4 million refugees (Findlay 2001: 275–8).

This unprecedented influx of migrants from Africa and elsewhere has also formed the bedrock for an extensive reordering of European and American religious life (Garber and Walkowitz 1999). In the following chapters, I shall demonstrate how many Africans who undergo these complex forms of migration have largely carried traits of their religious and cultural identities with them. In the final section of this chapter, I will tell 'two tales of one continent' that eulogize how Africa does not simply spawn immigrants cross-nationally and internationally, but also absorbs doses of immigrants/emigrants from other continents.

Two tales of a continent: Africa as a hotbed of immigration and emigration

I have shown above how Africa, historically, has been a 'breeding ground' for immigrants, both migrants within and outside the continent. This is hardly a one-way process. Just as Africans have joined the bandwagon of international migration, so has the continent served, historically and in the contemporary era, as a haven for emigrants from Europe, Asia, the Middle East and beyond. Most emigrants into Africa have created their own geo-ethnic immigrant enclaves, their own diasporas, and some are often now referred as 'white Africans', 'settlers' or have invented national and diasporic identities for themselves and their descendants. It is indeed this multidirectionality of migrants' mobility that characterize both historical and contemporary international migration, as well as diaspora formations.

Historically, both diasporas, that is Africans sojourning outside the continent and non-Africans settlements on the continent, have made their mark in their respective 'host contexts' or rather 'new homes' economically, politically, culturally, socially and demographically. They have produced economic movers and shakers, just as political juggernauts have emerged from among their constituencies. The African diaspora, in this case epitomized by the US President Barack Obama, who rose to the highest pinnacle of leadership and governance, an unprecedented development in US sociopolitical history. A diaspora or 'settler' community could even become so pervasive, usurp and wield political and economic power as the case of the erstwhile apartheid regime in South Africa vividly illustrates. The colonial rule eased Lebanese and Indian entry into Africa and assigned them a retail role in the colonial economy. They however became an economic force to reckon with and have remained so in many West African countries till date.

Prior to the post–World War II era of decolonization, white Europeans numbering up to 10 million persons were represented in virtually all parts of the African continent, especially South Africa (British and Boer); Algeria (French); Zimbabwe, formerly Rhodesia (British and Boer); Angola (Portuguese); and Mozambique (Portuguese) to mention a few. Many of these immigrants (settlers) left following the political independence of most African countries, but a substantial remnant of the European (white) immigrants that remained forms the European diasporas in Africa. South Africa records the largest white European diaspora community (now white African settler population). Descendants of the Dutch immigrants (Afrikaners) represent the oldest European-based culture, and the largest European ethnic group in sub-Saharan Africa.

South Africa has become characterized by a complex demographic profile and political-cultural history. As of 2010, the local African ethnic groups (comprising Zulu, Xhosa, Ndebele, Pedi, Sotho, Swazi and a host others) constitutes about 79.4 per cent (39,682,600) of the entire population of 49,991,300.[15] European (Dutch, French, German, Flemish, Portuguese, Italian, British etc.) immigrants since the late seventeenth century have produced 'white' diasporic communities (called settlers and white Africans), that make up 9.2 per cent (4,584,700) of the total population. As of the census of 2001, there were 4,293,638 whites and 1,409,690 white households in South Africa. Since 2003, the number of British migrants coming to South Africa has risen by 50 per cent. By 2005, an estimated 212,000 British citizens were residing in South Africa. An estimated 20,000 British migrants moved to South Africa in 2007.[16] The so-called Coloureds, a racial admixture of settlers, indigenous peoples and slaves; and Indian/Asian diasporic communities are made up of 8.8 per cent (4,424,100) and 2.6 per cent (1,299,900) respectively.[17] With the exception of the 'Coloureds', the immigrant and diasporic population in South Africa is at least 11.5 per cent of the total population.

There were also huge enclaves of white European immigrants or settlers in Zimbabwe, Namibia, Kenya, Angola, Tanzania, Malawi and in other Southern and Eastern African countries. Afrikaners migrated in their large numbers from South Africa to Zimbabwe, Kenya, Tanzania and Angola for obvious reasons. The nineteenth century started the wave of white settlers in Zimbabwe (Arnold 2008). Dutch, British, French, Portuguese, German, Flemish, Italian, Spanish and other European immigrants in Zimbabwe make up the white Africans of European ancestry or people of European descent living in Zimbabwe. More than half of white Zimbabweans, primarily of British origin, arrived in Zimbabwe after World War II. Afrikaners from South Africa and other European minorities, including Portuguese from Mozambique, also are present. Until the mid-1970s, there were about 1,000 white immigrants per year, but from 1976 to 1985, a steady emigration resulted in a loss of more than 150,000, leaving about 100,000 in 1992. Renewed white emigration in the late 1990s and early 2000s reduced the white population to less than 50,000.[18] These settlers dominated Zimbabwe politically and economically from the turn of the twentieth century until 1980.

Afrikaners and British diaspora communities (settlers) numbering over 30,000 live in Kenya's fertile Rift Valley. There were also other European (mostly British) diasporic settlements in Malawi and Zambia. At the brink of the country's independence in 1964, there were roughly 70,000 Europeans (mostly British) in Zambia (known as Northern Rhodesia before independence), most of whom worked in the Copperbelt region. This population made up roughly 2.3 per cent of the 3 million inhabitants at the time.[19] In 2010, the country's total population has increased tremendously and is now estimated at 13.2 million. The historical connection between Germany and Namibia, the latter an erstwhile German territory until World War I era, has continued to result in significant German immigration to present day Namibia (Sparks 1992; Katjavivi 1988). Besides, a huge Afrikaner population, from about 80,000 to 150,000, are estimated to live in Namibia. These indices above shows that the European diasporas in Africa can indeed be contrasted with the African Diasporas in Europe and the United States in a variety of ways, including the demography, civic role, political influence, their cultural socioeconomic impacts on the respective host communities.

Beside the European diasporas, there are also huge numbers of Arab (Lebanese, Syrian); Asian (Indian, Chinese) diasporas in different parts of Africa. The Lebanese, dubbed as 'colonial sidekicks', represent an important case study of Africa as a receiving area for non-African diasporas; Asians in East and South Africa are another example (Akyeampong 2000). Akyeampong (2000: 200–1) remarks that

> Just as colonial rule facilitated the movement of Africans within the wider empire, so it underpinned the entry of new, foreign commercial classes into Africa ... though not present in huge communities, the Lebanese were present in West Africa in numbers that exceeded the tiny European colonial presence. Unlike colonial officers, who came to Africa on 'tours of duty', Lebanese traders often came to settle, established families, and created Lebanese social networks.

The Lebanese diaspora in West Africa spread across Senegal, Sierra Leone, Ghana, Côte d'Ivoire and Nigeria (see also Leighton 1979; van der Laan 1975; Falola 1990: 523–53; Bierwirth 1999: 79–99). In the late 1980s, reportedly 60,000 to 120,000 Lebanese and Syrians lived in Côte d'Ivoire, although some observers gave a figure as high as 300,000.[20] The Lebanese business elite charted their path through the colonial and post-independent West Africa economies and successfully carved a niche for themselves. As Akyeampong (2000: 201)puts it: 'Through frugality, low-overhead costs by using the family as the unit of trade, enormous personal sacrifice, and shrewd business practices, the Lebanese in West Africa gradually emerged as a significant entrepreneurial class'. Owing to the privileged position that Lebanese and Indians enjoyed during the colonial dispensation, as middlemen and retail link between European wholesalers and African consumers; and their entrenched economic interests, they were usually on a collision course with local African merchants. Coupled with their unwillingness to assimilate culturally, Lebanese diasporas in Africa became victims of systematic discrimination and expropriation by several African governments (201). This was particularly so for the Indian diaspora as epitomized by the expulsion of Asians from

Uganda by President Idi Amin Dada in 1972 (Twaddle 1975). Africa has more than 3 million people belonging to the Indian (South Asian) diaspora. In fact, 8 per cent of the global Indian Diaspora is located in Africa. It is spread across all regions of Africa-Anglophone, Francophone, Lusophone, Arab Africa and Oceania (Dubey 2010; Oonk 2007). Indian diaspora communities on the African continent did not only exist in South Africa[21] but spread over 30 countries[22], particularly dominantly in East Africa (Kenya, Tanzania, Zanzibar and Uganda) besides South Africa.

I shall now turn attention to contextualizing the local scene, in this case, Ghana and Nigeria, from which most migrants nurture and embark on the journey to eldorado. This is expedient not only for the mere fact that the journey starts here, but more importantly, situating their economic, political, sociocultural histories makes the varied intentionalities of migration much more intelligible.

3

Situating the local scene(s)

West African migration and political economies

The local setting and context of migration in and out of Nigeria and Ghana is best captured within the wider pattern of migration in West Africa. Adepoju (2005) best encapsulates how the type, volume and direction of international migration in the West African sub-region are closely related to complex historical and political experiences and to economic structures. He demonstrates how the complementary economies of these countries, colonial histories, and sociocultural affinity amongst its peoples have made intra-regional migration inevitable. As Adepoju (2005: 26) notes:

> Migration between West African countries initially became identified with population movement aimed at restoring ecological balance and of individuals in search of food, better shelter and greater security, especially during the period of internecine warfare in the nineteenth century. In the pre-colonial era, movements now regarded as international migration, occurred over a wide area, restricted only by inter-ethnic warfare and fears of raids and slaving ... Commercial migration connected with trade also featured during this period, as in the colonial period.

The impact of colonial strategies is boldly imprinted on the migration circuit. Colonial rule strongly influenced the form and nature, and thereby the volume, motivations, sex, occupational and skill composition of migration (25). The colonial era invigorated a new framework for large-scale migration, deriving from the labour requirements for plantations, mines and public administration, beyond local supply. While colonial rule was seen to have altered both the causes and nature of migrations and reinforcing the linkages between internal and international migrations, the consolidation of boundaries at independence in the 1960s minimally hindered cross-border migrations; it ushered in an era of restrictions on so-called international migration (27–9).

Prior to the era in which African countries attained independence from imperial regimes, Africa was marginally implicated in both World Wars, which saw the conscription and deployment of able-bodied men to the war zones in Europe, Africa and elsewhere. The wars had dire economic consequences, strategic implications, and resulted in serious loss of manpower in Africa. Post-war reconstructions in Europe also served as a magnet for African immigration to the different colonial metropoles. The interwar and the post-war period witnessed the involuntary and voluntary movement of Africans across continental frontiers. While many returned home after both wars, others made new homes in the erstwhile war arenas. The late 1950s and early 1960s saw the steady increase of African presence in international landscapes following the brokering of political independence by several African countries.

Ghana was one of the first to become independent, attaining her political independence in 1957. Nigeria followed and procured her independence in 1960. The proliferation of independent African nations coincided with the establishment of diplomatic embassies in far-flung countries in Europe, the Americas and Asia. The demography of Africans swelled owing to the drafting of African diplomats and personnel. The urgency to produce qualified personnel to serve the budding African nation-states also stimulated intellectual appetites and the quest for higher education in citadels of learning abroad. Most Ghanaians and Nigerians who acquired higher education in Western countries returned home and formed the arrowheads of nation-building in their countries. The euphoria that visited this era of independent rule soon dimmed in the face of daunting local-global economic and political realities. Some national enthusiasts and their offspring would have to return to Europe and North America later on to circumvent the social-political uncertainty that loomed in their home countries.

Not too long after political independence, the economic nemesis occasioned by an unprecedented slump in tropical cash crop products in the world market, from the late 1950s, caught up with African countries such as Ghana and Nigeria, resulting in continual economic problems that were to characterize their political economies subsequently. Prior to independence, the Gold Coast's (now Ghana's) booming cocoa economy experienced economic depression between 1930 and 1940 with the steep fall in world cocoa prices. The country witnessed a sharp economic decline particularly between 1957 and 1966. As Akyeampong (2000: 205) notes, a steady decline from about 1958 in the world price of cocoa, Ghana's leading export, put an effective break on development projects.

Nigeria's economy in the first decade of its corporate existence was essentially a cash crop one with groundnut, cocoa and rubber serving as its major export earnings. The uninformed switch from an agriculture-based economy, with the sudden discovery of huge deposits of mineral resources soon shot her into international limelight as petroleum products became over 90 per cent of its export income. Thus, Nigeria witnessed an oil boom barely two decades after its inception, leading its then head of state, Yakubu Gowon, to remark that, 'The problem of Nigeria is not money but how to spend it.' The lackadaisical display of the national wealth became visible in social and political spheres. However, this period of relative affluence seems to have been short-lived with the decline in world oil prices, a development that had devastating consequences on national wealth. This debacle, coupled with sharp practices of increasingly corrupt elites, the insensitivity and lack of vision of successive military and civilian regimes, and their collaboration with foreign multinationals, led to an unprecedented nosedive in national standards of living. This precarious socio-economic state in Nigeria attracted world financial institutions (notably, the IMF). By recommending 'deregulation exercises', 'austerity measures' and 'structural adjustment programmes' as the only panacea for economic resurrection, these financial giants appeared to have trapped the country into an unending subservience with varied cosmetic loans and conditionalities. The gross misappropriation of these loans, coupled with the vicious insensitivity of the Nigerian leadership further helped to strangle and impoverish its citizens.

The Nigerian state witnessed tremendous socio-economic crises and political upheavals, particularly in the 1980s and 1990s. Reeling from the harsh realities of economic deregulation and the politics of subsidies, some Nigerians sought for new ways to escape this unprecedented malaise. One option that opened for some was to migrate elsewhere to less crisis-ridden contexts. Nigerians left the country in their droves from the late 1980s and early 1990s. Others escaped from political reprehension from draconian military dictatorships or bolted away from an oppressive atmosphere of economic hopelessness and social insecurity.

Ghana's political history through four republics was also characterized by stability or turbulence via civilian and military regimes (Awoonor 1990). Ghana's economic history post-independence has been even more turbulent than its political vicissitudes in that period (Jeffries 1989). The extensive expansionist and reconstruction programmes (7-Year Development Plan) introduced from January 1964 by Kwame Nkrumah, the first Ghanaian prime minister, was followed by significant improvements of infrastructure and social services, but also eventually resulted in an economic backlash owing partly to financial mismanagement. The post-Nkrumah governments inherited monumental economic problems as well as huge external debts. Rawlings accession to the World Bank and IMF conditionalities, the subsequent failure of two major economic reconstruction programmes, inflation, corruption and misappropriation of public funds pushed the country further into the economic abyss. The economic decline reached its apogee in the early 1980s, thus earning her a place in the IMF and World Bank's classified group of Highly Indebted Poor Countries (HIPC). Through the largesse from these institutions, Ghana started to enjoy cosmetic debt relief from the IMF and World Bank.

However, since the late 1990s, both African countries can be said to have entered into a new, gradual phase of economic reconstruction and political rehabilitation. The political climate has been relatively stable since then, in spite of lingering economic problems. The recent democratic dispensation is perceived by some commentators as taking giant strides in combating corruption and instigating a congenial sociopolitical environment for economic development, although a certain public scepticism is still being entertained on whether these policies of economic redress have had significant trickle-down effect on the masses.

Ghana and Nigeria share affinities in terms of political and socio-economic configurations. First, they experienced military coups in 1966 against the backdrop of economic stagnation and political jingoism. Due to these circumstances, waves of migrants and refugees traversed within African countries and out of Africa to Europe, North America and Asia. Second, Nigeria and Ghana generate large reservoirs of potential migrants who have a high propensity to migrate. Prior to the 1960s, Ghana took centre stage as a major recipient of immigrants from the West African sub-region. As Adepoju (2005: 32) notes, 'yet, until the 1960s, Ghana's high per capita income made it the "gold coast" for thousands of immigrants from Togo, Nigeria and Burkina Faso'. The case of Nigerian migrants in Ghana, prior to 1969, illustrates how, what began as labour migration to the cocoa growing and forest areas of Ghana later became commercial migration in diamond mining, trading and commerce (27).

In several West African countries, expulsions and deportations came to characterize national policies regulating the tide of immigration in the face of an economic nosedive. Ghana expelled non-nationals including Nigerians in 1969. The labour shortages that followed the expulsion of aliens adversely affected Ghana's cocoa industry and the economy in general. Production was at low ebb and cocoa pricing plummeted drastically. Currency devaluation and scarcity of raw materials shut the gates of several factories, thus constraining thousands of Ghanaians to look elsewhere for the golden fleece. 'In the late 1970s, Nigeria was the subregion's *Eldorado* for migrants' (31).

By 1975, the quest for oil-led expansion of road and building construction, infrastructure, education and allied sectors which attracted workers, both skilled and unskilled, from various West African countries heightened Nigeria's status as an important country of immigration. Most immigrants came from Ghana, Togo and Benin. They entered the country through both official and unofficial routes and by 1982, there were an estimated 2.5 million immigrants from West Africa living in Nigeria (30). In 1983, Ghanaians constituted 81 per cent of ECOWAS nationals legally resident in Nigeria (31). The huge emigration of Ghanaians from the late 1970s to Nigeria marked a major turning point in Ghanaian migration history. Ghanaians of various social classes, skilled and unskilled thronged to Nigeria for a 'better life'.

The economic tide in Nigeria turned in the early 1980s. Deteriorating living conditions, devalued national currency, employment embargo and hyperinflation partly resulted in Nigeria's revocation of Articles 4 and 27 of the Protocol on Free Movement of Persons in early 1983 and in mid-1985. This led to an unprecedented government expulsion of between 0.9 and 1.3 million illegal aliens, mostly Ghanaians. In June 1985, an additional 0.2 million illegal aliens were sent packing as the economic crisis deepened and unemployment intensified (Adepoju 2005: 32). This decision was perceived as a reprisal, in view of the earlier expulsion of Nigerian aliens from Ghana in 1969. This sudden marching order opened new avenues of emigration for Ghanaians afterwards. Some took advantage of the free movement within the ECOWAS countries, while a considerable number moved overseas to Europe, North America and Asia.

In this second wave of emigration, Ghanaians seemed to have paved the way for Nigerians who joined the bandwagon in their emigration to Western countries. By the mid-1980s the effects of a failing economy and one characterized by sociopolitical crisis has started to hit hard on Nigerians. Until the early 1980s, few Nigerian professionals saw emigration as a rewarding option because their working conditions were attractive and internationally competitive. At the exchange rate of one Naira to US$1.8 in June 1980, salaries were comparable with prevailing levels in low-income developed countries (Adepoju 2005: 33). The adverse economic conditions and dire political uncertainty funnelled large-scale emigration of both skilled and unskilled workers. Nigerian and Ghanaian professionals, of both genders, thronged to other African countries and far-flung countries in Europe, North America, Asia and the Gulf States. The apogee of the exodus necessitated the inauguration by the Nigerian government of a Presidential Task Force on Brain Drain to study the causes and consequences of the outflow and advice the government (34).

Two trends are immediately evident here. The earlier wave of emigration from Nigeria and Ghana in the immediate post-independence era (early 1960s and early 1970s) was dominated by diplomats, professionals and students seeking higher education. This emigration was transient, as many returned home to take up lucrative jobs and positions in the civil service and industries; joined the political elite, or took pioneering jobs at burgeoning ivory towers. In fact, during the era of oil boom, only a few Nigerians left their shores to settle elsewhere. This illusion of a Nigerian *El Dorado* was however short-lived, with the 1980s and 1990s witnessing economic and sociopolitical upheavals. The pattern of emigration became more complex as both skilled and unskilled joined the exodus.

Suffice it to mention that within these undulating periods of Nigeria and Ghana's political-economic mutation, the texture of Christianity also experienced considerable change and transformation. Main line churches were overshadowed in terms of their public visibility by African indigenous churches and new Pentecostal/charismatic waves.

Nigeria and Ghana began, in the 1980s, to experience an unprecedented explosion of Pentecostal/charismatic Christianities to the extent that it now constitutes one of their export commodities, albeit a spiritual one. Many Nigerian and Ghanaian Christians who migrated to other parts of Africa and beyond took their faiths with them. 'Associational life in the diaspora, in the form of churches and ethnic associations, provides an important social environment for survival and nurture of migrants abroad' (Akyeampong 2000: 208). Nigeria and Ghana can boast of producing the largest African immigrant spiritual supermarkets in Europe and North America. Their impact was also hugely felt in Western, Eastern, Central and Southern Africa. I shall turn to this dynamic in later chapters. The final section of this chapter will provide an overview of the immigration laws and policies that shape the demographic and religious influxes of Africans in Europe and North America.

US/EU changing immigration laws, policies and strategies

Immigration policies of destination countries, in this case, the United States and European Union, are hardly static. Immigration strategies mutate depending on: the prevailing sociopolitical problems; national security questions; and most importantly, economic needs and emergencies, especially the quest for sustained highly skilled manpower from foreign countries to complement an ageing workforce. As refugees are integral to international migration processes, legal rules on refugees constitute a significant part in the regulation of international migration. This section briefly explores the fluctuating US and EU immigration policies with a view to understanding how this is shaping the ebbs and flows of African immigration, particularly in the last decades. It is within these ecologies of migration that we better understand the relevance and resilience of religion within African immigrant and diaspora communities.

The United States of America

In the case of the US laws, policies and strategies, Arthur (2000: 7) aptly notes that 'for past and present immigrants, the laws regarding entry to and settlement in the United States are a continuum of qualitative and quantitative restrictions'. The immigration of Africans to the United States has been facilitated, in part, by the 1965 Immigration Act, the 1980 changes in laws related to refugees, the 1986 Immigration Reform and Control Act (IRCA), and the 1990 Immigration Act (7). The US Immigration and Nationality Act (INA), was created in 1952. Prior to this, a variety of statutes governed immigration law. The McCarran-Walter Bill of 1952, Public Law No. 82–414, collected and codified many existing provisions and reorganized the structure of immigration law. Though amended many times over the years, the Act remains the basic body of immigration law.[1] According to Immigration and Naturalization Service (INS), during the 1960s, the African immigrants comprised about 1 per cent of all immigrants who were legally admitted to the United States. The liberalized provisions in the Immigration Reform Act of 1965, coupled with prevailing economic, social and political exigencies have exacerbated the pace of immigration to the United States, particularly in the last few decades. It opened up the country to a massive influx of newcomers from Latin America, Asia and Africa.[2] By the end of the 1970s, the African immigrant's share of the total immigrant population increased to 2 per cent. In the 1980s and 1990s, they formed 3 per cent of those legally admitted (Arthur 2000: 2).

In 2009, there were 307 million people living in the United States, including 38.5 million who were foreign born, representing 1 in 8 residents. Between 2000 and 2009, the foreign-born population increased by 7.4 million persons, or by about 24 per cent.

Over half (53%) of all those foreign born were from Latin America; 28 per cent from Asia; the foreign born from Europe represented 13 per cent. About 4 per cent of the foreign born were from Africa, followed by about 3 per cent from other regions, including Oceania and Northern America.[3] In three states, the foreign born from Africa represented more than 15 per cent of the foreign-born population: North Dakota (22%), Minnesota (18%), and Maryland (16%). In 2009, the US foreign-born population total from Africa stood at 1,492,785, higher than Northern America (822,377) and Oceania (206,795) respectively.[4] Immigration from Africa shows a pattern similar to the foreign born from Latin America, albeit on a smaller scale. The non-immigrant admissions (1–94 only) to the United States from Africa rose from 405,951 in 2001 to 419,541 in 2010. The number of Ghanaians admitted increased slightly from 19,494 in 2001 to 20,996 in 2010; while that of Nigerians was far higher, with 39,108 recorded in 2001. There was a remarkable rise to 83,695 in 2010.[5]

In 2010, the total number of immigrant visas and non-immigrant visas issued for the African region was 39,181 and 205,365 respectively.[6] Out of these figures, 4,879 Ghanaians were issued immigrant visas, while Nigerians received 8,375. Ghanaians and Nigerians were issued 12,057 and 34,264 non-immigrant visas respectively. The total number of non-immigrant visas issued in Africa by nationality in the fiscal year 2001 of 348,935 shows a slight drop (303,851) in 2010.[7] The immigrant visas issued in the fiscal period of 2001–10 is 19,335 and a substantial rise to 39,191 in 2010.[8] While non-immigrant visas for Nigeria rose from 42,222 in 2001 to 64,279 in 2010, in the case of Ghana, it dropped from 19,995 in 2001 to 13,734 in 2010. This was again different in the case of immigrant visas, with Ghana recording an increase from, 2,201 in 2001 to 4,879 in 2010, and Nigeria recording 5,059 in 2001 and 8,375 in 2010. As we have noted earlier, these figures are only official figures which exclude irregular migrants, a number which is believed to be higher than official figures.

New African immigrants have joined in this immigration flow process through chain migration, family reunion, labour drives and employment preferences, refugees or asylees. As Arthur (2000: 2) notes, 'For many of the African immigrants, the journey to the US involves a transnational migratory pattern.' In a sense, the United States becomes the final destination point that many transients in Europe and Asia long for and work towards. Although immigration to the United States from Africa has increased in recent years, Africa nevertheless accounts for a relatively small percentage of immigrants to the United States.

A new twist has been witnessed with the establishment of the Green Card through the Diversity Immigrant Visa Program in the Immigration Act of 1996.

The Diversity Lottery is conducted under the terms of section 203(c) of the INA and makes available 50,000 permanent resident visas each fiscal year to persons from countries with low rates of immigration to the United States.[9] Although most immigrants come to live permanently in the United States through a family member's sponsorship, employment or a job offer, refugee or asylee status, there are many other ways to get a green card (permanent residence). This programme that allocates visas to countries with a low rate of immigration has attracted considerable interest from African countries. For instance, in 1995, Africa saw an increase of 153 per cent in issued US immigrant visas of 28,514 visas, a direct result of many African countries qualifying in the Diversity Visa category.[10] Of the African countries, Ghana and Nigeria top the list of individual applicants in any given year. In 2010, Africa again tops the list of countries, with the highest number of applications from Ghana at 8,752, followed by Nigeria at 6,006. In 2011, 6,002 and 6,000 applicants were registered from Ghana and Nigeria. Applicants registered for the DV-2012 programme were selected at random from 14,768,658 qualified entries (19,672,268 with derivatives) received during the 30-day application period that ran from October to November 2010.[11] The statistical breakdown by foreign-state chargeability of those registered for the DV-2012 program indicates the winning allocations as follows: Africa (50%); Europe (30.98%); Asia (15%); South and Central America, and the Caribbean (2.00%); Oceania (2.00%); and North America (0.02%). The country with the overall highest number of winners was Nigeria, followed by Ghana. This initiative aimed at further lineal diversification of the American population, although hardly a 'Father-Christmas gift' to eligible applicants, yet it has served to transform the demography of new African immigrants.

Zeleza (2002: 13) vividly demonstrates how the dynamics and directions of global mobility and African participation in international migration, particularly in Western Europe and North America, has become more pronounced, notwithstanding the imposition of stringent immigration controls by these countries. The adoption of restrictive immigration policies and the regional policy harmonization through the North American Free Trade Agreement (NAFTA) has partially impeded the flow of legal immigration and asylum flows, but has also indirectly transformed illegal immigration. The INS estimated that the total unauthorized immigrant population residing in the United States in January 2000 was 7 million. As of October 2003, there were about 8 million illegal aliens in the United States, assuming a continuation of the average 350,000 annual net increase that occurred during the 1990s.[12] Africans have benefited from the reconfiguration of US policies on refugees. The majority of Africa's refugees and asylum seekers are from Ethiopia, Somalia, Sudan, Eritrea, Ghana and Liberia (Arthur 2000: 9).

Generally, ample indicators point to the fact that Africans have contributed in no small measure to the American immigration quilt. Arthur (2000: vii) remarks that

> the cultural polyphony of Africans has become a noticeable aspect of the urban landscape of major metropolitan centres across the United States ... Largely invisible and unknown to many Americans, these Africans are becoming some of the continent's most educated and dynamic people.

Gordon (1998: 79–103) reveals that Nigerians alone now constitute 17 per cent of the African immigrant population in the United States.

The European Union

In 1958 France, Germany, Italy, Belgium, the Netherlands and Luxembourg joined to form the European Economic Community (EEC), and later a stronger economic network, the European Community (EC) in 1967. During the formative years of the EU, in the 1950s and 1960s, immigrants were primarily an extra workforce in most Western European countries. At that time, the economic situation and the labour market were in dire need of a cheap, flexible workforce that did not exist domestically. By the late 1960s and 1970s, immigration was increasingly becoming a subject of public concern, thus marking a radical shift from the permissive immigration policy to a control-oriented, restrictive policy. Restrained immigration was beginning to take root all over Western Europe at the end of 1973, when labour recruiting was halted abruptly in the face of increasing social tensions and fear of economic recession. In fact, the fortressization of European immigration policy is linked to the economic recession. In 1973, Great Britain, Ireland and Denmark joined the EC, and consequently its membership continued to enlarge.

A significant Europeanization of migration policy took off in the 1980s, when policy coordination became institutionalized in European interstate cooperation, the European Union. Since 1993, with the ratification of the Treaty of Maastricht, the European Community became the European Union. The Schengen Accord came into being on March 16, 1995 for seven countries: Belgium, France, Germany, Luxembourg, the Netherlands, Portugal and Spain. It was a definite attempt by these European states towards harmonizing their immigration procedures and regulating flows of people. The European Union set out the elements for a common immigration policy at the 1999 European Council in Tampere. Its adoption was confirmed by The Hague programme in 2004. In the last three decades, EU member states moved towards further cooperation at the supranational level and introduced increasing numbers of regulations at the EU level on migration related matters.

The Europeanization of migration laws and policies is tied to wider social, political, economic and strategic dynamics. Thus, the European integration process is implicated in the development of a restrictive migration and the social construction of migration into a security question (Huysmans 2000).

Africa appears to be the continent that matters most to EU policymakers working on migration. The prevailing perspective of the European Union concerning African migration is still focused mainly on security and prevention. The politicization of immigration has attained an alarming proportion in which immigrants and asylum seekers are portrayed as a challenge to the protection of national identity and welfare provisions. An important focus of the European Commission and of European Council policies has been to counter the entry of illegal migrants through the southern and eastern borders of the European Union. The security shift in EU migration policy contradicts the so-called global approach to migration. Also witnessed is the externalization of border controls, in which countries close to European coastlines (Morocco, Algeria, Tunisia, Libya and Turkey) have been encouraged to cooperate on specific security issues, including border management and readmission agreements. The adoption of uniform, rigid immigration laws by the European Union has turned the coasts of southern Italy and Spain into important points of entry into continental Europe. The influx has not abated in the face of the securitization of migration and externalization of border controls. One consequence is that it is increasing transforming Europe into a fortress.

The harmonization of EU immigration laws, policies and strategies has not been an entirely easy process. It is in fact a process that is still emerging, often laden with goodies, but amid tensions, contradictions and disagreements. Some European countries saw themselves historically as traditional immigrant countries, while others did not. The fact that not all EU countries such as the United Kingdom were part of the Schengen Treaty is another case in point. In spite of noticeable differences in immigration policies, what seems to be a common denominator is the fact that virtually all European countries and even the United States are undergoing unprecedented economic problems. This uncertainty no doubt has implications for immigrants and the migratory process. Here, I shall briefly contrast some EU countries, such as Germany and the United Kingdom, to show how immigration laws and strategies respond to their respective economies.

Germany

Germany with a self-acclaimed leitmotif as a 'non-immigrant country' started to experience a growing transformation and systematic diversification of its landscape since it began in post-World War II to open some windows to immigrants. The second half of the 1950s witnessed the inflow of immigrants with non-German ancestry. The quest for 'guest workers' led Germany to sign bilateral recruitment pacts with Italy (1955), Spain, Greece, Turkey (1960), Portugal (1964) and Yugoslavia (1968). From the early 1960s, Germany consciously recruited Turkish migrants as *Gastarbeiter* (guest workers), originally as a temporary measure, to cushion the remarkable deficits of her labour supply force generated by varied economic and demographic considerations. Turkey became the third country to sign such a treaty with West Germany, under which the Federal Labour Office was allowed to recruit temporary labour for work in German industries. This initial, transient migrant population translated over time into long-term/permanent communities, partly reinforced by reuniting families labour drives, asylum seeking, and chain migration. Today, Turks constitute the single largest non-national ethnic group in Germany, forming about 29 per cent of the total foreign nationals in Germany in 1997. By 1999, Turkish immigrants comprised 2,053.564 out of the total population of 7,343.591 that make up the foreign nationals in Germany.[13] The number of Turkish immigrants dropped in 2010 to 1,629,480 (24.1%).[14] Other larger national groups of foreigners derive from the European Union and East European States that came out from the former Soviet Union.

At the end of 1999, official records place the figures of foreign nationals at 7, 344,000 translating into approximately 9 per cent of the German population of 82, 037,011. A decade later, in 2009, the total foreign population fell further down to 7,130,919 (8.7%) of a total population of 81,802,257.[15] The total population of foreign nationals in Germany has dropped markedly in 2010 to 6,753,621.[16] Of this figure, 55.5 per cent comes from the 27 EU-countries (excluding Germany) and other Central, North, South and East Europe countries. These conservative official figures represent the legal immigrants but exclude the hundreds of thousands of asylum seekers, refugees and undocumented migrants that live in Germany. The German States with the highest foreign population are Nordrhein-Westfalen (1,868,770), Baden-Wuerttenberg (1,263,975) and Bayern (1,164,027). In 2008, there was a total of 682,146 arrivals as compared to 737,889 departures.[17] The difference of 55,743 is an indication of a drop in migrants' inflow into Germany.

The steady decrease in the inflow of migrants parallel Germany's population, which has witnessed decline since 2003. In July 2004, a new immigration law came into force, aimed at coping with certain issues: first, the integration of immigrants; second, the management of asylum; and the recruitment of foreigners to fill out the country's thinning domestic workforce (Benneh 2005: 94).

Most of the Africans that now constitute the African immigrant community in Germany seldom benefited from formal German 'guest worker' recruitment treaties and strategies with nations such as Turkey. Growing African migration into Germany particularly from the 1970s and 1980s had not been largely linked with any colonial ties, as Germany, unlike France and Britain, was not a significant shareholder in terms of colonial appropriation and expropriation. In fact, Germany was stripped off her few colonial holdings at the apogee of World War II. In spite of the general limitations and harsh immigration policies, which came to surround the entry of primary migrants to Germany, many nevertheless took advantage of a booming economy especially in the 1980s by joining in the ranks of highly skilled and unskilled migrants who moved over to greener pastures. Others have come to Germany on a temporary basis as scholars and students seeking higher education, personnel of the diplomatic corps, businessmen, and on grounds of reuniting families. The political and economic crises that characterize some burgeoning African democracies have also acted as a 'push-force' resulting in refugees, asylum seekers. To this complex mix of voluntary/involuntary migrants, I add the lucrative interracial and 'economics-driven' marriages of convenience. It is these varied, complex hues of migrants that now gradually populate the African community in Germany.

African immigrants form part of the minority groupings of foreign nationals with a population of 300, 611, representing only 4.1 per cent of the total foreign nationals and 0.4 per cent of the total population in Germany in 1999.[18] In 1999, the largest group of African nationals was Moroccans (81,450) followed by Tunisians (24,260) and Ghanaians (22,602). Others are Algerians (17,186), Ethiopians (16,470), Democratic Republic of Congo (16,090), Nigerians (15,351), Egyptians (13,811), Togolese (11,513) and other lesser groups from Somalia, Kenya, Cameroon, Tanzania, Liberia and so on.[19] About a decade later, in 2009, the number dropped markedly to 268,410. In 2010, the number of African immigrants stood at 271,431 forming 4.0 per cent of the total migrant population.[20] The largest number of West African nationals in Germany are from Ghana, Nigeria and Cameroon. In 2008, the number of Ghanaian-born nationals in Germany stood at 21,377, representing 0.3 per cent of the total German population. In 2009, it further decreased to 20,893 (7.8% of the total foreign nationals from Africa). Nigerian-born nationals stood at 17,903 (6.7% of the total foreign nationals from Africa.[21] Foreigners constitute a very small percentage of the population in the Federal States of the former East Germany. In the former Federal States of West Germany, more than twice as many foreigners are to be found in large conurbation areas than in rural areas, and almost three times as many in urban centres.

The United Kingdom

The description of the United Kingdom as a 'traditional immigrant country' is linked to its long history of immigration. The enactment of the British Nationality Act, 1948, marked a critical watershed event in the sociopolitical history of Britain and the erstwhile Empire. The legislation created a legal status, namely, 'Citizenship of the UK and Colonies', that embraced Britons and 'colonial' subjects under a single definition of British citizenship, while at the same time reinforcing their right to enter the United Kingdom. 'British subjects' and 'Commonwealth immigrants' could swim under a shallow euphoric current as 'citizens'. They could enter the United Kingdom relatively unrestrained, without visas. Consequently, the next decade and half following the legislation witnessed the entry of about half a million non-white 'British subjects' into the United Kingdom. The first post-war new Commonwealth immigrants (500 Jamaicans) arrived in London on 22 June 1948. Their arrival was unexpected (Hansen 1999: 90). The Labour government viewed these relocations and subsequent arrivals with great trepidation, and was in fact poised to discourage indiscriminate influxes. The Colonial Office partly responded by instructing colonial governments to use informal methods to discourage immigration. Ironically, this involved warning prospective immigrants of difficulties they would face finding accommodation and employment in the United Kingdom and withholding passports from those who lacked the funds for the passage or who were deemed unsuitable for regular employment.

As Hansen (1999: 94) indicated, 'The implications of the 1948 decision did not manifest themselves until the 1950s, the most obvious of these was the fact that those arriving from the colonies and independent Commonwealth countries landed in the UK as citizens.' Irrespective of the hostility and constraints that visited the legislation, the 1948 Act assumed a legal wellspring and constitutional revolution that transformed Britain into a visibly multi-ethnic society. Thus, Hansen concluded,

> the first wave of primary immigration (immigrants with no familial connections to the UK) led quasi-automatically to successive waves of secondary immigration (spouses and dependants joining their family in the UK). The BNA was the formal mechanism that legitimated the transformation into a multi-racial society, a development that has had inestimable impact on British society and politics. (1999: 95)

The Nottingham and Notting Hill riots in 1958 tilted national opinion decisively against immigration from the Commonwealth countries, particularly against non-white immigrants.

The Commonwealth Immigrants Bill of 1962 and the Immigration Acts of 1968 and 1971 restricted the entry of colonial subjects, including those from Africa.

> The significance of this legislation was heightened since for the first time, immigration policy was geared towards the distinction between the rights of the native-born population and those who had British-issued passports, and the rights of those who held passports issued by Commonwealth nations. These distinctions were further crystallized in 1965 with new voucher schemes that institutionalized the systematic and tight control of Asian, African, and West Indian migration. (Benneh 2005: 93)

However, by the time the Conservative government took concrete steps legislating to control migration influx in 1962, approximately 500,000 new Commonwealth immigrants had entered the United Kingdom, the majority from India and Pakistan. These individuals, and their spouses and dependants who joined them in the 1960s and 1970s, constitute the bulk of the UK's approximately 2.6 million members of ethnic minorities (Jones 1993: 12). In actual fact, the uniqueness of Britain's post-war migration experience, when compared with other EU countries, was one marked by the vast majority of UK's immigrants becoming citizens following the 1948 legislation. Thus, the politics of citizenship in the 1940s represents the spark that ignited the politicization of immigration, the criminalization of immigrants, and the subsequent vexing debates that have continued to shape the fluid nature, meaning and language of citizenship and nationality in contemporary Britain. The United Kingdom entered the EEC in 1972 and thus joined in the collective harmonization of EU immigration laws and policies. In 1985, stricter immigration policies were enacted to narrow immigration by limiting the residency rights exclusively to holders of British citizenship. Historical trends in terms of UK immigration policy exemplify consistency in narrowing the options for immigration.

The actual current population of Africans living in the United Kingdom is a matter of conjecture. Census and Home Office data suggests that the Nigerian, Ghanaian, Ugandan and Somalian and Sierra Leonean communities are the five largest in England, and perhaps in the United Kingdom. The 1991 census[22] recorded 202,842 people (0.4% of the population) in England who identified themselves as black African. People born in Nigeria (38,980), Ghana (28,909), Uganda (8,468) and Sierra Leone (5,161) accounted for 40.2 per cent of people describing themselves as black African during the 1991 census. A further 36.8 per cent of people describing themselves as black African were born in the United Kingdom. The Home Office data on the numbers of people entering the United Kingdom between 1992 and 1997 suggests that the population of black Africans may be much larger.

According to the estimates based on the 1991 census and taking into account Home Office entry figures for 1992 to 1997, people from Nigeria (and children of people from Nigeria) make up about a third of the black African population in England. Those from Ghana, as the second largest black African group in England, make up about another fifth (21%). These two West African communities account for about half of black Africans in the United Kingdom. Ugandans make up 7 per cent, Somalians 6 per cent, Sierra Leone 4 per cent, while the remaining 29 per cent of the black African population is made up of more than 20 other African nationalities, including North Africans (McMunn, Brookes, Nazroo 1999; Storkey 1997). While the majority of British black Africans are traditionally West African in origin, increased political instability since the 1970s has meant an increase in asylum seekers from Somalia, Ethiopia, Eritrea and, since 1980, Uganda. Africans living in England are concentrated in Greater London (home to three-quarters of Africans in the country) and also in Birmingham, Manchester, Leeds and Liverpool.

In 2002, the UK government launched the 'Highly Skilled Migrant Programme', which allows individuals with special skills and experience to immigrate to the United Kingdom. Although many Africans have benefited from this programme, most African people in the United Kingdom are frequently employed in work that does not reflect their educational qualifications (Elam and Chinouya 2000: 46). Income poverty rates among black Africans (45%) are second only to Bangladeshis and Pakistanis in the United Kingdom, compared to a much lower rate (20%) among white British people.[23] Ethnic minorities have higher unemployment rates than white British people.[24] Among African communities in the United Kingdom, high levels of education or social status are not always associated with non-manual or professional occupations or high incomes (Elam and Chinouya 2000: 46).

In 2008, more than 1 million African people entered the United Kingdom under a wide variety of circumstances and access arrangements, including: ordinary and business visitors, work permit holders and their dependants, student visas, applicants under the points based system, Commonwealth citizens with a UK-born grandparent and eligible for settlement, spouses or fiancées of UK residents, as persons seeking asylum at ports or in country, as persons who evade border or immigration controls.[25] The number of Africans granted entry into the United Kingdom should be understood against the backdrop of new general restrictive immigration rules and border agency controls. In February 2008, the UK Border Agency introduced a new Points Based System that rationalized many of the current entry routes to the United Kingdom. Today just under 2 million blacks live in Britain. The majority of this population are immigrants from the West Indies, but this population also includes a growing number of African-born immigrants. Indeed, the most recent population census of Britain shows that the African population in Britain is more highly educated than the general white population. Of the black population, 26 per cent have had at least some college education. This compares to 13 per cent of the white population in Britain.

EU economic climate and the plight of African immigrants

It would appear that any claimed vibrancy of the EU economies was short-lived against the backdrop of uncertainties and lingering crises. The EU unemployment rate started to climb in the mid-1970s and hit 10 per cent by the mid-1980s. Since the mid-1980s, the average EU rate has maintained its long time high level.[26] In December 2004, the EU25 unemployment rate stood at 8.9 per cent. Countries such as Germany and Sweden, which experienced relatively low unemployment in the 1960s and 1970s, are now high unemployment countries. For instance, the German unemployment rate rose in January 2005 to over 5 million (5,037,000) bringing the national average to 12.1 per cent (20.5% in the east and 9.9% in the West).[27]

The EU27 unemployment rate was 9.7 per cent in September 2011, compared with 9.6 per cent in August. Eurostat estimates that 23.264 million men and women in the EU27, of whom 16.198 million were in the euro area, were unemployed in September 2011. In the EU27, 5.308 million young persons (under-25s) were unemployed, of whom 3.290 million were in the euro area. Compared with September 2010, youth unemployment increased by 41 000 in the EU27 and by 71 000 in the euro area. The youth unemployment rate was 21.4 per cent in the EU27 and 21.2 per cent in the euro area.

These staggering unemployment figures, coupled with the proliferation of public strikes and youth demonstrations in Greece, United Kingdom, Portugal, France, Italy and Spain buttress the fact that the economic situation in many European countries is very dire. The politics of 'bail out' from enormous financial public debts is one that has drawn several EU countries towards economic survival or abyss. In fact, such economic uncertainties witnessed in Europe provides some kind of legitimacy for some governments to further tighten immigration laws, which restrict the in-flow of immigrants, but they also politicize the allocation of scarce jobs on the basis of citizen versus non-citizen, indigene versus foreigner. In this light, the rapid proliferation, public visibility and vocality of the far Right, anti-immigrant groups are reshaping the political landscape of several European countries considerably.

The persistent high rate of unemployment has dire implications for immigrants and foreigners, particularly the undocumented, ghost migrant population. Where job vacancies are available, discretionary tactics and preferences are employed in their allocation, to the detriment of even legal migrants. In Germany and the United Kingdom for instance, a German or British national would be the primary preference, and it is only when the position is not filled that attention will turn to applicants from other EU countries and then non-EU members such as from Eastern Europe. This prioritization of job places has become a fairly uniform process across EU countries. In the scale of preference, African immigrants would rank at the lower spine of the priority spectrum. Apart from a few highly skilled immigrants who compete for jobs in the now very competitive market, most African immigrants access low-paid employment in the major and sub-economic sectors, hustling for degrading, 'black' jobs that are shunned by indigenes and EU citizens. In fact, even these menial jobs are becoming scarce and hard to come by in the face of the lingering socio-economic crisis. In the United Kingdom, the commonest jobs that African immigrants resort to include working in nursing homes (often dubbed by them as BBC – 'British Bottom Cleaners',[28] within domestic services as cleaners, cooks, maids or childminders; and within security watch agencies as gatemen, day/night guards.

Many migrants would shun these and what would be regarded as related 'black' jobs back home. However, in the face of new socio-economic realities in Europe, migrants are constrained to take up these 'hard jobs' which are mostly abandoned by locals and the working class in the host context. Although a substantial part of salaries or monies accruing from some jobs do make financial sense, especially when converted into local foreign currencies and reinvested through remittances in the homeland, this new situation however creates enormous psychological stress and emotional strain for many of the migrants involved. Many would still need to cope with settling bills and pay off bank loans and mortgages in addition to coping with daily living costs and life vicissitudes in Europe. Describing his despicable situation, a member of an African-led church retorts:

> I hold a Masters Degree in Economics and Banking Management. I was Assistant Manager in a branch of the New Nigeria Bank PLC before I came over to Germany in 1992. It was a very nasty, harrowing ordeal that I do not want to remember ever again ... Today, I really regret taking such an action, but what can I do to unmake this? Would anyone at home believe that I clean toilets in a shopping centre here in order to survive? What I am paid in a month is barely enough to pay rents in the one-room apartment I share with a friend. In fact, I have to augment this with tips, often coins, emanating from the goodwill of shoppers who come to ease themselves in the toilets. We go for the almost expired foodstuffs and beverages in this shopping complex because they are very cheap. In spite of all these, we get messages from dependants and friends at home asking for one kind of financial assistance or the other. If my country was good (*improved economic situation*) ... I would not have come over here nor take up these dehumanizing jobs. It is really a shame but what can I do? After all, shit money does not smell. When things get better at home, I will definitely return, get married, raise a family and assist my younger ones with their education.[29]

Different shades of African immigrants, from highly skilled to less skilled, have swelled immigrant communities in Europe, the United States and elsewhere. While only very few of these may be hired to work within their specific professions either in citadels of academic learning or in firms, others have taken up menial and 'black' jobs as cleaners, labourers, security night/day watchers, taxi drivers, grape harvesters, house-helps, drug peddlers, street vendors and hawkers. In his book *Money Has No Smell*, Stoller (2002) paints an interesting portrait of the complex lives of West African immigrants who have come to North America in search of economic opportunity. He demonstrates how narratives of West African traders on the streets of New York City illuminate ongoing debates about globalization, the informal economy, and the changing nature of American communities. MacGaffey and

Bazenguissa-Ganga's (2000) multi-site ethnography, describes the lives of Central African transnational traders in Paris. In Europe, many female African migrants are also introduced into the lucrative transnational sexual labour trade, nude and pornographic business. Cities in Italy, Spain, the Netherlands, Belgium and other European countries represent the hotspots of these activities.

The vulnerability of African immigrants therefore becomes more complex as they are on the receiving end of two enigmas. Within Europe, they are most vulnerable to unemployment while at the same time the locus of public vendetta and animosity. In a sense, it could be argued that immigrants are usually the hardest hit of unemployment. Thus, the contentious politics of Europe's high unemployment partly result in the criminalization of immigrants as they assume the roles of guinea pigs and scapegoats in the public expression of frustration and disenchantment. The dwindling economies and failing welfare systems lead to public venting of anger on immigrants and foreigners, treating them as the unwanted Other. Immigrants often become the necessary evil responsible for all social and economic ills, and upon whom the blame is unjustifiably heaped for the ensuing crises. Sassen's remarks rightly counter this often mistaken perception:

> The majority of the contemporary European public would seem to be dead set against immigration, fearing they will be swamped by floods of immigrants they don't really need and cannot accommodate. And yet contrary to popular perception, Western Europe does need, and will continue to need, increasing access to foreign workers – for high-tech jobs, for global financial positions, and also for a proliferation of low-wage service jobs and other manual work…In fact this need to draw on foreign workers has been part of the unwritten history of Western Europe for the last two centuries … Immigration into Europe has never simply been an indiscriminate one-way flow from poverty to wealth, as many opponents would have it. On the contrary, migrants from particular cities and regions in one country tend to gravitate towards particular cities and regions … There is now a growing presence of immigrants who are not searching for a new home in a new country; but rather who think of themselves as moving in a global labor market.[30]

Shrewd politicians across Europe often engage in anti-immigrant rhetoric to lure public votes especially from the Right wing and the ranks of the unemployed. African (black) immigrants are much more vulnerable to random police checks, brutality and surveillance. In fact, one informant remarks, 'Every black African walking on the street is at first sight perceived a criminal, refugee or beggar until proved otherwise. We are perpetually and chronically disabled by our skin colour' (James Oba (pseudonym)). Fidelia Onyuku-Opukiri's[31] report on race related issues and police brutality in the United Kingdom is very pertinent here. Although some of her claims are controversial and cannot be verified, she nevertheless opens a Pandora's box on the persistence of the politics of institutional racism, and the effects on immigrants, refugees and asylum seekers. Onyuku-Opukiri remarks in her report:

> The British National Party (BNP) is a racist political party in the UK whose policy is zero migration. They believe that the in-flock of immigrants and asylum seekers are costing them jobs, housing, health, hospital places and financial problems etc. The activities of this party are to be compared with the American Ku Klux Klan. There is a major worry over the number of seats the BNP is currently holding in the British House of Parliament ... Their success is attributed to the people's fear of asylum seekers. This fear has been whipped up by sections of the media and fed on by some of the politicians. The number of racist offences is reported to have gone up by 400 percent while the number of arrest for racist offences is up by 300 percent ... the asylum seekers are currently in the front line of the persecution as the tabloid media continue to demonstrate in their campaign demonizing them as terrorists or potential terrorists. Sometimes, comments from the government and church hierarchy inflates the situation ... As a result, some locals now defy, hate and terrorize refugees in some parts of England.[32]

She also laments the escalating incidences of police harassment and brutality, a situation in which black African youths are largely at the receiving end. In her remarks:

> The 'stop and search' policy which was once supported by the government caused a great deal of racial tension in England which brought in a lot of complaints especially from black youths and their families. This in effect caused tension and lack of trust between the black youth, their families and the police. The government due to enormity of the complaints adopted a U-turn policy. But recently, there has been a return to the old policy due to the increasing rate of gun crimes. Stop and Search is now back on our streets and innocent black youths are always victimized. I speak as a mother who has a young son of 21 who gets stopped by the police at least once a month. Racist policemen and women use this opportunity to harass black men and women especially the young. Although gun crimes are a reality in our cities now in London, we experience drive by shooting such as is done in the USA.

It is expedient to mention that the distressing, adverse socio-economic and political climate painted above is not a totally despotic one for all African immigrants in Europe. There are certainly pockets of migrants that experience relative upward social mobility and can boast of good professional jobs. Some have even attained excellence and greater heights in business to become employers as well as captains of industries. Some are becoming integrated into the host European society through naturalization and other processes. However, a large cross-section of African migrants is less fortunate and remains perpetually in limbo. Nevertheless, the physical, emotional and psychological trauma and torture that many African immigrants undergo under these horrific circumstances hinted above further explains why immigrant religious communities such as African-led churches have assumed an abode of security and community. It is within this and other similar scenarios of uncertainty, insecurity, shattered hopes and forlorn dreams of migrants that the church appears to fill a vacuum. As my informant above remarks further:

> My best day of the week is Sunday when I am not on duty. The church is the place where you can forget these worries and problems. You are forced to dance away your sorrows and wipe your tears. They (*members*) are really good and friendly people there who are always ready to help and assist you ... I know one day these problems will become history because the God I serve is a faithful One.[33]

The role and place of the African-led churches as spiritual vacuum fillers, as spaces for socialization, and as engines for social, religious (spiritual) and capital formation deserves special treatment. African-led churches in Europe and the United States, in a limited sense, help to cushion pains and strains of unemployment by serving both as employers and as channels of information for job opportunities at both formal and informal economic sub-sectors of the society. Some are involved in the provision of spiritual and social services, thus transforming church vicinities as both religious (spiritual) and social centres, where religious rituals and extra-religious activities take place contemporaneously. I shall turn to exploring these dynamics in Chapter 6.

4

Historiography of new African Christianities in diaspora

Introduction

The historiography of the new African Christianities in Europe and North America can be divided into several historical epochs, with each phase characterized by distinctive features while also sharing affinities shaped by similar religio-cultural Weltanschauung, political exigencies and socio-economic milieux. The religious landscapes of the historical and contemporary African diaspora are shaped by pluralities with influences from Christianity, Islam and indigenous African cosmologies resulting in the African-derived religions and spiritualities. Each of these genres introduced and practised by Africans in diaspora have made a significant impact on the religious cultures of Europe and the Americas, just as both contexts have reshaped these religions and made them more relevant and appealing. This book focuses mainly on the new Christianities that are contributing to the religious diversification of Europe and North America. Prior to mapping the varied forms of African Christianities that dominate the demography of the new African religious diaspora, I shall provide brief glimpses of other religious geographies that make up the religious repertoire of the African diaspora. These are largely documented in the rich literature of the historical African diaspora and do not warrant any duplication here.

The historical African diaspora, partly epitomized by the African American community, has been integral to the shaping of the American religious mosaic. The obvious dehumanization process orchestrated through the trade in humans and the racial discrimination witnessed by the African diaspora in the late eighteenth- and early nineteenth-century America gave birth to a number of African American denominations from Methodist, Baptist and Presbyterian backgrounds (Woodson 1921). Some of the earliest initiatives by people of African descent and heritage include the African Methodist Episcopal Church, the African Methodist Episcopal Zion Church, the National Baptist Convention of America and the Presbyterian Church of USA. The Pentecostal Movement is by far the largest and most widespread religious movement to originate in the United States. Although the Wesleyan Holiness tradition influenced the Pentecostal movement prior to 1901, its origin is mostly traced to the Topeka-Kansas religious revival (Lincoln and Mamiya 1990; Sanders 1996; Pinn and Pinn 2003). Some of the earliest groups included the predominantly African American Church of God in Christ (1897), the Pentecostal Holiness Church (1898), the Church of God with headquarters in Cleveland, Tennessee (1906), and other smaller groups. The modern Pentecostal movement in the United States began in 1906 with William J. Seymour, a black Holiness preacher (Martin 1999).

The historical and cultural significance of indigenous African religious traditions is partly discerned in their plurality and multi-vocality both in Africa and the African diaspora. Most religions of sub-Sahara Africa have been transmitted into new geo-cultural contexts through migration, tourism, and new communication technologies. The African diaspora resulting from the trans-Atlantic slave trade profoundly influenced the cultures of Brazil, Cuba, Haiti and the rest of the New World, partly leading to the development of African-derived religions such as Santeria (Lukumi, Macumba) in Cuba, the Candomblé Nago in Brazil, Vodun, Yoruba-Orisa traditions and other West African rooted traditions across the Americas.

These religious forms have continued to proliferate in the diasporic context, with the scope of practitioners and clientele widening multi-ethnically and multiracially. The twentieth and twenty-first century proliferation of groups of Orisa practitioners outside of West Africa continues to attract millions of adherents of Yoruba and Santeria religious practices (Clarke 2004: 5). Ifa priests and devotees now include Yoruba, Africans, African Americans and non-Africans alike. 'African-derived religions have entered a new phase with the growing presence of western adepts. These have become part of an evolving tradition' (Bellegarde-Smith 2005: 5).

The growth of indigenous African religions in the United States and Europe has been characterized by the proliferation of virtual-religiosity in which most Orisa and Ifa priests exist, operate and communicate through their internet websites with old and new clientele as well as with the wider public. Interestingly, an internet browse of such religion-based websites reveals faces of white American or European rather than black African people assuming the role of chief priests and founders of African-derived religious traditions such as Ifa and Orisa. In this way, they cease to be religions in which people's membership is limited by birth to being traditions to which non-indigenes can convert. With the proliferation of indigenous religious forms in Africa and the African diaspora, Africa has become fully part of a global cosmos in religious terms.

African Islam was spread to the diaspora through migration. Within the context of the historical African diaspora, enslaved Muslims from parts of

HISTORIOGRAPHY OF NEW AFRICAN CHRISTIANITIES

Africa brought their religion to North America. Two such religious groups that eventually emerged to challenge segregation in America and colonialism in Africa were the Moorish Science Temple (Timothy Drew) and the Nation of Islam (Wallace Fard, later known as Farrad Mohammed). Contemporary migration has brought many African Muslims to Europe and North America where they have joined other Muslim immigrants in furthering religious diversification of the host societies. For instance, Somalis, Sudanese and Senegalese Muslims have migrated to Europe and North America particularly in the 1980s and 1990s. Muridism, an integral part of the Sufi Order, has spread around the multi-sited migration network and evolved (Salzbrunn 2004: 489).

From the above, we have shown the significance of the religious variable in the context of the historical and contemporary African diaspora. Indigenous religious traditions, Islam and Christianity were, and continue to be, significant as a motor for African diaspora formation, in the way African immigrants organize, reconstruct and interpret the cosmos and their lives within it. In this chapter, I shall further explore, through various phases of history, the import and resilience of new African Christianities in diaspora; and demonstrate how and to what extent religious, social, cultural, political and economic realities of specific host contexts impact and shape the raison dêtre, modus operandi and worldviews of African-led churches in Europe and the United States.

Many Africans who undergo the complex forms of migration described earlier have carried, as hand baggage, traits of their religious and cultural identities with them. This development has helped in transforming the demography of African immigrant communities and forms the bedrock for a reordering of their religious lifeworlds. The United States represents one of the largest 'religious supermarkets of the world', as well as one of the most ethnically diverse countries. Until recently, the huge repertoire of new African religious communities that have made their abode in the United States and found it a promising mission field has escaped scholarly gaze. However, recent mappings of this phenomenon have begun to provide informative vignettes that enrich our understanding of the complex tapestry of the American religious landscape.

Although numerically, Muslim immigrants from the North African countries of Morocco, Tunisia, Algeria and Egypt dominate African immigrant groups in a country like Germany, their religious communities are less visible within the German public sphere.[1] Rather, immigrants from Ghana, Nigeria and the Congo have gradually inserted themselves into German religious maps through the gradual expansion of AICs, African-led Pentecostal/Charismatic churches and ministries, mission-related churches, African groups and African pastors existing within German churches, freelance evangelism, interdenominational fellowship groups, house cells and para-church organizations.[2] This variety, which is characterized by multiple denominational genres, has run to over 350 churches located mainly in cities in Germany.[3] These religious repertoires draw their clientele from both Africans and non-Africans, although significantly more from the former than the latter. Africans who dominate these groups are largely emanating from Western Africa (Ghana, Nigeria, Liberia, Togo) and Central Africa (DRC, Zaire), while a few members from Southern and Eastern Africa can also be identified.

Typology of African-led churches in diaspora

African-led churches have come to represent a very significant factor in the contemporary life of the new African diaspora in Europe and the United States. Beginning in the 1920s, when they first appeared in Great Britain, they have increasingly made their presence known and felt in European and American religious landscapes. The Nigerian and Ghanaian Christian initiatives represent two of the largest, most widespread. Other less visible Christian communities are constituted by Zimbabwean, Congolese/Zairean, Cameroonian, Kenyan, Liberian and Sierra Leonian immigrants. They reveal a complex variety in terms of their historical origins and development, social composition, geographical distribution, polity, ethos and liturgical orientations. This religious repertoire can be distinguished under two broad categories: that is, religious communities that exist solely as branches, parishes or mission posts of their mother churches headquartered in Africa; and those which were established independently by Africans living in diaspora. Through their headquarters and branches in Europe and North America, the latter category is expanding to Africa and other parts of the world.

In terms of their histories of emergence, belief systems and ritual traditions, a working typology that aggregates the characteristic features of these genres can be outlined as: Mission churches (Methodist, Catholic, Coptic, Orthodox); African Instituted Churches (AIC type such as the Aladura, Kimbanguism, Tokoist); Charismatic/Pentecostal; groups existing within foreign-led churches (such as the African Christian Church, Hamburg under the *Nordelbian Kirche* in Germany). There is also an increasing number of African clergy within or outside mainstream churches ministering solely to African groups. Supportive ministries, fellowship groups and house cells (interdenominational) are a common feature of the new African religious diaspora. This section sketches the historical trajectory of new African religious communities in diaspora. Historical periodization is quintessential for understanding these religious developments in perspective. Undoubtedly, it is impossible for a single book or a sole researcher to capture this diverse religious ferment in one lifetime. This section therefore makes use of works of scholars and researchers who have contributed robustly in the constructive of 'telling the stories' of new African diasporic religions and their communities.

Mapping religious geographies

First phase: The African Churches Mission in Liverpool (1922–64)

One of the earliest initiatives was the African Churches Mission (ACM) established in the south end of Liverpool in 1922. Marika Sherwood (1994) best captures the history of ACM, ostensibly the first African-led church that took root in Europe in the early twentieth century, founded by the Nigerian-born Daniels G. Ekarte in Toxteth, one of the slums in Liverpool. Ekarte, from the Scottish Mission in Calabar-Nigeria, received early financial support from churches in West Africa. Influenced by Mary Slessor (1848–1915), who engaged in pioneer missionary work in Calabar, Ekarte had carried out extensive mission work with riverboats along the creeks of Calabar. Following a spiritual experience in 1922, Ekarte commenced services in private rooms, open-air services with mixed audiences of different cultural persuasions. This practice often brought him into the harsh gaze of local police authorities. Ekarte also undertook frequent visits to Africans on ships, in lodging houses and hospitals. After switching between several temporary religious spaces, he established a permanent mission home. With local financial support, a permanent space was acquired through a three-year lease agreement, and Ekarte officially became pastor of the ACM in July 1931. From its inception, the nucleus group established a bond with British Christians, who provided Ekarte with a church building in Liverpool to hold meetings.

In the 1930s and 1940s, Ekarte became a popular and well-respected figure within both black and white communities, and the ACM grew larger assumed the role of social centre catering to the multifarious needs of many in the immediate community.

In 1934, 380 men and women were registered with the Mission and 148 children were on the Sunday School list. By 1936, membership had risen to 558 (Sherwood 1994: 32ff.). In 1938, the mission worked with about 1,000 men and women and approximately 3,000 children.[4] Apart from the Sunday morning and evening services, the Mission embarked on other activities such as Scouting, music and secondary school classes for the black children. Free meals and temporary accommodation was provided for the poor and homeless (both black and white) at the expense of the Mission. The Mission became the local centre for the needy. Ekarte's activities went beyond the Mission house as he also visited the poor and the needy in their homes, in hospitals and in police cells (Sherwood 1994: 40). In defence of Africans living in Liverpool, he often engaged in spirited correspondence with many anonymous, racist letter writers who expressed ill-feeling about the growing influx of 'Negro men, women and children' and intermarriages. Ekarte took on both religious and extra-religious roles as he became involved in social, philanthropic, humanitarian as well as overtly political activities.

The sociopolitical and economic milieu of Liverpool is important in understanding the circumstances under which the ACM was born, and how the environment impacted on its growth and development. Liverpool's prosperity in the mid-nineteenth century depended largely on slave economy. The black (African) resident population in Liverpool increased considerably during and after World War I. One of the effects of this war on Liverpool was the rapid upsurge of unemployment and the abysmal, squalid conditions in which the poor and unemployed lived, coupled with an escalation of racial tensions. Another highly volatile issue which Liverpool society had to contend with during the war era was that of bi-racial marriages between Africans, African American seamen and soldiers with English women and the resultant population of half-caste children. Such a development heightened the existing racial hostility. This was the sociocultural, economic and political scenario into and within which the ACM emerged (Adogame 2003: 24–41).

One inevitable feature of the post–World War II years throughout Europe in general and Britain in particular was the presence of what came to be called 'GI Babies',[5] 'Brown Babies',[6] 'illegitimate babies' or 'foundlings', the result of intimate relationships between black American GIs stationed in England and British girls. The ACM and its activities under Ekarte came to light as it struggled to deal with one of its attendant consequences, that is, the 'illegitimate' children. Official restrictions imposed by US Army authorities prohibited intermarriages. Despite attempts to discourage such relationships, however, many Anglo-American babies were born in England. After the war, majority of the soldiers had to return home without their new babies and their mothers. Only a small number of mothers married the fathers of their babies. Some of the mothers lost face in their communities and had to leave home. Others saw their black babies as a social stigma and gave them up for adoption or had them placed in orphanages. Such a situation no doubt had adverse social, cultural, political and economic consequences for the foundlings, their families and the host British society. This development attracted newspaper headlines such as 'Fatherless children test racial liberation of Britons' and 'Foundlings of Two Wars'.[7] As a story headlined 'Britain's Brown Babies: Illegitimate Tots a Tough Problem for England' reported:

> Many of the GI fathers of the newly born babies in England wanted to marry their mothers but Army officials blocked thousands of such marriages by

their refusal to grant permission. The results have been babies without names. British adoption societies balked at accepting the colored youngsters and they became a problem for the government. To date Laborite officials have ducked the situation. The problem is being partly solved by the tiny church missions such as the home run by a bearded African Minister, the Rev. G. Daniels Ekarte, in Liverpool. He hopes to establish a Booker T. Washington Children's Home and is seeking government aid for the project.[8]

Brian Joseph Lawrenson, born to a black American soldier and a white English woman, was one of the children raised under the pastoral guardianship of the ACM.[9] Brian's mother left him to the care of the church in September 1944, barely 3 months after his birth. He lived under the tutelage of Daniels Ekarte until the age of 5 years, when Social Services in Liverpool forcibly removed him to Olive Mount Children's Hospital on 3 June 1949.[10] According to Lawrenson, the mission was

> a fitting situation to raise 'Brown Babies' who were the offspring of white English women and black American General Infantry Soldiers (GIs).... In God's own providence he did provide for me, not through his ordered means of providing for children, that is with the care and love of one's biological family, but under the protection of the African Churches Mission, Liverpool Fazakerley Cottage Homes and foster parents.[11]

Apart from the single case of one white child named Gladys Cooper,[12] all the children at the mission home were the so-called brown babies.

His engagement in the struggle for equal wages and better working conditions for African seamen in Liverpool put him ostensibly on a collision course with the local authorities and the city's shipping companies, and visited dire consequences on Ekarte and the ACM. His interest in transforming the Mission into a Children's Home as well as rehabilitating women with 'coloured illegitimate babies' was largely hampered by financial constraints. The distrust and suspicion felt by the local authorities, of an African who believed fervently in 'racial equality, self-help and who openly castigated those responsible for the rape of Africa', led to the failure in his long-term objectives of providing better educational facilities for black youngsters, a permanent home and a better equipped social centre for abandoned children and the downtrodden in British society. Following the inauguration of the National Health Service in England, the Liverpool City Council ordered the mission home to close, and for all children to be relocated to other orphanages in the city. On 3 June 1949 the Mission house was closed, the children forcefully transferred to the city's children home. Ekarte was barred from any further contacts with them. Heartbroken by the treatment meted to him by the Council, Ekarte died on

12 July 1964 barely two weeks after he was relocated from the Mission to a Liverpool Council house.[13] Lawrenson described Ekarte as

> a very articulate man, and from what I could remember knew every black person in the city. Elizabeth Roberts was his housekeeper, and she along with some of her own family fed, clothed, washed and generally cared for we children ... The Pastor was a man who was devoid of any material consideration for himself. He never owned a car or a bicycle, and although he was dressed acceptably you would need a vivid and weird imagination to call him 'Flash'. If there was ever a man who was innocent of the crime and sin of 'filthy lucre' it was Pastor G. Daniels Ekarte.[14]

Ekarte was very popular locally because of his mission work. Writing from Hoylake on the Wirral, Nella Armah said:

> I first went to his African Churches Mission the day it opened, when I was a schoolgirl. Even then I realized here was a man prepared to devote his whole life to the welfare of others ... He has been described as 'the African Saint' and I can truly say that to a great many coloured people in Liverpool he was just that. Words can never describe the loss the coloured people have suffered by his death. He will never be forgotten among us.[15]

Ekarte became and remained a hero in the eyes of many Africans and a suspect in the eyes of many others. The life of the Mission continued as a struggle for survival until the building housing it was demolished on the order of the local authorities in 1964. The Mission did not die with Ekarte; services continued to be held under new leadership until the late 1970s, when it gradually fizzled out. The successors of Ekarte's pioneering African mission were the AICs in the 1960s.

Second phase: African Instituted Churches from the 1960s and 1970s

The 1960s was the period when many African countries attained political independence from European colonial hegemonies. During this era, a new crop of African immigrants charted new routes into the diaspora. These were no longer enslaved Africans, seamen, domestic workers or soldiers of the interwar era. This new stream of immigrants largely comprised students sent or commissioned to pursue further studies abroad, civil servants, businessmen/women, and diplomats deployed to newly established African embassies and consulates in foreign countries. As they settled in the new contexts, many became involved in religious activities that either led to the establishment of new branches of their home churches back in Africa or even the founding of new ones. The most popular of the African-led churches established in Europe in the 1960s and 1970s was the Aladura, one of the most widespread AICs. The Aladura literally translated as 'the praying people' or 'owners of prayers' emerged mainly from western Nigeria during the 1920s. They are so called due to their penchant for prayer, prophecy, visions and dreams, and other charismatic features. Churches that fall under this umbrella are the Christ Apostolic Church (CAC), Cherubim and Seraphim (C&S), Church of the Lord-Aladura (CLA), Celestial Church of Christ (CCC), and Evangelical Church of Yahweh (ECY) as well as their various appendages.

The Aladura have come to represent a very significant factor in the contemporary life situation of the African diaspora. Its debut and presence grew from the establishment in London of the first branch of the CLA in 1964, C&S in 1965, and CCC in 1967. Other Aladura churches, such as the CAC and ECY followed. Today, branches as well as offshoots from these churches abound in different parts of Europe and North America. Thus, the planting in Europe of a brand of Christianity genuinely influenced by African culture can be traced to the 1960s, first in the United Kingdom and afterwards in continental Europe and the United States. Nigerians represent one of the largest African-led immigrant groups in the United Kingdom, and the Aladura were the most visible indigenous religious initiative.

Essentially, the expansion of Aladura churches in Europe in the early 1960s was the work of Nigerian students abroad, and of people on business and official assignments who had no intention of permanently living away from their homeland. When a few members of each group found themselves in one city or local community, they began to meet and worship together in private rooms and residential homes. As their numbers increased, the groups became inter-ethnic and international in outlook. Thus, the nucleus groups of the respective churches met for worship services, fellowship or cell meetings and Bible studies in private homes and later grew into branches scattered all over Europe today. Branches of these churches have now been established in the United Kingdom, Germany, Austria, the Netherlands, Italy, France, Belgium and Spain, to mention a few. AIC membership in Europe encompasses dichotomies of skilled and unskilled; documented and undocumented; temporary and permanent; male and female; and adult and children migrants. Some of these churches had already experienced schisms in their histories prior to their establishment in Europe. Thus, various factions now exist in Europe and the United States. The original composition of these religious communities in diaspora has altered with the arrival of families and the birth of children (first and second generation), thus resulting in a major shift to long-term immigrants or settlers. The new membership development has far-reaching implications for these communities, and facilitates the religious networking process that became expedient for these groups.

A second AIC category, of the Aladura extraction, in diaspora is those churches that emerged in Europe either by severing from an already existing denomination or that which emanates from the charismatic quality of a leader. An example of the latter is the Aladura International Church founded in London by the Nigerian-born Olu Abiola. Many African Christians who come to Europe often try to find and identify with mainstream churches or denominations similar or related to their churches back home. As soon as they discover these churches, the spiritual tepidity or the experience of being unwelcome confronts them. Many African Christians abandon the historic churches due to the disaffection they experience, establish their own churches, or turn to a number of new churches that are the products of African initiatives and under African leadership. Olu Abiola, who later founded the Aladura International Church, described his experience in this way:

> As an ordained minister of the Church Missionary Society of Nigeria (Anglican), I attended and worshipped at one of the Church of England near my home the very first Sunday after my arrival in London. But to my surprise, I was told at the end of the service by the officiating minister that I will be much at home with my own kind and he directed me to a Black Pentecostal Church.[16]

In the same vein, John Adegoke, the Spiritual Leader of C&S in Birmingham, was a member of the Anglican Church in Nigeria when he came to London in 1964. He had attended Church of England services for about a year. When the first meetings of the C&S Church were held, he experienced this as a breakthrough. He remarked:

> Any Nigerian will find the church here different from what he expected. The missionaries came to Nigeria, faking people to live like Christians. But here in England people do not live like Christians, many things are contrary to Christian principles. Sunday is not literally taken as the Christian Sabbath. Nobody has time for the Sunday service, whereas in Nigeria the services are long. You begin to wonder. After suffering for one year, I found people who were interested. I found myself there.[17]

One consequence of this development was a greater identity of African Christians with churches that were more likely to express their interests and sentiments. Many Africans, including ordained priests and ministers of mainstream churches, changed religious affiliation, usually from a mainstream church to an AIC or Pentecostal church. Churches such as the AICs, and more recently the African Pentecostal/charismatic churches, have come to fill this spiritual vacuum and offer 'a home away from home' for many disenchanted Africans.

Following the nascent histories of the Aladura variety of AICs in Britain, scholarship has chronicled their growth and expansion, and also the emergence of other brands of AICs in continental Europe. Gerrie Ter Haar (1998) provides a pioneering scholarly analysis on the import of African Christianity on the European soil and the first to situate this new phenomenon within the religious history of Europe. Drawing from her rich ethnographic data on African congregations in the Netherlands (the Bijlmer district of Amsterdam) and concentrating on one independent church from Ghana, *The True Teachings of Christ Temple*, the oldest of the African congregations in the Netherlands, Ter Haar attempts rather ambitiously to capture the wider situation of African Christians in Europe in the early 1990s. This tendency became one of the pitfalls over which her work was criticized for overgeneralization (Gerloff 2000a: 506–8). Gerloff's review unearths another basic presupposition of Ter Haar's book, an assertion she makes that 'African Christians in Europe are first and foremost Christians and only secondly Africans', and that their new identity does not lie 'in their being Africans', and that the issue of being black is not 'of much importance' to them, and indeed that a stress on Africanness would only be counter to their self-interest as a 'communitas of crisis' which desires to become integrated into mainstream Dutch Christian society.

Gerloff (1992) was perceptive in highlighting this sharp presupposition, based on her own research experience with black (Afro-Caribbean) churches in Britain. Nevertheless, she seems to have taken the other extreme point of departure, suggesting that African Christians were first to be seen as Africans before being seen as Christians. The controversy that ensued on the notions of African and Christian identity can be better understood against the backdrop of the academic orientation of both scholars, but much more located on our intentionality of scholars and researchers vis-à-vis the kind of questions they pose to respondents and the feedback that is solicited in each case. While the notions of 'African' and 'Christian' identities have remained highly contested, I contend that the identity of African immigrants is much more complex. At the very least, African Christians in diaspora see themselves both as African and Christian contemporaneously. The tendency to prioritize any identity strand depends on the circumstances and on who is being spoken to. In fact, such a juxtaposition of notions and perceptions of identity as being 'African' and 'Christian' is hardly incompatible. No single individual is made up of just one identity, but rather, of a kaleidoscope of fluid identities. Besides, to limit the negotiation to continental and religious identity is to grossly undermine the inherent complexities. National, ethnic, clan, town, village, diaspora, gender, age, class as well as new identities through naturalization processes exist side by side with these rather broad continental and religious umbrellas. I shall return to the dynamics of identity formation and negotiation in chapter seven. But suffice it to say that in spite of some critical inadequacies inherent in Ter Haar's book, it undoubtedly attracted public attention, commentary and further scholarly zeal on the religious dimension of African new immigrants, such as African Christians, first in the Netherlands but also across Europe, the United States and elsewhere.

Following on the heels of Ter Haar, my earliest religious ethnography in Europe mapped the spread of the Celestial Church of Christ (CCC) in the Diaspora-Europe with especial focus on Great Britain and Germany (Adogame 1998; 1999: 58–69). The planting of CCC branches in Europe at the initial stage followed a similar pattern to other AICs. It was introduced by Nigerian students abroad, or people on business and official assignments. As the membership increased, the recognition of CCC authorities in Lagos was sought through the invitation of the Pastor-Founder to visit the Harton Street Parish (Deptford, Southeast London) which was then the only existing parish outside Africa. In July 1975, Alexander Bada, then Supreme Evangelist made his first visit to the United Kingdom on behalf of the Pastor-Founder. In 1979, Philip Ajose's was deployed to Harton Street Parish, London as General Overseer of the Overseas Diocese (comprising Europe, United States and Canada).

With these developments, the creation of an overseas diocese incorporating parishes outside Africa became formalized. By 1996, the number of parishes had risen to 68 with United Kingdom 26, United States 26, Canada 2, Austria 3, Germany 4 and France 7, respectively.[18] New CCC parishes were also established in Italy, Belgium and Switzerland. Though official church figures in 1999 put the number of CCC parishes in the United Kingdom at 26, many members estimated the total number to be 50. This number includes CCC branches yet to be officially registered or recognized as full-fledged parishes at the time.

Just as in the case of Britain, CCC was introduced through Switzerland into Germany by students of Nigerian origin. The wife of a Nigerian Ambassador to Switzerland was holding meetings with some Celestians then studying at Bern. When Paul Olaniyan and his wife went over to Germany for further studies, they met some Nigerian students who were also Celestians, and together they founded the first parish in Munich in 1974.[19] The Munich parish was the second CCC parish established in Europe after the Harton Street Parish in London.[20] The nucleus parish at Munich comprised of mainly Nigerians and thus services were conducted in Yoruba and English. However, as the membership increased to include other Africans and some Germans, their services were conducted in three languages namely Yoruba, English and German. At least two Germans were claimed to have been baptized into the Munich parish shortly after its inception there in 1974.[21] By 1990, the membership strength had increased to between 50 and 80, comprising Africans (mainly Nigerians, Togolese, Ghanaians and Beninoise), Caribbeans and Europeans (mainly Germans). New CCC parishes were established in Stuttgart, Frankfurt, Aachen, Bremen and Wuppertal, respectively.

My in-depth research from 1995 on the AICs in Europe has gone beyond the CCC to capture the history and development of the CLA and other churches.[22] Other scholars, from varied disciplinary perspectives, have advanced research work on the AICs in Europe and the United States. For instance, Hermoine Harris (2006) did an anthropological study of C&S in London. Her ethnographic work helps to provide a much-needed update of C&S activities following her debut over four decades ago. Benjamin Simon (2010) analyses sermons of three African Initiated churches from an ecumenical and missiological perspective – the Eglise de Jésu-Christ sur la Terre par son Envoyé Special Simon Kimbangu (Kimbanguist Church), the Church of the Lord-Aladura Worldwide, and the All Christian Believers' Fellowship, in the German context to demonstrate how the churches 'develop in a missionary direction and how they can become ecumenical partners'. Damien Mottier (2008) explores The City of Zion, one of the numerous African churches in France, founded in 2000 by a Congolese prophet. The church was made up of members from the West Indies and Francophone African countries. This anthropological research coupled with a documentary film, *Prophète(s)* (2007) forms part of his PhD research on African churches in the suburbs of Paris. In this film, *Placide* a young man from Ivory Coast comes to Paris with the sole intention of evangelizing France. The three examples above shed some light on religious developments among the AICs in Britain, Germany and France respectively. Other scholars are mapping the development of AICs elsewhere, for instance, in Northern Europe.

Ramon Sarró and Ruy Llera Blanes (2009: 52–72) give useful glimpses of the flux of Christianities across the Lusophone Atlantic by providing some ethnographic data on the diasporic expansion of Angolan and Congolese prophet-based movements: the *Eglise de Jesus-Christ sur la terre par son envoyé special Simon Kimbangu* (Kimbanguism) and the *Igreja do Nosso Senhor Jesus Christo no Mundo* (Tokoism) in Luanda and Lisbon. They assert that Methodist, Presbyterian, Pentecostal and Catholic churches in Portugal have benefited enormously from the flow of African (and Brazilian) immigration (Sarró and Blanes 2009: 58).

Kimbanguism and Tokoism first arrived in Lisbon in the 1980s and 1990s. Initially, they settled in areas of Greater Lisbon. The Kimbaguist church was particularly attractive to young Bakongo men and women who migrated from Angola to Congo (then Zaire), and later to Portugal. The Tokoist church in Lisbon (larger than the Kimbanguist church) displays a more varied sociological background: members from the North to the South of Angola and many youths from the Angolan diaspora.

Another variant of African Christianity which had its foothold in diaspora was the Coptic Orthodox Church planted by migrants from Egypt (Masri and Habib 1982; Ibrahim and Ibrahim 1998:129–61). A tenth of the over 10 million Copts migrated from the mid-1950s and 1970s to North America, Europe, Australia and the Arab world to escape from religious discrimination and persecution in Egypt during the last half of the twentieth century. They established churches, cultural centres which became places of worship, retreat and social gatherings. The earliest Coptic churches established in the North American diaspora were in Toronto (1964), Los Angeles (1969) and in Jersey City (1970). Bishops and priests were consecrated by Pope Shenouda III in Cairo for specific religious services in the diaspora. About 60 Coptic Bishops have been assigned to govern dioceses within and outside Egypt such as in Israel, Sudan, Western Africa, Europe and the United States.

Some of the notable women scholars who have described AICs and gender in the diasporic context are Deidre Crumbley (2008, 2010), Mojubaolu Okome (2007) and Amele Ekué (1998). Crumbley explores religion, gender and power in the context of African diaspora religion in the United States. She interrogates the spread of AICs into developed countries and comparing their rise on both sides of the Atlantic – in Africa and its diaspora. Okome conducts research on African immigrants in New York City focusing largely on gender, leadership and power in the AICs in Nigeria and the United States, exploring how women in West Africa and the United States are important engines for community empowerment. Ekué offers a reinterpretation of African women's religious experiences, as well as the impact of religious resources in transitional situations, in this case Germany.

On the whole, AICs have continued to proliferate in Europe, the United States and elsewhere where they are contesting religious space and power within the new contexts. As Jenkins (2002b: 25) aptly remarks:

> Many African immigrants … come from nations in which Christianity is enjoying an upsurge of passionate enthusiasm scarcely precedented in the whole history of the religion. Independent and prophetic African churches are now firmly rooted in American cities, from which they plan ambitious evangelistic expansion. To take one critical example that has attracted next to no media attention, consider the thriving Nigerian churches based in Houston, many of which stem from the prophetic healing tradition known as Aladura. Conceivably, these African-derived churches could soon represent a significant new phase in the history of American urban revivalism.

While AICs seem to have been the harbingers of new brands of African Christianity to Europe and the United States, it was Pentecostal/charismatic groups that cemented this implantation with alacrity. I shall now turn to the most recent phase in the history of African-led churches, an era characterized by significant growth of Pentecostal/charismatic churches.

Third phase: African-led Pentecostal/Charismatic Churches from the 1980s

The religious geography of African-led churches in diaspora is most spectacular from the 1980s and 1990s. Europe and America are increasingly undergoing religious transformation and diversification with the most recent entry of African-led Pentecostal/Charismatic movements. What started with a few churches in the late 1970s is now characterized by a complex religious plurality. The Pentecostal/Charismatic churches represent the most visible variety in the contemporary geo-religious landscape and it is with this genre that African-led churches have witnessed the most remarkable geographical spread and mobility in diaspora.

Their histories of emergence can be located under three broad categories. The first contains churches that exist in diaspora as branches of a mother church headquartered in Africa. This includes large churches from Africa such as the Redeemed Christian Church of God, the Deeper Christian Life Church, the Living Faith Christian Ministry (a.k.a.Winners Chapel), Mountain of Fire and Miracles Church International, Christ Embassy with international headquarters in Nigeria; the Church of Pentecost International, the Lighthouse Gospel Church, International Central Gospel Church with international headquarters in Ghana. African-led churches from Southern and Eastern Africa are less visible in diasporic and public spaces (when contrasted with West African-led churches for instance), partly owing to historical antecedents, political histories and economies of home countries, international patterns of migration and demographic spread of Southern and Eastern African immigrants within and beyond the continent. However, one of the prominent, rapidly proliferating examples is the Forward in Faith International Ministries (ZAOGA in Southern Africa). In the early 1960s, the FIFMI was founded in Bindura, Zimbabwe by Ezekiel Guti. FIFMI began in Europe in the early 1980s with the establishment of the church in London. They now lay claim to branches in major cities of the United Kingdom including, London, Manchester, Birmingham, Belfast, Glasgow and Cardiff. Outside the United Kingdom, FIFMI has spread not only to Portugal, France, and Germany, Austria and Poland, but also to North America, Asia, Australia and elsewhere.[23]

The second coterie consists of churches founded by new African immigrants to the United States and Europe; these churches establish their headquarters in the diaspora and from there they are expanding to Africa and elsewhere. There are several African-led churches which started in various parts of Europe such as the Christian Church Outreach Mission International led by the Ghanaian-born, Abraham Bediako, with international headquarters in Hamburg, Germany; the Kingsway International Christian Centre led by the Nigerian-born, Matthew Ashimolowo, with headquarters in London; and the World Conquerors Christian Centre led by the Kenyan-born, Climate Irungu, with headquarters in Edinburgh. African-led churches have also extended their domains into Eastern Europe including the former USSR. An example is the Embassy of the Blessed Kingdom of God for All Nations (formerly known as the Word of Faith Bible Church) founded and led by the Nigerian-born, Sunday Odulaja, in Kiev (Adogame 2008a; Asamoah-Gyadu 2005b). The latter is an exception in the African-led churches in Europe in that it has a majority non-African membership. More than half of the membership is Ukrainian and Russian.

Lastly, there is the proliferation of para-churches, prayer/fellowship groups, supportive or interdenominational ministries. They are characterized by somewhat loose, flexible, non-formalized organizational hierarchies and administrative structures in which freelance evangelists and short-term missionaries from Africa embark on frequent visits to a network of churches overseas under the rubric of evangelism and intra-religious networks. Ministries associated for instance with individuals such as Abubakar Bako, Omo Okpai are characterized by less institutionalized hierarchies and structures of operation. Such freelancing is carried out within and between African and other Pentecostal/Charismatic church circles under the rubric of evangelism and intra-religious networks.

Philip Jenkins' *The Next Christendom* (2002) calls attention to the shifting contours of Christianity, particularly as they are shaped by the generally neglected religious communities of North America and Europe. As if to echo some of Jenkins' observations, *The New York Times* of 13 and 14 October and 2003, featured two stories: 'The Changing Church: Faith Fades Where It Once Burned Strong' by Frank Bruni, and 'Where Faith Grows, Fired by Pentecostalism' by Somini Sengupta and Larry Rohter (Bruni 2003; Sengupta and Rohter 2003). Bruni's article focuses on the decline of Christianity in Europe during the last quarter century and the shift in its centre of gravity to the Southern hemisphere. As Bruni (2003) notes: 'Christianity has boomed in the developing world, competing successfully with Islam, deepening its influence and possibly finding its future there. But Europe already seems more and more like a series of tourist-trod monuments to Christianity's past....' Although the focus on church-oriented religiosity in these stories was on Europe, the United States situation is perhaps only a little different. In the midst of this decline, the article refers to the appearance of African-led churches in the religious landscape. As Bruni further remarks: 'Christianity's greatest hope in Europe may in fact be immigrants from the developing world, who in many cases learned the religion from European missionaries, adapted it to their own needs and tastes, then toted it back to the Continent.' One example used in these reports is the Nigerian-born Matthew Ashimolowo and his Kingsway International Christian Center (KICC) located in East London. The KICC is believed to be the largest single Pentecostal congregation in London with about 3000 participants in each of the three scheduled Sunday worship services.

Similar to these new religious developments in Europe, the United States is also currently witnessing a rapid proliferation of African religious influences both within and beyond Christian and Islamic communities. In a *Chicago Tribune* front-page report, for example, Julia Lieblich and Tom McCann wrote about the RCCG. The story describes the Nigerian-based Pentecostal church's efforts to spread its evangelistic form of Christianity to America. Lieblich and McCann note: 'For years American missionaries brought Christianity to Africa. Now African Christians say they want to export their own brand of ecstatic worship and moral discipline to the United States, a country they believe has lost its fervor' (Lieblich and McCann 2002: 1).

The proliferation, mobility and public visibility of African-led AICs, Pentecostal/charismatic and other genres in local, global and transnational spaces, which caught the early gaze of media practitioners, has also proved a rich goldmine for researchers and scholars. Owing to its inherent fluidity and complexity, the religious phenomenon has been approached from a multidisciplinary (religious studies, sociological, anthropological, historical, theological and missiological) perspective. First, some pioneering edited volumes that focus on the place and significance of religion in international migration and among new African immigrant communities often devoted ample space to African-led Pentecostal/charismatic movements alongside Islam and neo-indigenous religious movements (Adogame and Weisskoeppel 2005; Olupona and Gemignani 2007; Adogame and Spickard 2010; Adogame 2011; Ludwig and Asamoah-Gyadu 2011).

Afe Adogame and Cordula Weisskoeppel (2005) and other edited/co-edited volumes by the author (Adogame et al. 2008; Adogame et al. 2008; Adogame and Spickard 2010; and Adogame 2011) are sustained attempts to contribute to the wide-ranging debate on African religious communities in diaspora. The book, Adogame and Weisskoeppel (2005) was interdisciplinary in scope and content, with contributions from scholars of religion, sociologists, anthropologists, Africanists, scholars of migration and diaspora focusing on recent, but often neglected developments of religion within recent migration trends and offering insights to theoretical and methodological debate by contrasting different case studies. The contributions largely represent a rich variety of empirical data, facts and findings, analyses from recent fieldwork among African migrant communities in host countries such as Germany, the United States, Norway, Finland, Israel, and the United Kingdom. The contributors dealt with a wide spectrum of religious groups within the Christian and Islamic religious traditions: Muslims from Sudan and Somalia, Copts from Egypt, Sufis from Egypt, Sudan and Germany, Eritrean Christians, African (Ghanaian and Nigerian) Pentecostals/Charismatics/African Initiated Churches in Germany, Israel, Great Britain.

Jacob Olupona and Regina Gemignani (2007) resulting from in-depth research on a broad range of communities, represents a pioneering, comprehensive attempt at mapping the religious dimensions of new African immigrants that enrich our understanding of the complex tapestry of American religious landscape. These multidisciplinary insights demonstrate that the demographic expansion and mobility of African religious communities, particularly in US gateway cities of New York, Los Angeles, Chicago, the San Francisco Bay Area, Atlanta, Miami, and Washington DC, is quite phenomenal. Although the book has limitations in terms of scope and detail, to the extent to which it has succeeded in mapping this dynamic phenomenon hitherto masked by social marginality and obscurity, it opens up a goldmine for further research (Adogame 2008c).

The emerging field is also witnessing monographs that follow a geographical or thematic scope. Recent notable works include those by Regina Jach (2005), Jehu Hanciles (2008), Claudia Währisch-Oblau (2009), Moses Biney (2011) and Mark Gornik (2011). Gornik explores the recent development of African Christianity in New York City. Drawing especially on ten years of intensive research into three very different African immigrant churches: the Presbyterian Church of Ghana in Harlem, the Church of the Lord (Aladura) in the Bronx, and the Redeemed Christian Church of God International Chapel, Brooklyn, Gornik sheds light on the pastoral, spiritual, and missional dynamics of this exciting global, transnational Christian movement. In fact, there is a growing scholarly literature on African religions (Christianity, Islam, Indigenous religions) in diaspora in form of book chapters, article contributions in international peer-review journals, encyclopaedias, dictionaries and so on. Some notable works of scholars include those of Rijk van Dijk (1997; 2001), Afe Adogame (see publication list from 2003–10), Stephen Hunt (2001, 2002), Roswith Gerloff (2000, 2003, 2004), Birgit Meyer 2004, Wisdom Tettey (2007), Geraldine Mossiere (2007, 2010), Girish Daswani (2010), Roy Kerridge (1995), and Jack Thompson (1995) to mention but a few.

While I appear to have a robust focus on AICs and Pentecostal/charismatic churches in this chapter, they are obviously not the sole players in the religious diaspora field. In fact, mission-related churches or African congregations within European-based churches represent visible actors within the religious 'supermarkets' in Europe and North America. This religious mosaic of the African diaspora is further characterized by African groups, clergy and laity existing within foreign churches. Examples include the African Christian Church, Hamburg under the *Nordelbian Kirche* in Germany, African groups within the American and European mainstream churches such as the Episcopal, Anglican, Methodist, Lutheran and Catholic. The Methodist and Presbyterian Churches of Ghana, the Church of Nigeria (Anglican Communion), the Catholic Church of Zimbabwe and Nigeria offer a tremendous window into this paradigm. The Church of Nigeria (Anglican Communion) alongside other African provinces of the Anglican Church is beginning to explore a missionary episcopacy (Chua 2010). There are growing numbers of Nigerian Roman Catholic and Anglican priests in the United States, Tanzanian Lutheran and Ghanaian Methodist priests in Germany, Presbyterian priests in the United States. African priests and ministers in these churches are sometimes employed by the host churches but have the African congregations as their primary constituency. This phenomenon has started to attract scholarship in the United States and Europe.

Moses Biney (2011) explores the complexities of the social, economic, and cultural adaptation of the Presbyterian Church of Ghana in New York, based on personal stories, notes from participant observation, and interviews. Biney aptly demonstrated that Ghanaian Presbyterian congregations in New York are more than mere 'ethnic enclaves' or safe havens from American social and cultural values. Rather, they help maintain the essential balance between cultural acclimation and ethnic preservation needed for these new citizens to flourish. Mattia Fumanti (2010) and Dominic Pasura (2008; 2012) have investigated the activities of Ghanaian Methodists and Zimbabwean Catholics in London respectively. Their works are responding to the growing recognition of the significant presence of African migrants in Britain. Focusing on Ghanaian Methodists in London, Fumanti explores the significance of transnational and religious networks between Ghana and the diaspora. Pasura's multi-sited ethnography of the Zimbabwean diaspora in Britain explores the ways in which different spatial settings shape diasporic identities and cleavages. He explored the phenomenon of religious transnationalism using the case example of Zimbabwean Catholics in Britain.

The conscious missionary strategy by mother churches in Africa of evangelizing the diaspora is a relatively recent one. Diaspora has been a key aspect to their response to European mission. The 'reverse flow' initiative, which I shall return to in Chapter 9, entails sending African missionaries abroad. The moratorium call was designed among other things to awaken the Third World peoples to their responsibility, creating new goals and of formulating a viable evangelical strategy towards Europe (Kalu 1980: 365–74).

This 'exportation' of clergy and missionaries on 'reverse-mission' from Africa to the diaspora demonstrates the stature of Africa as an emerging global theatre of Christianity. The fact that policymakers and funding bodies are recently investing and committing huge public funds for research projects on new African religiosities and spiritualities in Europe and the United States lends credence to their gradual coming of age and attainment of a local-global stature. Some examples are the New Opportunities for Research Funding Agency Co-operation in Europe; Templeton Foundation; Pew Trust; Arts and Humanities Research Council; German Research Foundation, Volkswagen Foundation.

5

A phenomenology of African Christian communities in diaspora

Introduction

This chapter provides a phenomenological expose of the demographic, socio-ethnic constitution, polity and organizational structures typical of several African Christian church communities in the diaspora, but also in their original homes of origin, Africa. It explicates how these religious groups are negotiating their religious worldviews – varied ways in which belief patterns and ritual structures are oscillating between resilience, transformation and change – in the face of cultural, political and socio-economic realities. Such a conjecture paves the way towards emergent theologies among African Christian communities in the cultural milieus of Europe and the United States and against the backdrop of their transnational linkages to and exchanges with Africa.

Demography and Social-ethnic configuration

Most African-led churches which came to be established in diaspora from the 1960s were the initiative of a few individual students, or people on business and official assignments who had no intention of residing permanently abroad. This group made up of a few members who met and worshiped together in 'house cells or fellowships' and later transformed into full-fledged branches with acquired or leased properties as religious buildings. In some cases, a new branch sought official recognition or affiliation with headquarters in Africa. The demographic change of the migrant communities has slightly altered this original composition in the last few decades. The arrival of migrant families and the birth of children (first and second generation) has led to a major shift to becoming long-term migrants or settlers. This no doubt has far-reaching implications on the status and growth of some new African religious communities.

African-led churches have demonstrated determination to make global links and make non-Africans as targets in their membership drives. Most of the churches lack a cross-cultural appeal thus leaving their membership predominantly African. The socialization process of African migrants whereby they mix and interact mainly with fellow Africans is another barrier towards the realization of a multiracial group. In fact, some of them are simply labelled as ethnic or national churches. However, there are few others that have transcended racial-ethnic boundaries to include non-Africans in their membership. The existing non-African element is largely owing to bi-racial couples and friendship; but also sometimes as a result of personal evangelism. This membership structure is likely to be transformed and altered in the future if the churches continue to make inroads into the new religious landscape. The social anatomy of the churches is complex and variegated. The majority of members are not illiterates, but elites of their countries or those who have ventured out in search of the golden fleece. In most recent times, the churches' membership has been characterized by skilled and unskilled factory workers, the unemployed, asylum seekers and refugees. With such a socio-ethnic structure, African churches in diaspora largely remain the locus of identity, community and security primarily for African immigrants (see Chapter 7).

Organizational structures and the hierarchization of a religious polity

The governing, hierarchies and organizational structures of AICs and Pentecostal/charismatic churches in Africa and the African diaspora are as diverse as the religious groups themselves. They vary from groups with loose structures to those where the day-to-day running is anchored on the leader, his wife and his family and or his peers, to those with complex polities and administrative structures. Any attempt to map the structures of all these diverse religious entities will be tantamount to 'painting with broad strokes'. However, I shall use three examples to briefly illustrate these hierarchical and organizational complexities within some of the more institutionalized groups. First, I will draw upon two churches, contrasting an AIC-type, the Celestial Church of Christ (CCC) with a Pentecostal-type, the Redeemed Christian Church of God (RCCG), both with headquarters in Lagos (Africa); and a third example, a Pentecostal-type, the Christian Church Outreach Mission (CCOMI), with international headquarters in Hamburg, Germany (Europe).

These examples do not typify the general structures, rather they simply illustrate church polity and leadership mechanisms.

Celestial Church of Christ

Generally, CCC organization is structured around the centralized authority of the Pastor-Founder. As both spiritual and administrative head, the pastor has unchallengeable authority on all matters, and legitimizes this authority through his personal charisma. This tendency has continued after the demise of the Pastor-Founder with successive leadership evincing such charismatic potentialities noticed in the Pástor-Founder. CCC internal organization provides a complex hierarchical structure that could be classified into the upper and lower cadres (Adogame 1999: 99). The lower provides a vertical progression along three separate but corresponding axes—leader, *wolider/wolijah* (prophet/prophetess) and elder. Though not necessarily equal in rank, the three lines correspond with one another at the terminal posts of superior senior leader, superior senior *wolider/wolijah* and superior senior elder. They represent the highest rank in the hierarchy to which members may normally be elevated by promotion. The line of leaders is exclusively for males, while the other two are characterized by both male/female axes. Consequently, members who attain these levels do not expect automatic promotion to the higher ranks.

Progression from any of these three 'lower-apex' ranks to the upper hierarchy is largely dependent on either of two ways. On one hand, the pastor, in whom resides all authority, may at his sole discretion, make direct appointments to any rank including that of assistant evangelist, honorary assistant evangelist and above. On the other hand, where vacancies occur in the higher ranks, selection from the corresponding ranks of superior senior leader, superior senior *wolider*, and superior senior elder is made after due consideration of the candidates' eligibility by the pastor assisted by a special committee of the Pastor-in-Council (CCC 1980: 49–50). Parish committees could also make suggestions to the pastor for the promotion of members to the three leadership lines. However, for the upper echelon, it is the pastor himself who calls to the unction (the action of anointing someone with oil or ointment as a religious rite). Both the top and lower hierarchies may further be categorized into two distinct but parallel paradigms as 'administrative' and 'prophetic'. By virtue of his status, the pastor embodies both structures contemporaneously. Every local parish is expected to be headed by both hierarchies, that is, where the shepherd comes from the leader or the elder axis, the assistant must necessarily come from the line of *wolidah* (prophet), and vice versa. Therefore, these two 'governing' and 'spiritual' structures appear to be delicately balanced.

Generally, women's mobility in the hierarchical echelon is limited. They cannot go beyond the terminal posts of the lower hierarchy due to prohibitions and taboos. Female members are forbidden within the precincts of the sacred space for 8 and 41 days during menstruation and after childbirth respectively. Such women undertake purification rituals as a necessary prerequisite for re-admittance into the church building. Women are also restricted from participating in certain ritual activities within and outside church services such as conducting services, preaching sermons, reading Bible lessons, making announcements, reciting the benediction, and leading men in prayers. However, they may pray or read Bible portions during the sermon at the preacher's request. Female members may perform spiritual functions among a female congregation during outdoor evangelism. The status and role of CCC women in Africa and the African diaspora presents an ambivalent situation in which the spiritual/political streams of empowerment are perpetually challenged by their lack of mobility to the top hierarchy and ritual prohibitions.

The CCC worldwide is run through its international headquarters in Ketu-Lagos, Nigeria. The CCC Supreme Headquarters is located in Porto-Novo, Benin Republic by virtue of the church's birth there. The Pastor-in-Council, under the ultimate authority of the pastor, represents the highest body of government. It comprises the diocesan heads and deputies, the board of trustees, and members appointed by the pastor who serves as chairman (CCC 1980: 45). A board of trustees is appointed at the sole discretion of the pastor and charged with custodianship of all land and other church properties. They are also vested with sole authority to represent the church in all matters of relationship with the state, religious and other organizations.

The CCC organizational framework is divided into dioceses of West Africa—Nigeria, Benin, Togo, Côte d'Ivoire, and Guinea—and those of overseas countries in Europe and North America. Fewer parishes exist in southern, central and eastern Africa and in India (New Delhi) and the Asia Pacific. Except for the Overseas Diocese, each seems to have been created to correspond to individual countries where there is a significant membership. At the level of each diocese is a Diocesan head and a general committee which administers and oversees the activities and decisions of the state, zonal and district headquarters and various parochial committees of individual parishes (CCC 1980: 39). State headquarters exist under a diocese, except in the Overseas Diocese where they are categorized into territories. In dioceses like Nigeria, several zones, districts and parishes within a federal state are organized under the state headquarters and a state/regional administrative evangelist is in charge. Parishes, a local congregation within the district, are further grouped geographically under zones. A number of zones make up a district. Each zone is put in charge of a zonal evangelist.

The leadership of a parish is under an *Oluso-agutan* (shepherd) and his deputy. The shepherd-in-charge of a parish is seen as the pastor's representative in that parish. A balance between spiritual and administrative domains is ensured in each parish. The parish's day-to-day affairs are run by an elected parochial committee, and sometimes a committee of elders constituted usually with a gender balance.

Redeemed Christian Church of God

The RCCG's authority structure is rather complex. The overall leader is called the General Overseer (GO). The current hierarchical structure follows the following order: The General Overseer, The Governing Council, Deputy General Overseer, Mother-in-Israel, Assistant General Overseers, Elders, Assistant Elders, Secretaries, Provincial Coordinators, Directors, Assistant Secretaries, Provincial Pastors, Assistant Provincial Pastors, Zonal Pastors, Area Pastors, Parish Pastors, Assistant Parish Pastors, Deacons/Deaconesses, Ministers, Workers, the Faithful (Congregation), and Seekers/Visitors.

The church maintains two headquarters, one national and the other international with the GO's office overseeing both. Under the GO's Office are six administrative blocs attached to the national headquarters: Fellowships; Parishes; Areas; Zones; Provinces; and Regions. The national headquarters oversees all branches in Nigeria. These branches are grouped into five administrative sections called 'regions'. Below the unit of regions are a number of provinces. Lagos region, for example, has 11 provinces. This regional administrative structure illustrates the church's geographical spread. The next administrative unit is the 'zones'. A province is a collection of 'zones'. A zone, in turn, consists of 'Areas'. An area comprises a number of parishes. A parish is made up of 'Home Fellowships', the smallest unit in the church. The RCCG is structured in the following order: Office of the General Overseer, International Headquarters, National Headquarters, Regions, Directorates, Provinces, African RCCG Zones, Europe Regions, RCCG Areas North America, Parishes, and Home Fellowships.

The structure at the international headquarters is less complex than at the national headquarters. The GO coordinates all activities involving foreign missions, outside Africa, through the International Office. Other RCCG branches in Africa are grouped into regions, each headed by a regional coordinator. The regions include the West Coast, Cameroon, Ethiopia, East Africa, and South Africa. RCCG parishes worldwide are organizationally structured into 'Areas', with each 'Area' subdivided into 'Zones' for administrative purposes. Each zone is assigned a coordinator. Each country is divided into zones, states and provinces are grouped together to form a zone. In 2008, there were a total of 22 zones in RCCG North America, 19 in the United States and Caribbean and 3 in Canada. At the RCCGNA Annual Convention held in Dallas (Texas) in 2003, over 120 parishes were listed.[1] In September 2008, 334 parishes were listed on the RCCGNA official website.[2] RCCG's religious cartographical maps of North America quite consciously illuminate the demographic spread of parishes but also how the terrain has been mapped and partitioned for missionary, evangelistic ends.

Christian Church Outreach Mission International

CCOMI developed a complex hierarchical structure that has a transnational outlook akin to the CCC and RCCG. At the topmost echelon of the organizational structure is the International Executive Board (IEB) that cuts across geographical and gender divides. Next to IEB is the International Ministerial Board, an umbrella body composed of pastors and ministers of CCOMI branches worldwide. There are also the National, Regional, Districts, and Local Ministerial Boards. Thus, CCOMI branches in each respective country are divided accordingly along this structure for administrative convenience. The hierarchical structure and administrative system is headed by the Bishop, General Overseer of all branches worldwide. The international headquarters in Hamburg, Germany is regarded as the CCOMI Central Assembly while all other branches comprise the CCOMI Global Assemblies.[3] The Central Assembly is administered by three pastors and four ministers, one female and six males. All are Ghanaians apart from one of the ministers, Boris Bromm, who is German. Although the IEB has a representative each from Ghana and Holland, the top hierarchy is currently dominated by Germany.

Generally, the segmentation and internationalization of CCC, RCCG and CCOM's governing, administrative organs and structures of hierarchy along multiple geographies is pertinent. The institutional actors embedded in each local church structure constitute a complex web of relationships characterized by transnational networks, travel and visit exchanges, grass-roots initiatives, special religious events, and through their appropriation of new media technologies. Thus, their organizational and hierarchical structures partly underscore their transnational nature, links and relationships.

The complex ways in which these church communities are governed is often woven around theological constructs or legitimized through biblical and church historical precedents. But even how the hierarchy is structured and the organization shaped is through ongoing negotiation processes located within and beyond the context that they emerged. Some structures are modelled in such a way as they clone or synchronize existing church organizational structures and in some cases caricatures and replicates functional business structures and models of democratic and authoritarian political governance. Thus, to have a firm grasp of how they are led, ways in which they govern themselves, parameters for day-to-day living and interactions with members and the wider society, it is important to see how and to what extent 'religion matters' to them, but also how the local contexts shape processes of theologizing their lifeworlds.

The God of immigrants or immigrant God? Unpacking religious worldviews and ritual cosmos

African Christian communities in diaspora present a robust religious demography as they continue to mushroom across Europe and North America. The explanations for their emergence, expansion and visibility are quintessential in understanding their spiritual worldviews and emerging theologies. While their complex pluriformity, their sociocultural identities and fluid membership structures render the task of exploring their theologies very tenuous, it is useful nonetheless, to isolate some outstanding ingredients that most likely shape these emergent theologies. As most of these religious communities are relatively new in Europe and North America, having started within the last three decades, their evolving theologies emerge out of ongoing contestation between resilience, transformation and change. A proper grasp of the action-orientedness of African religions provides a window for understanding the shape and texture of these cosmologies, especially when transmuted to new sociocultural contexts. Most often, defining African religions from its belief system is akin to putting it upside down. Religion is usually not thought out in the agora of theology, but lived out in the marketplace of Africa. Their theology is not in books but in their heads, thoughts, utterances and day-to-day actions and life modes. In the diaspora, there is a certain resilience of the action-orientedness of African Christianities. This should however not be misconstrued or understood out of context. The common depiction of African Christianities by scholars as 'this worldly', 'conservative', and as providing mainly literal interpretations of the Bible is rather simplistic and fails to capture the internal religious dynamics. Scholars need to examine their belief paradigms and ritual worlds more closely in order to unpack their belief and ritual particularities, rather than relying on grandiose, external considerations.

Theologies are emerging from and built around the long *dureé* of migration – the home of origin as a point of departure, the transitory journey to El Dorado, the arrival at temporary/final destinations, the circumstances shaping their lived experiences of adaptation or resistance to integration, and even the imagination, illusory thoughts of return migration. African immigrants often take 'their religion or aspects of it' as hand baggage. Thus, the religious worldviews and ritual enactments of African Christian communities that will be described in this section need to be understood against the backdrop of the particular life circumstances of immigrants; the specific social, cultural, economic, political and religious realities of the host context that shape their existence and lifeworlds; and how and to what extent these has enabled them to contemplate, write, sing, eat, dance and follow their theologies.

In actual fact, theologies are acted out from simple exchange of pleasantries 'How are you?' and the response it evokes among Ghanaians, such as 'By God's grace'; or Nigerians replying: 'We thank God', 'God dey!', 'E go better!', 'We go survive!', 'To God be the Glory!'; or further as some Kenya-led churches are accustomed to responding: 'I am blessed and mightily favoured'. Such wide-ranging responses elicit narratives woven around day-to-day life experiences. That is why a casual, flying greeting such as 'Hi' is often frowned upon and not well received as this is perceived as unconcern about another person's welfare. It is indeed a matter of conjecture how and in what ways such theologies of 'everyday life' partly verbalized by African Christians can enrich 'classroom' theologies common among many Western Christians.

In the new geo-cultural context, African-led churches are in constant negotiation between old and new worldviews, split between tradition and modernity, maintaining and constructing old and new identities. They assimilate notions of the global; make conscious, concerted attempts to reinterpret and reconstruct via religious ideologies, symbols and praxis, the cosmos that surrounds them. African-led churches are conduits for member's self-insertion and integration into the new cultural environment. They also represent, self-evidently, channels for reinventing and maintaining local, religio-cultural identities. I shall now turn to examining this negotiation process between resilience, change and transformation through the prism of religious cosmology and ritual praxis.

One index of affinity and continuity between African-led churches in diaspora and their respective indigenous cosmologies is the belief in the reality of supramundane forces and the ritual orientation towards these paranormal entities. This frame of thought is resilient to the ritual sensibilities of African-led churches within and beyond their immediate context of emergence (Adogame 2005d: 503–7; 1999: 115f). There is the stark recognition of a dual cosmic space that is intricately intertwined. The reality of the numerous malevolent spiritual powers is not a bone of contention in the epistemologies of African Christianities. However, the medium of and ritual strategy for control is what has changed. Most of these continue to wage 'spiritual warfare' on the enigmatic forces through elaborate prayer rituals, prophecy, trance, visions and dreams. Although they vary in matters of specific ritual emphases, the

AICs and Pentecostal/charismatic variety in particular are perpetually awash with ritual enactments.

Most African Christians in diaspora, (un-)consciously, retain and sustain the belief in indigenous aetiologies of diseases, illnesses and evil, although they may have been enlarged through biblical and other frames of reference. Nothing is left to chance or taken for granted, be it childbirth, naming, marriage, infertility, academic examinations, promotion, unemployment, acquiring visas and residence permits, xenophobia, death, dreams, accidents, sickness, poverty, loss of property, homelessness and so on. Virtually all events or actions perceived as 'unnatural' and 'abnormal' are often subjected to spiritual scrutiny and extrapolation. Therefore, illnesses that defy medical prognosis are easily interpreted as 'spiritual attack'. As far as they are concerned, natural problems can be resolved through natural and spiritual means, but 'spiritual' problems can be diagnosed and solved only through 'spiritual' means. Barrenness or premature death is usually not treated as a natural occurrence. A person who experiences a prolonged state of unemployment reads spiritual meanings into his difficulties. In all circumstances, these AICs and Pentecostal/charismatic churches hold fervently that an afflicted person must be healed, and the beleaguering malevolent powers invalidated at the same time. A few examples from the AICs and Pentecostal/charismatic churches will illuminate these affinities between indigenous religious cosmologies, ritual attitudes and orientations. I shall demonstrate how each is negotiating between resilience, transformation and change in the new context.

Aladura ritual worlds

AICs such as the Aladura describe themselves as bona fide Christian churches that emerged to supplant the lukewarm religiosity of mission-related Christianity. They attest to the increasing secularization of the world, a development which their 'divine mission' is set out to counteract. In a matter-of-fact way, they express this claim to a special spiritual task or 'mission'. We cite here examples from the CCC, C&S and CLA, the most widespread AICs in diaspora. CCC self-identification as *Oko igbala ikehin* (the last ship/vessel/boat for salvation) best exemplifies the fusion of this-worldly and other-worldly orientations in their understanding of *igbala* – salvation (Adogame 2000a: 8). Aladura take the Bible as the pivot on which their entire belief code and ritual world is anchored. CCC tenets are outlined succinctly in their constitution, which states the belief of the church that the name, organization of the church, its doctrines, beliefs and rituals are derived primarily from the inspirations of the Holy Spirit. 'Members are strictly forbidden to engage or participate in any form of idolatry, fetish ceremony or cults, black magic and charms.' (CCC Constitution 1980: 29ff.; Adogame 1999:130–1). The total condemnation of 'juju' and 'charms' is stated in C&S's original constitution[4] The Devil embraces any extra-Aladura ritual, not only Yoruba deities and medicine, but freemasonry, Rosicrucianism, the Reformed Ogboni Society, spiritualism – the whole array of contemporary occult practitioners (Harris 2006: 91).

In spite of these claims to the primacy of the Bible and a total repudiation of what Aladura perceive as 'unchristian' and 'unbiblical', their ritual cosmos is evidently suffused with features that demonstrate some affinities with a Yoruba religious worldview. The dialectics between Aladura's self-image as a Christian Church sui generis that refuses any connection with traditional religious thought and praxis on the one hand, and the public perception of their rapport with Yoruba religio-cultural matrix on the other raises the politics of cultural identity (Adogame 1999). As far as Aladura are concerned, faithful observance of biblical injunctions and church norms ensures health, wealth, good fortune and salvation. Failure to observe them correctly places one's health in jeopardy by making one vulnerable to malevolent agencies. The Aladura are quite explicit in their criticism of any member or group that attempts to introduce what they would call 'un-Aladura' or 'unchristian' doctrines and practices. Rufus Ositelu puts it plainly:

> Our rules and regulations, our beliefs and practices are quite explicit. The Holy Bible is our dictionary and reference point. Those who devise other means for problem resolution without calling on the name of our Lord Jesus Christ are not for us but against us. Within every group, there are always Judases. These are the people that give us a bad name. When we see such cases, we immediately call them to order and pray that God removes Satan's scales which have blindfolded them.

This statement is suggestive of the dichotomy between official and popular religiosity. While Aladura leadership considers straying from prescribed codes of belief and rituals as against church regulations, the hermeneutics of beliefs and ritual may be interpreted differently at times on the level of popular religion.

Aladura churches generally emerge from within Yoruba geo-cultural precincts and founded by prophetic figures who were themselves Yoruba by ethnic extraction. The Aladura worldview echoes Yoruba understanding and polarization of the cosmos into *orun* (heaven/sky as the abode of the spiritual entities) and *aye* (the world/earth of human habitation). In fact, *aye* is a sacral entity because it serves as a centre for the dramatization of spirit beings. It is a delineated space occupied by two pantheons of paranormal forces, *Orisa* (400 supernatural powers of the right) and *ajogun* (200 supernatural forces of the left), engaged in a timeless and sustained competition for its domination. Human beings are caught up in this cross-fire between the benevolent and malevolent spiritual forces. However, the protection and escape from these 'spiritual conflicts' is the recourse to divination and propitiation of the *Orisa*. The *Orisa*, including Orisa Nla, Orunmila, Ogun, Shango, Yemoja and Esu, are largely benevolent to humans so long as their precepts are jealously kept (Abimbola 1994). Their wrath is incurred when their precepts are flouted, and when they are not adequately propitiated. On the other hand, the *ajogun* such as *iku* (death), *arun* (disease), *ofo* (loss) are inherently malevolent. The spirit forces that make up this genre are preoccupied with total human annihilation. Figuratively, *aye* assumes a 'marketplace' and the journey through it to the final destination – 'home' (the spirit world/heaven) – is characterized by life's vicissitudes (Adogame 2000a: 3–29).

Basically, the Aladura share a similar mentality in their belief tradition, employing an indigenous hermeneutic of spiritual power but casting it within new conceptual frames of reference. The bedrock of their belief system is the pre-eminence of benevolent powers – God, Jesus Christ, the Holy Spirit, the legion of angels. The bestowal, manifestation and appropriation of *agbara emi mimo* (power of the Holy Spirit) form the nerve centre of Aladura spirituality. The Aladura wage 'spiritual war' on the enigmatic forces through elaborate prayer rituals, prophecy, trance, visions and dreams. Aladura liturgical tradition is a highly expressive action characterized by a heavy dose of rituals enacted to resolve individual and collective existential problems. Each segment of the ritual worship is seen by members to be full of religious symbolism and meaning. These objects are not ends in themselves but are the means to achieving some ritual ends (Adogame 2000b: 59–77).

'Witches do not need visas to Europe': Negotiating resilience and transformation

The resilience of Aladura cosmology and ritual praxis is evident in the diaspora. Efforts are made to ensure continuity, and church members retain the same practices as they face the same dangers. Witches, wizards and sorcerers shuttle across geographical boundaries unrestrained. As an informant remarked, 'Witches and sorcerers do not require any visas to come to Europe from Africa. Some reside here, and others can come over as frequently as they have nocturnal assignments to accomplish.' (Adogame

2004b: 505). Institutional racism and all other xenophobic tendencies experienced by migrants are located under the portfolio of Satan/Devil. In other regards, many Africans find their sojourn in Europe rather more complicated than they had envisaged. Prior high hopes of 'making it' on arrival in Europe, to use Nigerian parlance for 'material success and upward social mobility', are dashed. In fact, Europe becomes personified as Satan's stronghold and perceived as the 'Dark Continent' in dire need of spiritual regeneration. Life is particularly difficult for some African immigrants, because of declining European and US economies, retrenched welfare systems, cultural gaps, xenophobia at individual and institutional levels, acute unemployment, police harassment and brutality, dashed hopes, stress, loneliness, extended family expectations from home, and mounting unpaid bills and mortgages. Under these distressing conditions, many Africans find spiritual, psychological and material succour in the church. Through elaborate rituals, a sense of identity, security and protection is provided for members (Adogame 2004b: 505).

The church conveys its power over malevolent forces by employing metaphors from common parlance in reference to Satan (Adogame 1998a: 159). During ritual service, Satan is accused as having stayed too long within the society and has become an illegal immigrant that must be deported immediately to where he belongs. This is akin to the experience and anxiety of illegal immigrants among them who are always conscious of their status and the uncertainty that goes with it. At the end of the service, members 'praise God believing that the deportation order has been issued to Satan, the illegal immigrant, the one who is not supposed to be here but has been tormenting people for too long'.[5] This metaphorical repositioning of Satan or the Devil encompasses the discourse on individual and institutional racism. An informant's testimony and the subsequent thanksgiving ritual during a Sunday worship service will suffice here:

> I came to Germany in 1983 with our two children. It was a family reunion with my husband who studied earlier and is now residing here. A few months after I arrived in this country, one of my main worries was how our children will fit into German schools without any prior grasp of the German language.... During discussions with German family friends on one occasion, the couple told me in a highly discouraging tone that my children could never adjust and cope in a German high school nor attend a German university. 'At best they will end up in a *Hauptschule* but certainly not the *Realschule* or *Gymnasium*' they added. I took this comment with exception and discussed with my husband afterwards. It was a trick of the devil and I refused to claim it. So I took it as a prayer point to the church. I fasted and prayed as I have never done before, asking God to arrest the

plans of this 'spirit of racism'. My inner mind told me this was a spiritual attack in the making, so I depended on my God for a counterattack. I told my God that my children will not only succeed in this Deutschland but will excel to the chagrin of the Devil ... To God be the Glory! Our son and daughter went successfully through high school and they have both gained admission into German universities.[6]

The remarks of the German couple, on the one hand, may not necessarily mean any ill-will, but simply explain how the educational system works. On the other hand, they could be interpreted as being laced with racism. But inherent in this testimonial is the conviction that these comments were overtly racial. As a result, the informant took them very seriously and even read in religious and racial meanings. Her reaction could be understood by reference to the local context.

Probing my informant further on why and how she inferred this conclusion from the couples' statement, she retorted:

Can you imagine that the couple was convinced that our children can never do well in German schools? What kind of prophecy is this? This is definitely not coming from God but the Devil. The society continues to think that African (black) children have a lesser intelligence than whites. You see, my children have proven the direct opposite...I really think all white people must begin to change these stereotypes.

Ostensibly, the comments of the German couple were understood and interpreted as the device of Satan. The fact that a single remark during a conversation over coffee could generate such concern is significant in understanding the resilience of indigenous cosmology.

Another informant's narrative of his multiple encounters with a frightening, black cat in a Germany city best shows the pertinacity of belief in the reality of malevolent spiritual entities and the resilience of indigenous religious worldview in a context where such sensibilities have assumed the stance of fiction, fairy tales and superstitious narratives in the eyes of the public. As he describes his traumatic experience:

I was walking along a lonely street to my apartment one cold evening. A solemn screeching sound behind me attracted my attention. When I looked back, there was this black, fiercely looking cat walking towards me. When I stopped it stopped moving, when I continued walking it kept pace with me. Abruptly, I detoured and took an alternative route to my apartment. It continued to trail me until when I suddenly took to running. Then, it disappeared into thin air. I was shocked stiff because I did not understand why such a black cat would trail me. I shivered all the way home and told my wife about the gory experience. We simply prayed about it and I became relieved. I thought this was going to be my last ordeal ... Two days later I was in my study working late into the night when I heard a 'bang-bang', like a heavy knock on my window. I stopped working and listened with rapt attention. Within a split of a second, the knocks came more repeatedly. I stood up and drew the window blinds open. Behold, a big black cat was standing outside gazing directly at me. I believe it was the same I saw on the street few days earlier. The mere sight sent me into frenzy and I instantly drew the window blinds and woke my wife up from sleep to share my new experience. This must be a spiritual attack from witches or sorcerers. We immediately fell on our knees and prayed that God should avert any impending danger. We told God, 'In this Deutschland, the evil one shall not see us nor confront us'. Thank God, the next Sunday I mentioned it as a prayer point in the church, prayer warriors and members took it up in prayer. We are happy that since then we have not had this experience again.

The above narrative might generate scepticism among Europeans. Many would certainly not draw any spiritual interpretation out of this. However, for my informant, his family and his fellow church members, this experience was not to be taken at face value. It is common belief that witches and wizards attend their nocturnal meetings in the form of birds, 'black' cats or other disguised identities. This was essentially the mental picture presented by my informant when I probed him further on the mentality associated with cats and the colour black. In Yoruba traditional context, the colour black is associated with darkness, sexual passion, secrecy and excrement as well as the colour symbolizing witchcraft and sorcery (Adogame 1999: 200). The translatability of indigenous worldview renders the encounter with the 'cat' intelligible to my informant in concrete, spiritual terms. Thus, the reaction and interpretation demonstrate how and to what extent indigenous religious sensibilities are translated into new geo-cultural contexts but more importantly how their ritual attitude, actions and cosmos continues to be shaped by it.

This resilience is not peculiar to the AICs, it is also common within African Pentecostal/charismatic belief paradigms and their ritual maps of the universe. I shall draw on three case examples from the Living Faith Tabernacle (LFT) a.k.a. Winners Chapel, the Redeemed Christian Church of God (RCCG) and the Mountain of Fire and Miracles International Ministries (MFM) to demonstrate members' preoccupation with 'spiritual mapping' and the rhetoric of spiritual terrorism in two geo-cultural contexts.

Spiritual terrorism within and beyond borders: Pentecostalism and ritual emplacement

The texture of spiritual terrorism that is revealed in African Pentecostal movements shows a kind of adaptation of Christianity to the existential needs of Africans. The epistemology and negotiation of spiritual warfare makes sense in African Pentecostal ritual sensibilities. It is the rapprochement with indigenous cosmology and ritual praxis that distinguishes it within global Pentecostalism(s), and accounts largely for its horizontal and vertical expansion and relative success. These churches represent some of the most widespread neo-Pentecostal groups emanating from Africa. Their etiologies of disease and illness as well as ritual orientations are similar, although each has its own doctrinal and methodological emphasis.

Winners Chapel

Elaborate rituals in the LFT or Winners Chapel are packaged to handle spiritual terrorist attacks such as sickness, unemployment, social insecurity, death, emotional stress, hunger, poverty, barrenness and virtually all of life's vicissitudes. During participant-observation in a Lagos branch in 2002, I randomly selected 25 members to interview on what attracted them to the church. Of these, 18 claimed to have assumed membership after an 'encounter with Christ'. Five interviewees claimed to have sought protection from traditional healers all to no avail. Ten informants remarked that they were tormented by the devil and therefore came into the church in search of solutions. These 10 informants at the time of the interview were already graduates in different disciplines and had been unemployed for a number of years. Seven respondents said the devil had denied them of the fruit of the womb and were thus attracted to seek a solution where 'the Living God dwells'. Others claimed to experience bad dreams periodically. In such dreams, they disclosed that strange things always occurred, and they were being chased by the devil for destruction. Of the members, 12 were ready for marriage but 7 are yet to find their life partners and 5 were having problems with pre-marital sex and pre-marital relationships. As another member testifies:

> On the night of December 30 2001, I woke up with a holy anger in me because I was in a bank with nothing to show for it. I told God in a prayer that I want a change and I was led to multiply my present monthly tithe by three. Also, in the month of November, when there was a call for sacrificial offering, I gave the whole of my November salary, and then during Shiloh in December, when the call for prayer request was made, I told God that I

needed a job in an international oil company, and if not in an oil company, I want it in a reputable bank. To the Glory of God, between Shiloh and now, I've secured a job in an international oil company and two offers from two reputable banks. I give God all the Glory.

A cursory look at these narratives above shows that although the existential problems vary from one person to the other, yet the general interpretation links all problems to one major actor, the devil. They were attracted to the church due to their belief that the church is capable of dealing with the devil in the spiritual battle they are confronted with. Winners Chapel is preoccupied with waging war against the terror of Satan and his cohorts. This is achieved through elaborate prayer rites, rituals of healing, deliverance, fasting, anointing, spiritual baptism and night vigils. As Bishop Oyedepo (1992: 99), the founder/leader of Winners Chapel remarked:

> Many people hate to hear the word 'battle' mentioned for any reason. Whether you like it or not, whether you are conscious of it or not, battles are a part of our existence. We are all involved in warfare; we are born into it ... our victory in every battle is guaranteed in all ways and in every place. Interestingly, we are not the force behind this victory; God is. He causes the triumph. So, we are only instruments in His hands that He uses to fight against His arch-enemy. We are called into warfare, and thank God, we are at the same time, called into triumph ... Battles are real to life, salvation notwithstanding. That you have battles does not mean that you have missed God, it only means you are on the path of destiny.

Oyedepo noted elsewhere,

> The devil is a mind-blocker. He organizes programmes to blind your mind, because he knows that when your mind is blinded, your destiny is blocked and your future becomes uncertain ... the devil is very crafty! You can't catch him easily, except you are spiritually smart. (Oyedepo 2000: 140)
>
> The end time army is a conglomeration of a strong people set in battle array-men who will run like horses, climb walls like men of war; men that if they fall on the sword cannot be wounded ... Sickness and disease will be so far from their dwelling places. They won't know the meaning of pain at all, but will enjoy heavy immunity by the presence of the Holy Ghost. (160)

These discourses were vivid illustrations of what the Winners Chapel has come to represent for its members in Africa and the diaspora.

Redeemed Christian Church of God

RCCG members also engage in deliverance rituals, healing rituals, night vigils, prayer and fasting rituals, and thanksgiving rituals (rites of passage) in order to counteract Satan's evil machinations. They claim that the warfare motif in the Bible provides humans with ample instruments with which to thwart the enemy's plans. In the new Christian dispensation, this spiritual engagement and warfare motif is legitimized with biblical credence in Ephesians 6: 10–17:

> Finally, be strong in the Lord and in his mighty power. Put on the full armor of God so that you can take your stand against the devil's schemes. For our struggle is not against flesh and blood, but against the rulers, against the authorities, against the powers of this dark world and against the spiritual forces of evil in the heavenly realms. Therefore put on the full armor of God, so that when the day of evil comes, you may be able to stand your ground, and after you have done everything, to stand. Stand firm then, with the belt of truth buckled round your waist, with the breastplate of righteousness in place, and with your feet fitted with the readiness that comes from the gospel of peace. In addition to all this, take up the shield of faith, with which you can extinguish all the flaming arrows of the evil one. (NIV)

Another often cited reference which gives weight to the warfare motif is II Corinthians 10: 3–4 which states: 'For though we walk in the flesh, we do not war after the flesh for the weapons of our warfare are not carnal but mighty through God to the pulling down of strongholds...' (NIV). There are several other biblical references that use the rhetoric of the devil as the enemy, thus highlighting the expediency of spiritual warfare. Adeboye (2002: 76–8) isolates ten methods of warfare, various ways in which God fights the enemy on behalf of members. For the RCCG, this military-cum-spiritual offensive and strategy can only be achieved through total dependence in God by faith. It is a spiritual warfare that can only be fought spiritually and not through any mundane means. Adeboye (68ff.) recommends:

> Do not wait for the enemy to hit you first; hit the enemy first. Every true child of God must be a terror to the devil and his agents. You must learn to take an offensive stance. If you don't get rid of the agents of the devil in your life, they are likely to get rid of you ... You are to resist the devil steadfastly in the faith. Go on the offensive as soon as you know the enemy is around. God says our defense is sure. This defense is impregnable, so we are supposed to be aggressive ... Demons recognize and tremble at the name of Jesus Christ.

RCCG and LFT offer spiritual power to overcome and heal the maladies of poverty. Banners, personal testimonies, sermons, hymns, and gifts of the Spirit bear testimony to the centrality of power in their spiritual discourse and praxis. There are frequent references to the spirit or demon of disease, illness, barrenness, death, doubt, adultery, poverty, lying and drunkenness. Adeboye (2002: 65, 93) writes:

> Everyone has enemies. The enemy can be sickness, sorrow, failure, poverty, death, other people or whatever is warring against you. The enemy tries to put the cuffs on you and rob you of the joyful life God has intended for all His children to live ... Money is a defense. I pity those who say they don't want to hear about prosperity. I pity anybody who talks about nothing but prosperity. I pity anyone who preaches everything but prosperity. I am going to prosper. Poverty is a terrible thing. Your prayer should be that poverty should be a stranger to you.

The paraphernalia of the devil has become enlarged to include anything that prevents the attainment of good health and wealth. This lends credence to the multiple understanding and translations of poverty. It is also against this backdrop that the mechanics of the prosperity gospel can be better understood and interpreted. Thus, there is a remarkable difference in this conceptualization as compared to understandings of prosperity gospel within American and European Pentecostalism.

The terrorism motif and theology assumes a more complicated dimension with the distinction made between two interrelated plains of spiritual warfare. The horizontal axis, referred to as the 'ground-level warfare' involves dealing with the various spirits that inhabit people (demons), while the 'cosmic-level warfare' is the vertical axis dealing with different shades of higher-level spirits. In every society they argue, the horizontal warfare contends with the issue of ground-level demonization, and the indwelling spirits or demons may be of varying kinds including family spirits, occult spirits, and 'ordinary' spirits such as those attached to fear, death or homosexuality. Demons are believed to work at ground level in ways appropriate to the society in which they operate. The vertical warfare includes territorial spirits over cities, regions, and nations; institutional spirits such as those assigned to churches, governments, educational institutions, occult organizations and non-Christian religions; spirits assigned to oversee and encourage special functions, including vices such as prostitution, abortion, homosexuality, gambling, pornography and war. Ancestral spirits are also assigned to work with specific families. The cosmic spirits are apparently in charge of ground-level spirits, although both are tightly interconnected.

In spiritual warfare, African Pentecostals generally engage the spiritual mapping technique in discerning and identifying cosmic-level spirits and the geographical areas, institutions, vices and objects that they rule over as a step towards developing strategies to oppose and defeat them. The power encounter concept that is central to the spiritual warfare discourse is reminiscent of scriptural encounters such as that between Moses and Pharaoh (Exodus 7–12) and between Elijah and the prophets of Baal (I Kings 18). Healing and deliverance from demons are perceived as power encounters. While African Pentecostal/charismatic Christians believe in the reality of these enigmatic forces that constitute terror, most Western Christians would be sceptical not only about their reality of their existence but most importantly, about what to do about them.

Mountain of Fire and Miracles Ministries

The MFM, a church founded in Lagos by Daniel Olukoya in the late 1980s and with demographic expansion in Africa and the African diaspora, has made a significant mark in global Christian circles through its ritual emphasis on deliverance, healing, and spiritual warfare. In fact, MFM, through its preoccupation with the epistemology of demons and extensive appropriation of warfare rhetoric, carves out a niche for itself in African Pentecostal discourse.

An explication of MFM's demonology and deliverance rhetoric shows the prevalence and continuity of local epistemologies of spiritual constitution and agency in MFM's Christian ritual cosmology, thus accounting for its popularity and swelling clientele, particularly within the Nigeria religious milieu, but also beyond into the diaspora, such as in the United Kingdom (Adogame 2012).

MFM's self-recognition best eulogizes the tendency of engaging rituals as a 'military strategy' in which 'an army of aggressive prayer warriors are being prepared in this end time'. Olukoya affirms,

> As God's children, we are supposed to do all our things militantly. We read the Bible militantly, speak militantly, evangelize militantly and pray militantly because God is not a civilian but a soldier … The Lord Himself is a man of war. So when you pray, you are employing a very powerful military strategy … Militant prayer must have power and fire in it.[7]

Existing church literature and sermon genres are replete with an extensive appropriation of warfare rhetoric such as 'warfare prayers', 'battle cry', 'bullets of fire', 'spiritual terrorists', 'deliverance by fire', 'sword of deliverance', 'prayer warriors', 'sword of deliverance', 'divine revolution', military strategy, militant prayers and so on. Such phrases are suggestive of how their belief structure is shaped, but also how this impacts their ritual system. This can be clearly exemplified within the context of their ritual space, written texts, and oral prayer genres and in the various prayer ritual strategies.

In a sermon titled 'Prayer as a Military Strategy', Olukoya highlighted 'militant prayer points' claiming that members 'must pray fervently, effectually, and with spiritual violence'.[8] A few stanzas illustrating this kind of invocatory ritual will suffice here:

> I paralyze every evil hand pointing at my blessing, in the name of Jesus
> I withdraw every satanic instruction targeted against me...
> Every evil river dry up, every evil shrine working against me, be roasted...
> I refuse to be subdued by the forces of darkness...
> I nullify every night arrow fired against me...
> Devil, you are a liar, you cannot capture my destiny...
> I break every agreement made between my parents and Satan on my behalf...
> I break every covenant formed between my enemies against me...
> Every stronghold of wickedness fashioned against me, let the fire of
> God burn them to ashes...
> Every ritual and sacrifice working against me, be neutralized...
> Every evil bird delegated against me, fall down to the ground and die...
> I refuse to dwell in the building constructed for me by my enemies...
> I paralyze every spirit of wastage, I shall not borrow...
> *I command confusion and disagreement between my hardened enemies...*

The aggressiveness and literal militancy with which prayer rituals are enacted and targeted against enemies suggests a disregard of the biblical injunction that Christians should love and pray for their enemies (Matthew 5: 44f). To this critique, however, Olukoya would respond that the target of the verbal, spiritual war is the Devil (Satan) and not human beings, although Satan could also manifest through humans themselves. MFM's extensive prayer repertoire indicates the importance of invoking God, the name of Jesus, Holy Ghost, and angels in order to demolish and claim victory over Satan and its cohort. Such phrases as, 'Fire of God,' 'the blood of Jesus', 'Holy Ghost Fire', and 'Angels of God' therefore assume spiritual weaponry.

If God is for us, who can be against us? Theologizing survival, hope and mobility

The lived experiences of African Christian immigrants shape their spiritual/religious lives, just as theologies are constructed from these experiences and the reservoir of indigenous religious worldviews retained by them in their 'new homes'. The ways in which immigrant's experiences shape their religious lives, and in which their spiritualities speak to and condition their day-to-day experiences and expressions is illuminated by their narratives partly woven 'between and betwixt' themes of survival and security, adaptation and mobility. Such narratives are verbal contestations of a growing fortressization of Europe characterized by the adoption of stringent, restrictive immigration policies and the politicization of US immigration laws and policies. The immigrant is not concerned primarily with adaptation and integration but with economic, social, cultural and psychological survival. Thus, religion can be a significant part of a 'survival-security' strategy followed by an 'adaptation' strategy. Religion can reflect the suffering and the problems of the immigrants, and in some cases offering them an escape route and or a ghetto.

What makes African immigrant Christians tick, or what shapes their theology of hope, empowerment and survival is not simply the ordeals in the host context (diaspora), but more importantly also the incessant pressures from the home of origin. These ordeals and pressures can be of varying kind and scope. These may include social and economic strains, the pursuit of legal documentation (visas, residence permits), hostility of neighbours, xenophobic tendencies within the host context, social and familial pressures from nuclear and extended family members and friends back home for favours, to send money (remittances) or other forms of assistance through unexpected phone calls and emails, the fear of witchcraft, suspicion of envious or jealous family members, friends, neighbours, and the struggle to succeed while away from home.

Immigrants' actions are to be understood in terms of their own goals, strategies established first in order to survive, and after that, to adapt or not to adapt to the new social milieu. There is a certain link between theology of hope and theology of empowerment in the diaspora. This brings to the fore the symbolic significance of a song/chorus that most African Christians hold dear to their hearts. By rendering the song, the church vicinity becomes a space in which the theology of hope and security is sung to visibility.

Because He Lives, I can face tomorrow
Because He Lives, All fear is gone
Because I know oh, oh, He holds my future
And life is worth the living
Just because He Lives!
Because He Lives, We can face tomorrow
Because He Lives, All fear is gone
Because We know oh, oh, He holds our future

And life is worth the living
Just because He Lives!

In conclusion, coupled with the prevailing expressions of dashed or rekindled hopes, frustration and disillusionment, there remains the consciousness that 'Witches do not require any visas to come to Europe and the US from Africa ...' The latter underscores the fact that indigenous epistemologies such as these are rarely discarded by most African Christians in diaspora. Rather, such beliefs and the ritual attitudes and sensibilities that accompany them are retained and reinterpreted in the face of new challenges that characterize the new context. Several immigrants are still confronted with similar, sometimes more devastating, life vicissitudes as in their original home contexts. Thus, this ambivalent sense of hope, on the one hand, of self-rediscovery, empowerment, and socio-economic mobility is juxtaposed with a profound feeling of hopelessness, frustration, and uncertainty, thus creating an enabling environment in which several immigrants reproduce beliefs, recreate socio-religious identities, and re-enact rituals.

6

African Christianities as social, cultural and spiritual capital

Introduction

One basic feature in comprehending the social dynamics of migratory processes is that each migratory movement can be seen broadly as a consequence of interacting macro-, micro- and meso-structures (see Chapter 1). This macro/micro dichotomy is akin to Portes et al.'s (1999: 221) distinction between *transnationalism from above* (activities 'conducted by powerful institutional actors, such as multinational corporation and states') and *transnationalism from below* (activities 'that are the result of grass-roots initiatives by immigrants and their home country counterparts').

The proliferation of African Christian communities in Europe and United States can be located broadly at the intersection of micro- and meso-structures and the mechanisms of migratory processes. Ostensibly, religion serves as an important source of 'social', 'cultural' and 'spiritual' capital among African immigrants. This is one framework in which issues of agency and changing worldviews become intelligible. In a sense, we could locate immigrant religious communities within the coterie of migrant industry. Depending on the specific circumstances, such people can be both helpers and exploiters of immigrants. Religious groups can help build and break individuals and societies because of their bridging and bonding behaviour. However, the intertwining nature of these multiple structures may make a clear dividing line between them very problematic. This chapter explores how African Christian communities, as strategic actors and benefactors, in diaspora are involved in the processes of religious, social and cultural capital engineering. This is partly achieved through strengthening and establishing relationships, norms and values as means towards realizing a new state of social inclusion/exclusion; but also through networks that mediate access to the host cultural context, new opportunities, resources and information. Before undertaking this venture, it is expedient to delineate our usage of social, cultural and religious capital as these concepts themselves have attracted varied connotations and differing definitions, albeit vague sometimes. These concepts are now fairly well established in theoretical and policy discourses although there are various formulations and contestations around their appropriation and measurement.

Conceptualizing capital

Capital is assuming the role of being a buzz word and a marketplace concept in academic and public discourses, with a growing utility that is trans-disciplinary in outlook. Alongside the more general application of social, cultural and religious (spiritual) capital, its liberalization is further epitomized in the varied appropriation as symbolic capital, intellectual capital, human capital, financial capital, civic social capital, political capital, economic capital, institutional capital, power capital, 'big society' capital, sport capital, food capital, recovery capital and health capital to mention but a few. Nonetheless, the primary focus of this chapter is on the more popular usages of the concept – social, cultural and religious – and how they play out within African Christian communities in the triangular contexts of Africa, Europe and North America.

The discourse on social, cultural and religious capital has gained wide currency in the United States, far over and above the conceptual treatment in the United Kingdom and Europe in general. Corwin Smidt's *Religion as Social Capital. Producing the Common Good* (2003) is a significant contribution to debates about civil society and civic renewal in the United States, addressing the relationship between religion and civil society through an exploration of the interconnectedness between religion, social capital and democratic life. However, as the UK Office of National Statistics (ONS) report cautions about the applicability of the concept,

> Much of the research is carried out in America and the concept has tended to be exported wholesale to the UK which ignores the cultural context of its conceptualisation. Caution needs to be applied in comparisons where the cultural context of social capital is ignored. (3)

Generally, the discourse on social capital in the United Kingdom is firmly established in the political lexicon and has generated a lot of interest within Government research, statistics and policy areas. The ONS, Home Office, Department of Health and Department for Education and Skills are all carrying out research to measure and analyse the impact of various aspects of social capital (5). Social capital has well-established relationship with the outcomes policymakers are concerned with, namely: economic growth, social inclusion, improved health and more effective government (4).

Social capital

Social capital as a core concept in social science refers to the advantage created by a person's location in a structure of relationships. It is perceived as the resources available to one through the networks that they hold or the tendency to increase the confidence and capacity of individuals and small groups to get involved in activities and build mutually supportive networks that could hold communities together, or in some cases render them asunder. It consists of the networks, norms, relationships, values and informal sanctions that shape the quantity and cooperative quality of a society's social interactions. Thus, the central idea of social capital is that social networks are a valuable asset (Field 2003: 12). Three leading figures made seminal contributions to the emerging concept of social capital: Pierre Bourdieu, James Coleman and Robert Putnam.

The concept that underlies social capital is old but it was perhaps Pierre Bourdieu who gave the first cohesive exposition of the term in 1972. In *The Forms of Capital* (1986), Bourdieu distinguishes between three forms of capital: economic capital, cultural capital and social capital. He added symbolic capital to this categorization later on. Bourdieu defines social capital as 'the aggregate of the actual or potential resources which are linked to possession of a durable network of more or less institutionalized relationships of mutual acquaintance and recognition' (Bourdieu 1983: 249). He places the source of social capital, not just in social structure but also in social connections.

Social capital is also viewed as a set of 'moral resources' that lead to increased cooperation among individuals. According to James Coleman (1990: 302–4),

> Like other forms of capital, social capital is productive, making possible the achievement of certain ends that would not be attainable in its absence … For example, a group whose members manifest trustworthiness and place extensive trust in one another will be able to accomplish much more than a comparable group lacking that trustworthiness and trust.

Coleman provides some specificity to the very constitution of social capital. He posits ingredients of social relationships that include social capital in terms of the elements of social obligations and expectations, norms and sanctions, social support and being tied to voluntary associations (Coleman 1990: 311–13).

Coleman conceptualizes social capital as a structural variable, as something that only exists between and among certain individuals within a particular context. Social capital is socially embedded in particular relationships. Such relationships were not limited to the powerful, but could also convey real benefits to poor and marginalized communities.

In his influential study, *Bowling Alone* (2000), Robert Putnam provided a useful, related definition. For him, 'social capital refers to connections among individuals – social networks, and the norms of reciprocity and trustworthiness that arise from them' (2000: 19). It has to do with the collective value of all 'social networks' and the inclinations that arise from these networks to do things for each other. Putnam (1993: 169) defined social capital as 'features of social organization, such as trust, norms, and networks that can improve the efficiency of society by facilitating coordinated actions'. He reasserts, 'Communities of faith (when they work well) are acknowledged to be primary hubs where social networks and normative values and practices can be accessed within an atmosphere of reciprocity and trust' (Putnam 2000: 66–7). Putnam posits two main components of the concept: *bonding social capital* and *bridging social capital*. 'Bonding' refers to the value assigned to social networks between homogeneous groups of people, and 'bridging' to social networks between socially heterogeneous groups. Bonding social capital tends to reinforce exclusive identities and maintain homogeneity; bridging social capital tends to bring together people across diverse social divisions. Each form is helpful in meeting different needs. Bonding social capital is good for undergirding specific reciprocity and mobilizing solidarity, while serving as a kind of sociological super glue in maintaining strong in-group loyalty and reinforcing specific identities. Suffice to add 'linking' (power relations, types of participation and role in civil society) as a third type of social capital. 'Linking' capital refers to alliances with and connections to individuals or groups perceived to wield political, economic or spiritual power. This can be related to power over resources needed for social and economic development.

Communication is needed to access and use social capital through exchanging information, identifying problems and solutions and managing conflict. Putnam's distinction is useful in highlighting how social capital may not always be beneficial for society as a whole, though it is always an asset for those individuals and groups involved. Putnam recognizes that faith communities in which people worship together are arguably the single most important repository of social capital. A consideration of these contexts suggests clear ways in which the economy and quality of social capital is relevant to African Christian communities in Europe and the United States.

In a research project aimed at developing an overall framework for the measurement and analysis of social capital, the ONS provided a useful literature review.[1] In spite of the definitional confusion about what constitutes social capital, there is some consensus within the social sciences towards a definition that emphasizes the role of networks and civic norms (Healy 2001). The key indicators of social capital include social relations, formal and informal social networks, group membership, trust, reciprocity and civic engagement. Social capital is generally understood as the property of the group rather than as the property of the individual. We should be cautious about ignoring the effect of social capital at an individual level, and especially, of disregarding the importance of networks of relationships as a prominent source of social capital (see Halman and Luijkx 2006).

Cultural capital

Cultural capital is a fairly general sociological concept that brings into focus the question of cultural values as they relate to things like: what constitutes knowledge, how knowledge is to be achieved and how knowledge is to be validated. The concept has gained wide currency since Bourdieu first articulated it. Bourdieu and Jean-Claude Passeron first used the term in *Cultural Reproduction and Social Reproduction* (1973) in an attempt to explain differences in educational outcomes in France during the 1960s. It was later elaborated and developed in terms of other types of capital in *The Forms of Capital* (1986). According to Bourdieu, 'Cultural capital acts as a social relation within a system of exchange that includes the accumulated cultural knowledge that confers power and status' (1986: 47). Bourdieu distinguishes three subtypes of cultural capital as: embodied, objectified and institutionalized. He locates a set of cultural experiences, values, beliefs as representing a form of cultural capital.

Bourdieu's treatment of immigrants and their amount of linguistic capital and habitus is illuminating. His later ethnographic work develops the concepts of capital and habitus, and explores further the role of agency. His theory of habitus encompasses both structural considerations and agency, and his incorporation of culture and cultural capital into his framework of social class and social reproduction demonstrates that he clearly does not reduce everything to economics. His notion of capital and fields is also perhaps useful in understanding how people of African nationalities / ethnicities, such as African immigrants, may try and exchange the cultural capital of their national/ethnic backgrounds with that of 'American', 'German', 'French', 'British' or simply 'European Union' to attempt to gain a higher position of respectability and mobility in the social hierarchy. Whether this is realizable or attainable at the end is a different question altogether. However, it raises the politics of citizenship and naturalization in a way that exposes the arbitrariness of what is African, European or American, and how it is determined and negotiated by those in the dominant as well as the fringes of European and American societies (see Chapter 7).

Religious/spiritual capital

Generally, religious capital is associated with the investment an individual makes in his/her religious faith or organization. The investment is the time and physical work involved with the religious faith, as well as the personal investment in ideology, doctrine and practice. The value that individuals place on religion influences, their levels of religious participation, and their commitment and belief. Religious capital is the practical contribution to local and national life made by religious and faith-based groups. Spiritual capital energizes religious capital by providing a theological identity and worshiping tradition, but also a value system, a moral vision and a basis for faith. Spiritual capital is often embedded locally within religious and faith-based groups, but it is also expressed in the lives of individuals.

Although I have treated each of these genres – social, cultural, religious/spiritual capitals – separately above, this chapter does not necessarily perceive them as mutually exclusive. Our focus on African Christian communities and their tendency towards capital formation will hardly compartmentalize them as disparate domains. I shall explore them as interconnected with one form dovetailing in another genre in practical terms. The concept of spiritual and religious capital is similar to the more general concept of social capital because it is a resource based on relationships that individuals and religious/faith-based groups can access for their personal well-being, but can also donate as a gift to the wider community. Both religious capital and social capital include investments and participation in networks and activities.

In general, the advocates of the concepts of social, cultural and religious capitals have often over-emphasized their benefits and understated their negative dimensions. In actual fact, social capital is not a panacea, it has a downside, hence more of it may not necessarily be better. It could be counter-productive, it is considered to get depleted if not maintained. Churches, religious communities, faith-based groups, religious NGOs, fraternal organizations, internet social networks create exclusionary but also inclusionary social capital. Prior to exploring this ambivalent negotiation of capital formation among African Christian communities, I highlight some inherent disadvantages that could go with the building of social capital.

The downsides of social capital

The same ingredients of social capital that enable productive benefits have the potential to cause negative externalities. The importance of paying attention to the negative factors of social capital was perhaps first documented by Portes (1998) but now is synonymous with our understanding of social capital theory. Potential downsides of social capital can include fostering behaviour that worsens rather than improves economic performance; acting as a barrier to social inclusion and social mobility; dividing rather than uniting communities or societies; facilitating rather than reducing crime, education underachievement and health-damaging behaviour (Aldridge et al. 2002). The kinds of groupings and associations which can generate social capital always also carry the potential to exclude others (Hunter 2000).

Portes (1998) identifies four negative consequences of social capital: exclusion of outsiders; excess claims on group members; restrictions on individual freedom and downward levelling norms. He believes that these consequences and the unequal nature of access to social capital must be balanced against an optimistic view, if social capital is to be useful as a tool for societal analysis and transformation. In exploring the downside of social capital, Quibria (2003) highlights four potentially destructive dimensions of networks, norms and reciprocities, especially focusing on urban and ethnic communities. First, social capital that opens up opportunities for the members of the network, which is often based on ethnicity, religion, language and profession, can at the same time constitute an enormous barrier to entry for others outside the network. Second, while a close-knit group can be a source of economic dynamism for its membership, it can also dilute personal incentives to work hard, as in the case of a community that is substantially supported by welfare. Moreover, group membership of the community can enforce strict conformity when it infringes on individual freedoms, and can thus create pressure for submission to mediocrity. Finally, network and group coordination can often lead to the establishment of negative norms and values that are self-reinforcing, such as teenage pregnancy and drug addiction.

Xavier Briggs (2004) discusses two faces of social capital: social capital as an individual good; and social capital as a collective good. He suggest that the dark side of social capital, especially the potential for exclusion, is very evident in social capital as a collective good, a resource possessed by a social system that helps the system as a whole to solve problems. For instance, community norms can be tied to religious beliefs and symbols and to ethnicity, in ways that exclude others. Bonding social networks can reinforce and deepen ethnic and class distinctions and conflicts. So there is high potential for exclusion in relation to social capital.

The above exploration confronts us with the crucial concerns of this chapter about whether, how and to what extent new African Christian communities in diaspora generate social, cultural and religious capital while in the midst of cultural flux in Europe and the United States. Ample data illuminate the fabric of social, religious and cultural capital among the various new African Christian communities in diaspora, and their ability to transfer, transform and continually negotiate their religious and cultural identities in new host contexts. It is to this that I now turn.

African Christianities as social capital

In order to understand the involvement of religious groups in public life, Casanova (1994) posits that one needs to look at the three domains of the public sphere: the state, the political society and the civil society. Voluntary organizations and members of the associational life in civil society advance the socialization of individuals and cultivate values and mores regarding communal life, such as reciprocity, trustworthiness and friendship. Putnam (2000) recognizes that faith communities in which people worship together are arguably the single most important repository of social capital. Allen Hays (2001) suggests four processes through which church congregations may contribute to social capital. First, in mobilizing resources that might not otherwise be mobilized to address community problems. Second, in raising consciousness about community problems among people who would not otherwise be aware or engaged. Third, in creating linkages between social groups that would not normally exist; and lastly in empowering social groups that normally have little influence. Smidt (2003) makes a valuable contribution to the ongoing discourse on the place of religion in civil society and its role in fostering social capital. The book documents a vast array of religious institutions in the United States, their roles and capacities in generating social capital and promoting civic engagement. Alex Stepick et al. (2009) focus on the intersection of religion and civic engagement among Miami's immigrant and minority groups in examining the role of religious organizations in developing social relationships and how these relationships affect the broader civic world. Whether we see social capital as a possession of individuals or as inhering in networks has a huge impact on how we operationalize and then measure the concept.

Generally speaking, hardly any attention, as yet, has been devoted to the unique role that African Christianities may play in building social capital. In spite of the growing literature on African diaspora religiosities, not much attempt has been made to capture how religious communities are generating social, cultural and religious capital. Attention needs to be given to the dynamics of African Christianities in generating social, cultural and spiritual capital so as to illuminate pathways in which the economy and quality of capital formation is relevant to African Christian communities in Europe and the United States. What role does religious involvement in these communities play in promoting stocks of social, cultural and spiritual capital? To what extent do these religious communities contribute to bonding and/or bridging social capital? What is the downside of social capital among African religious communities? How do African faith-based groups contribute to the institutional infrastructure of local communities through working with and supporting local-global networks?

African Christian communities contribute enormous bridging, bonding and linking social capital, but also confront barriers to development and civic engagement. Their spaces of worship are not simply religious places, they are also spaces of socialization where business, politics, education, music, home country and food cultures, even gossips are engaged and negotiated. Such spaces often transcend socio-ethnic, race, class, gender and intergenerational boundaries. People meet others from different backgrounds, they share activities and build trust in one another, albeit temporarily.

African-led churches facilitate bridge-building and links-building with others, thus generating local-global networking trends, new forms of association, and engendering trust in shared community initiatives. Their landscapes of worship can also be a source of conflict among members, between the leadership and the followers, but also between these religious communities and their neighbourhoods.

African Christian communities in Europe and the United States both empower and disempower their members. The inequalities of power, such as in the subordination of youths and women, can also inhibit the generation of social capital. The choice of appropriate liturgical language for worship services, approved dress codes, moral instructions, prescribed respect modes for elders and authority, and gender role differentiation often engender conflict. The orientation and attitudinal differences between first-generation parents/elders, and second- or third-generation children/youth often provokes inter-generational conflicts. To attempt to answer the questions posed above, one requires a framework for measuring processes of capital formation. Some features discussed below will provide some glimpses on how African Christian communities facilitate or inhibit social, cultural and spiritual capital engineering.

African Christian communities are forums that 'bridge' and 'bond' together people across different social, ethnic, gender, class and intergenerational echelons. While these communities are predominantly African in a demographic sense, this is only a continental category. Their membership is characterized by a complex fusion of ethnic, national, religious, social, cultural, gender, class, and intergenerational identities (see also Chapter 7). The value that most African-led churches assign to bringing these peoples together under the same roof, and in forging and maintaining networks between these homogeneous and heterogeneous groups of people, has immense potential for bridging and bonding capital. Thus, in bridging and bonding social capital, African Christian communities have the tendency to forge and reinforce inclusive and exclusive identities; maintain homogeneity and heterogeneity; mobilize loyalty, solidarity and undergird reciprocity or the lack of it. The tendency to create avenues where people share similar sentiments and religio-cultural identities could also result in a kind of systemic ghettoization of these communities, and serve as a forum for fuelling ethnically or nationally related intrigues, strife and bickering among members. Ethnically based churches with a single ethnic language as the medium of worship, such as Twi, Akan, Yoruba, Igbo, Shona-speaking churches in Europe and the United States, have a tendency to perpetuate and reproduce ethnic, national cleavages and fissure. In the process of maintaining ethnic-based communities, they unconsciously exclude people of other African ethnicities and nationalities irrespective of other proximities by marriage, cultures, peer-groupings and friendship.

In the case of linking capital, some African Christian communities in Europe and the United States often pay courtesy calls and build links to policymakers, members of parliament, politicians, community leaders to garner legitimacy, support and recognition as bona fide churches, faith-based organizations or in fact in lobbying for spaces of worship. They also build links to business entrepreneurs for financial support and sponsorship of their programmes; and to religious entrepreneurs for spiritual mentoring. Such linkages enable individuals and communities to speak directly to those with formal decision-making power rather than have their views filtered via 'vendors', 'lobbyists' and 'brokers'. For instance, RCCG Jesus House in Brent Cross, North London – the largest RCCG parish in the United Kingdom, hosted the Prince of Wales as part of celebrations to mark his 59th birthday. He was accompanied by his wife, Camilla, the Duchess of Cornwall. Other dignitaries in attendance included the Mayor of Barnet, Councillor Maureen Braun, some local MPs, and the Bishop of London – Rt Rev Richard Chartres. The historic visit of such a prominent figure as the Prince of Wales and others is indeed a linking capital booster for the RCCG's public image and ecclesiastical legitimacy in Great Britain. As the RCCG reports, 'Emotion was let loose on November 14 in London when Prince of Wales, Prince Charles celebrated his 59th birthday at the RCCG, Jesus House'. [2] The host senior pastor, Rev Agu Irukwu, felt the prince's visit was good for everyone. 'I felt the privilege and honour of hosting Prince Charles was not just to Jesus House and RCCG, but also the wider black community.'[3] The Prince of Wales commended the great contribution made to the British society by a great number of churches operated by black people. As he remarks:

> I can't tell you what a joy it is to worship with you today. All I can tell you is that there is nowhere I would rather be on my birthday ... I want you to remember that it is highly appreciated by me and more and more by other people ... In your church, you are doing the things that Jesus would do if he walked the streets of London today. You are all a marvellous example of how so many people whose families originate from the Commonwealth, have yourselves brought new life into the Christian Church in the UK

thereby completing the cycle started by missionaries from Britain so many years ago. So we have that to thank you for ...'

It was reported that Prince Charles even went further to initiate a possible collaboration between the RCCG and his charity initiative, The Prince's Trust. This instance of linking capital provided here is not an isolated example but a common initiative forged by the RCCG and other African-led churches to demonstrate their clout in religious, political and civic realms. But probably the most important and studied aspect of religious social capital is volunteering, because of its capacity to generate social, cultural and spiritual capital.

Volunteerism

A social capital approach is better adapted to understanding the outcomes of religion on other parts of life, for instance in areas of volunteerism and civic engagement. The volunteer labour potential of church members is enormous. Much of the preparation and execution of church programmes and activities such as worship services, midweek services, night vigils, bible studies, children services, out-door evangelism, conventions, retreats are volunteered by members. It takes considerable time to arrange, clean up meeting halls prior to and after events. Members volunteer to 'baby-sit' children, wash dishes, clean toilets and ensure that church vicinities are kept tidy, especially in cases where the same worship venue is rented or shared by various groups. Thus, different departments such as the crèche, youth ministry, hospitality and welcome, after service coffee/tea provision, housing, music, choir team, technical, evangelism, prayer warriors, protection of vulnerable groups, security, buildings and maintenance are mostly run on volunteer basis. Members volunteer expertise and identify area(s) where they can contribute to the growth, smooth running of their religious communities. In fact, most local pastors or leaders of African Christian communities in Europe and the United States do not receive monthly salaries or stipends, they volunteer their services. Against this backdrop, some serve the communities on a part-time basis, combining their religious vocation with a paid job. In some other cases, pastors or leaders cannot earn salaries or stipends owing to the poor financial situation of the local church. Some local churches struggle to pay their monthly rent or lease and utility bills. Under such circumstances, some pastors often have to rely on the goodwill of the membership.

Church attendance is associated with increased volunteering, and religious beliefs can influence the meaning of volunteering in people's lives. For several African-led churches in Europe and the United States, church belongingness is hardly a Sunday-Sunday ritual. The entire week is usually dotted with programmes including the Sunday morning worship service, evening service, week-day morning prayer, mid-week service, night vigil, bible study fellowship, prayer night, deliverance night, healing service, fasting week, choir practice, church workers meeting, vestry meeting, visiting members, house warming, baby showers, child christening and outdoor events, new job thanksgiving event, birthday celebrations, marriage and wedding anniversaries to mention a few.

Religious capital is built through member's enormous time investment and in the physical work they are involved in within their respective communities. In spite of busy daily job and school routines, members volunteer and set aside time to attend several church functions and programmes that often range from one to several hours or even days. Experientially, African Christians, as compared to most European and American Christians, are more likely to spend more time in church services or religious programmes. While many Western Christians are used to average church service duration of a quarter to one hour, some African church worship services could run for a couple of hours. As members battle against increasing unemployment, new socio-economic realities of the host context, negotiating a delicate balance between time apportioned to church activities, secular employment, studies, family responsibilities often generates a great deal of tension. While the church leadership rely on members' support in planning and executing programmes, and may even pronounce mandatory attendance to some church events, others are largely voluntary. Member's commitment and participation in church activities is mostly perceived as a sacred duty and service to God and humanity that must be encouraged. Although, many African Christians have created new homes in Europe and the United States, the new feature of 'religious believing but not belonging; and belonging but not believing' which now shapes the demography of European churches is hardly imagined or contemplated by them.

Religion as a body of beliefs, values and norms motivates believers to volunteer in community affairs to provide social services such as health care, soup kitchens, education and helping the poor (Ugar 2007: 154). African Christian communities in Europe and the United States act as communication networks that foster religious but also in some cases civic volunteerism. Religion also provides a source of common identity to its followers and creates bonds between them. The belief systems and teachings of many African-led churches play a crucial role in enhancing or hindering social capital formation. A spiritual kinship system is engendered in these communities with the appropriation of a distinctive language of reference to one another as 'brothers' and 'sisters' or in some cases simply as 'brethren', in day-to-day conversation. Such inclusivity has the tendency to draw boundaries between 'brothers/sisters in the Lord' and the 'Others'. The distinctiveness of some of their beliefs, especially their orientation towards evangelism, the emphasis in the reality of the superterrestrial forces and the ritual attitude against malevolent forces, makes them somewhat inward-looking and in turn prevents achieving a much more global appeal of their worldviews. Religiously motivated volunteers employ communitarian language not only for self-reference, but to describe their involvement and to appeal to some sense of the common good. 'Religion also provides a symbolic language enmeshed in the grammar of the society by speaking the language of the masses and utilizing the cultural capital' (Smidt 2003).

As church members, people give money voluntarily to their communities and devote their time even to secular efforts. Tithing is perceived as a solemn covenant between God and his people (members). Some of the oft-quoted biblical references to legitimize this practice states:

> 'Will a man rob God? Yet you rob me. But you ask, How do we rob you? In Tithes and Offerings. You are under a curse – the whole nation of you – because you are robbing God. Bring the whole tithe into the storehouse, that there may be food in my house. Test me in this and see if I will not throw open the floodgates of heaven and pour out so much blessing that you will not have room enough for it. I will prevent pests from devouring your crops, and the vines in your fields will not cast their fruits, says the Lord Almighty. Then all the nations will call you blessed, for yours will be a delightful land, says the Lord Almighty'. (Malachi 3: 8–12)
>
> Remember this: Whoever sows sparingly will also reap sparingly, and whoever sows generously will also reap generously. Each man should give what he has decided in his heart to give, not reluctantly or under compulsion, for God loves a cheerful giver. (II Corinthians 9: 6–7)

Proving God with tithes is cast as a faith principle. This principle has a special significance to the tithe. In tithing, you therefore need to be proving God. While most African-led churches strongly enjoin its members to engage in tithing, members are not compelled in a matter-of-fact sense. The liturgical structure makes ample space for the collection of tithes. Prior to this stage, the oft-cited references are recited as a way of calling members to wake up to their responsibility. They believe that unfaithfulness in the area of tithing can make a member lose lots of God's blessings, because he is perceived as stealing directly from God. The failure to pay tithes is believed to automatically bring curse upon a member and his/her business.

Tithes and offerings is a revolving theme in sermon texts and in church publications. The principle of reciprocity which 'tithe and offering' represents is further honed into members' ears with the frequent rendition of biblical injunctions by singing and dancing: 'Give and it will be given to you. A good measure, pressed down, shaken together and running over, will be poured into your lap. For with the measure you use, it will be measured to you' (Luke 6:

38). The importance of tithes and offerings is evident in members' adherence to it both in their giving as well as in their testimonies about tithing. The enormous financial resources generated through tithing are primarily geared towards catering for the welfare of church leader(s) and employees, as well as for the poor and the needy.

In addition to the communitarian language and experience that their faith brings to them, it also provides civic skills for those who participate in its structures. The concern of African-led churches with social and political issues in Africa and the diaspora vary from context to context. So is the civic agendas and direct engagement with civil society they may pursue beyond their immediate church vicinity, stretching far beyond the pastoral realm. The relationship between time volunteered for spiritual/religious concerns and civic engagement depends on the context, and individual circumstances. The immigration status, the ratio of legal versus undocumented, of the leader/pastor and the church members is also an important determining factor of whether and how far the church community will be favourably disposed towards and incorporate civic engagement into their modus operandi, or focus their everyday praxis on individual spiritual concerns, and even towards their original home countries.

In Europe and the United States, churches and faith-based organizations register under government corporate affairs departments. In the United Kingdom, most African-led churches register with the charity commission as charitable, non-profit organizations. Thus, many African-led churches and faith communities are at 'the vanguard of charitable initiatives' (Stepick et al. 2009: 3); and actively promote civic engagement through micro finance programmes, supporting thrift shops, providing soup kitchens, warm clothing and blankets to the vulnerable during winter season, language classes, tutoring for children and youth. They also provide training geared towards self-employment and poverty alleviation, youth and women empowerment, and making contributions to the welfare of their constituency through a multiplicity of spiritual and social resources. Characteristic attempts of African Christian communities to lift themselves out of poverty are savings and credit schemes, where well-trusted principles of reciprocity assist people to establish small businesses. The strength of the churches lies in their spiritual and social capital, which is strongest at the grass-roots level (Imunde and Padwick 2008). For instance, the MFM Greatway Microfinance in Edinburgh was set up in 2008 to target low-income women's empowerment in the Edinburgh branch of MFM. It has helped many women out of chronic poverty.[4] Through services such as loans, savings, insurance and remittances, many women involved have become self-reliant and have built their own economic base, besides and to complement that of their husbands. Some have started small-scale businesses, even buying and selling within the church precincts.

Some of the African-led churches have been a focal point of leadership development and empowerment. A case in point is the Nigerian-born Matthew Ashimolowo and his KICC located in East London, renowned in global Christian circles for planning and executing large religious programmes such as crusades, conventions and training programmes. Besides, internal youth and leadership empowerment initiatives include the Kings Kids, KICC Champions, Singles Ministry, Men's Ministry and Women's Ministry. The catchword for KICC's annual Christian Conference, the International Gathering of Champions (IGOC) is 'Raising Champions, Taking Territories'.[5] The IGOC is 'renowned for equipping Christians with the insightful and practical knowledge they need to lead successful lives'. The successful planning and execution of most of these programmes largely rest on the volunteering of KICC members and other stakeholders.

The initiative that was started by Ashimolowo in 1991 gathers more than 180,000 Christians from over 40 nations for more than a week at each instance, for what is now known as Europe's premier Christian conference.[6] Local and international evangelists and leaders participate in this annual ecumenical event. African American evangelists and Pentecostal leaders who have participated include Eddie Long, Thomas Jakes, Keith Butler, Juanita Bynum and Donnie McClurkin. They appeared alongside African Pentecostal preachers such as Enoch Adeboye, David Oyedepo, Dipo Oluyomi, Mensah Otabil and Robert Kayanja.[7] Such forums often parade a mix of leaders and members from both constituencies. The conference is also an avenue for the commodification of sermon texts, gospel music, songs, films, anointing oil, documentaries and programmes of participating leaders and churches made into books, diaries, almanacs, souvenirs and audio-visual products.[8] The Winning Women's Conference hosted by the wife of the pastor, Yemisi Ashimolowo, attracts over 4,000 women annually.[9] The conference provides 'days of empowering teaching that equips women with the keys to winning in all aspects of their lives'. The line-up of gifted ministers bring messages that inspire and encourage women of different ages to handle the myriad challenges of life. Such conferences common among African-led churches are not simply forums for religious networking and spiritual rejuvenation; the varieties of programmes and teachings also promote leadership engagement, empowerment and civic engagement.

Trust, trustworthiness and reciprocity

Social capital can be understood at two separate but interrelated levels. One is the individual level pertaining to the degree to which individuals are 'community minded' with a sense of the common good. The other level is more inter-subjective and structural, and relates to the absence or existence of trust between individuals in a society. In a way, voluntary organizations in the civil society play an important role in transforming anonymous masses into communities, and trust lubricates cooperation for mutual benefit (Smidt 2003). Religious institutions play a distinctive role within the specific local contexts of Africa and the African diaspora because those settings that previously generated trust and sustained broad social networks have deteriorated badly: unions, blue-collar workplaces, cultural associations, families, governments and so forth. The dwindling of European and US economies, soaring unemployment, failing welfare systems, and the tightening of immigration policies has contributed to eroding any trust that many immigrants have for host governments, politicians and policy makers. Owing to their vulnerability, immigrants, particularly the undocumented, would often see the police and security agents as potential foes and people never to be trusted. It is against this backdrop that leaders, pastors of African Christian communities fill a major vacuum, a spiritual next-of-kin in a largely hostile social environment. Members repose much trust in and respect for their church pastors and leaders. As a result of this trust, they can confide in them their private family matters, disclose actual immigration status, share immigration stories, dashed dreams, rekindled hopes and lived experiences in diaspora. They can also support their pastors and leaders with material (money) and moral resources.

Trust is closely linked to social capital, either as a direct part of it or as an outcome. This trust and trustworthiness evokes reciprocity, confidentiality, and anonymity must not be disclosed. But this trust could also be betrayed. As a result of this fervent trust, some leaders and pastors do play on the ignorance and humility of members and exploit them to their own advantage. Such confidence that members have on the pastor/leader could be abused with leaders attempting to carve out religious empires for themselves or misappropriating church finances to the detriment of members, and thus leading to personality squabbles and betrayal of trust.

> The values of reciprocity are reinforced by the directions and sanctions of the Holy Spirit, who speaks in prophecies, dreams, visions, and "tongues", through prophets and individual church members, to correct erring members, and to re-assert the principles of social justice. (Imunde and Padwick 2008: 5)

There is perhaps a thin line between when religion becomes a source of cooperation rather than a source of conflict. Religious exhortations can reduce tensions in some, but also increase them in others. It can help to heal divisions within the fold, but it can also exacerbate them especially when long held mutual trust has been eroded. As core elements of social capital, reciprocity and trust do not simply rest with the pastor/leader and his followers/members, they are more generally associated with family and church networks. The number and types of exchanges between family, peer and church members within the various networks, and shared identities that develop, does influence the amount of social, material and spiritual support an individual has, as well as giving access to other sources of help.

Family and church networks

The family and community are crucial in migration networks. Family linkages often provide both the financial and the cultural capital which make migration possible (Castles and Miller 1993: 27–8). What kinds of actors or agents are involved in religiously relevant, transnational networks, and what kinds of ties or links describe the relationships that these networks assume? Religious and social networks of new African immigrants in Europe and North America are basically composed of kin and church members. Social capital is a vital concept that allows us to analyse the benefits obtained as a result of family, church or individual networks in the everyday activities of people (Ebaugh and Chafetz 2002: 34). Family and church networks assume social and cultural capital through the immense, vital knowledge, information, experience that are shared and constantly transmitted between network members in order to ease their multiple everyday activities such as travelling, getting jobs, education, housing, changing their legal/illegal status, sending remittances home, obtaining inexpensive health-care services, buying and shipping cars and the like. 'Immigrant concentrations are also commonly the sites of social capital formation utilized in the adaptation to the host society. Immigrant congregants man exchange food, loans, and help with finding housing, rides, job referrals, childcare, and other services' (Ebaugh and Chafetz 2000).

Owing to the vulnerability of many immigrants, particularly the undocumented ones, family and church networks help immigrants who are confronted with difficult situations. African-led churches become brokers (meso-structure) between the majority of their members and the wider society. In some cases, being a functional church member functions as an 'identity card' that guarantees moral, material as well as spiritual support in case of need. African Christian communities play a significant role, albeit an ambivalent one, in fostering and sustaining inter-ethnic relations on the one hand; but also in facilitating the integration, or the lack of it, into European and American cultural and social life. Within their church vicinity, immigration, language instructions, cultural adaptation seminars are provided as part of their social programmes. In fact, border crossing may be one of the arenas in which individual and church networks become social capital. Church pastors and leaders also cultivate social capital through their sermons and actions.

The anonymity of undocumented immigrants is often maintained within these religious communities. In fact, the stories of illegal migration and unapproved residence permits are sometimes legitimized as sacred narratives. Pastors encourage members (undocumented immigrants) not to 'look at their past histories or present predicaments, but look forward to God's future plan for and with them', 'I do not care how you came to this country. It was not by any mistake, but by God's perfect design. God brought you to this country for a purpose'. Such phrases are not uncommon in sermons rendered during worship services. Information abounds through family, peer, church networks about cheap, affordable housing, accommodation and health care. Lessons of how to cope in the new context are freely available. Attitudes and knowledge that will make members adapt and succeed easily in the new context are consciously promoted. The church as a social, cultural and spiritual capital becomes more intelligible if we consider the church arena both as a religious space and a space for socialization where negotiation occur between the resilience of cultural and religious identities and the urge to assimilate notions of the global. The social capital that is generated within African Christian communities in Europe and the United States has a local, global twist. The capital that is cultivated has implications not only for the immediate, local church community. It does have impact for the wider host community and a transnational reach.

Social capital and transnational religious networks

The triangular focus of this book on African Christian communities in Europe, the United Sttaes and Africa evince a multiplicity of links and networks that are religious, economic, political, social and cultural at the same time (see Chapter 10). Within these different geo-contexts, African-led churches mutually shape and influence each other with regard to worldviews, ritual structures, personnel, lived experiences and through flow of resources. When we ask what kinds of resources flow along ties between network nodes, we are asking about the content of network interactions, in this case, what resources flow across national borders that have a bearing on religious institutions, personnel, objects, beliefs and ritual practices. There is a common tendency to think only of monetary flows in form of remittances from immigrants in the receiving country to kin, neighbours, friends and communities in their original home context. The transnational nature of contemporary societies largely renders this picture much more complex. Levitt (1998) introduced the concept *social remittances* and defined it 'as the ideas, behaviours and social capital that flow from receiving to sending communities'. She was quite apt in broadening the concept 'remittances' to include nonmaterial as well as financial phenomena. She recognizes that immigrants bring with them to the host society a set of norms, practices, and varying degrees of social capital, which she calls their 'resources' (Levitt 2001). In the course of their lives in the receiving country, they adapt and effect changes in these resources, which, in turn, become the content of social remittances sent back to their original home communities.

When I examine the transnational religious networks of African immigrants in Europe and the United States, I do not only find the variety of material and social remittances of which Levitt speaks but also varying degrees of bi-directionality in flows of different kinds of resources. Drawing from Levitt's typology of social remittances – normative structures, practices and social capital, I shall demonstrate the complex, varying degrees of bi-directionality in flows of different kinds of resources generated by African Christian communities in diaspora.

Monetary and material resources

African Christian communities exchange monetary and material resources not only within the triangular contexts of Africa, Europe and North America. The organizational structure of these churches makes this process easy to conjecture. Their internal religious characteristics and self-financing dynamics and strategies act as stimuli for growth and spread in Africa and in the diaspora, but also in a manner that reconfigures and impact on the global religious economy. As their financial structure and economic base vary in scope and modus operandi, the example of the RCCG will suffice here. Each individual RCCG parish is linked to the Lagos International headquarters, through an evolving hierarchical administrative structure.[10] At the central organizational level, local parishes are required to make monthly financial remittances through administrative zonal headquarters to RCCG International headquarters. This includes 10 per cent of total Tithes and Offerings of all RCCG fellowships, 30 per cent of Tithes and 10 per cent of Offerings of all parishes dedicated by the General Overseer or not. Each local parish is expected in addition to submit a comprehensive financial report for proper financial accountability. For instance, within the RCCG North America (RCCGNA), each parish is required to send a portion of its monthly income to the Finance Coordinating Center in Houston. The funds accumulating there are used to assist new, young or weak parishes that need financial help for a time, and also for international missions.[11] While the RCCG's primary source of revenue is tithes and offerings, other sources include Sunday worship offertory, thanksgiving offerings, special programme offerings, donations, vows, pledges and special levies on projects such as building constructions. The huge monies generated from these diverse sources and events form the church's economic bedrock.

The RCCG expansion in diaspora is now characterized by parishes founded out of the initiative of local parishes in Nigeria. Such local parishes did not only establish new branches in diaspora, but also take financial responsibility by sending a missionary pastor and providing facilities and infrastructure for the new parish. Such coordinating pastors sent directly from Nigeria also have their salaries and honorarium paid from the local Nigerian parish especially in the infancy of the new parish. The evidence calls for a further re-examination of any explanations that privilege ecclesiastical externality and extraversion in explaining the success of African new Christianities.

When an immigrant religious congregation is in its infancy years and members mostly new arrivals, money and material goods flow from home to host country religious institutions. This flow of money, material goods, technology is also from the host to the home contexts, and from one host context to another. Typically, technology such as computers, websites and so on. flow to the home country but some other types of religious and cultural objects such as books, tapes, anointing oil and other religious paraphernalia continue overtime to flow to Europe and the United States or flow bilaterally. In a sense, the introduction of material goods may serve also to alter religious norms, worldviews and practices (Ebaugh and Chafetz 2002: 176).

Far more than monetary flows, Ebaugh and Chafetz (2000) aptly points out that, 'early in the history of most immigrant congregations, religious norms and practices are imported and reproduced as faithfully as possible'. An issue that is perhaps more problematic to speculate on is the extent to which this importation process continues at more mature stages of institutional development, and the extent to which innovations, often developed as part of the process of adaptation to the host community are exported back to religious institutions in home countries (cf. Levitt 2001).

Normative structures:
Theological ideas, values and beliefs

One crucial challenge for African Christian communities, generally poised for demographic expansion (mission) in the West, is to forge new expansion strategies, demonstrate public (social) relevance, and repackage rhetoric and narratives of evangelism in such a way that would appeal to sensibilities of potential clientele within the new host society. This is more so the case against the backdrop of perceived secularizing tendencies that has characterized Western societies and churches in Europe. Most African-led churches ensure that theological ideas, values and beliefs are sustained and rehearsed in their branches universally through the appropriation of bible study manuals, Sunday school devotional materials, prayer books, hymn/song books, holy water, incense, anointing oil, annual ritual calendars, liturgical order of service and other religious paraphernalia. Recorded audio and video tapes of leader's sermons and major church programmes, Christian home videos are very popular and circulate within Africa and the diaspora.

MFM branches worldwide seem to ensure and demonstrate resilience, continuity, and consistency in most of their beliefs and ritual praxis.

> The importation of churches like MFM into Europe involves not just personnel, buildings, or a renewal of Christianity, but also additional belief systems that may or may not be familiar to the mainstream population. These worldviews are often effectively reproduced within the religious setting through socialization procedures, which occur in the spatial-temporal locus of the church. (Larm 2008)

It is believed that the General Overseer devised a strategy, inaugurating a 'compliance team', what Olatunde described as 'Ministry Shoppers', who make impromptu, unannounced visits to MFM branches around the world as a means of ensuring member's and branch's compliance with church beliefs and practices, but also in sustaining loyalty to the church leadership.[12]

The RCCG International headquarters in Nigeria provides ongoing normative resources to its diaspora by centrally controlling doctrine and all or most of its core religious personnel at the global level. RCCG use of universal literature for liturgy, bible study, Sunday school manual, commodification of audio and video tapes with recordings of Pastor Adeboye or other leader's sermons is a way of maintaining their specific Christian identity and worldview. While they use the Sunday school manual in all RCCG parishes all over the world, the prerogative of the local pastors on the sermon theme brings in innovation. The RCCG have largely appropriated electronic and print mediums in the transmission and propagation of their religious messages. Electronic gadgets are utilized in church programmes as well as by members in a matter-of-fact fashion. Sermon texts by the General Overseer have been processed and commodified in book form, audio-video cassettes. They are distributed to all parishes worldwide. The RCCG Internet project has helped to bridge geo-distance, thus linking and maintaining continuity of all parishes with the international headquarters. Special programmes are transmitted online and can be viewed simultaneously and instantaneously. RCCG's use of email and interactive communication helps to build social capital. It does bridge members together, although it may not necessarily bond them.

The resilience and transformation of indigenous religious cosmologies is not unconnected with how African Christian communities respond to social change. Theological ideas, values, and beliefs are not simply adhered to hook, line and sinker, but are critiqued and negotiated with existing theological ideas and values in the new local host contexts. The RCCG posit a conservative *widerspruch* (criticism) of modernity that is starkly rooted in the Bible. It challenges cross-dressing, piercing, 'punkish' dress codes, homosexuality, gayism, lesbianism, gay-marriages, gay-bishops and priests, single parentage, pre- and extra-marital sexual relations, alcoholism, smoking and even the use of mobile phones during church services. The church not only criticizes these acts and modes of behaviour as 'ungodly' but also enacts rituals to counteract these 'vices' within the wider society. There are regulations concerning the use of mobile phones during church worship services. The church recommends that members switch them off discretionarily during rituals. As a bold notice at the entrance of one of the church building states: 'Please switch off your mobile phones. The only urgent call expected here is the voice of God'. This is an indication of how the RCCG negotiates modernity.

In sum, the relative intensity and reciprocity characteristic of resource flows in the transnational religious networks I have been describing makes the exploration of 'agency' and 'changing worldviews' within African immigrant religiosity both complex and illuminating. African religious communities have been shown to be involved in reciprocal exchanges of different types of resources with their parent churches in Africa or in the diaspora. African Christian communities in Europe and the United States provide regular but infrequent material and financial resources, and are involved in the provision of social capital to the home based churches and vice versa in circular fashion. An examination of resource flows in transnational religious networks demonstrate that, in addition to money and material goods, there are a number of other resources that circulate. While most flows are 'remittances' in the sense that they originate among immigrants and their religious communities and flow to home communities and other host destinations, there are also ample cases of reciprocity. Reciprocity could be financial as we have demonstrated, but it could also be in terms of material goods – religious paraphernalia such as books, audio-visuals and other ritual objects, normative structures and even ritual practices. This underscores the significance of examining ongoing, bi-directional resource flows, not just remittances, when considering well-established, but as well as new, immigrant communities such as the African one and their transnational networks.

7

Negotiating identity, citizenship and power

Introduction

The discourse on identity, its scope, structure and modes of negotiation remain contentious. Is identity a given out there or is it a figment of construction? Is it used as a descriptive or analytical term? How helpful is it to talk of identity in the singular without pluralizing the concept? As a highly contested concept, the identity discourse has even assumed new dimensions especially in postmodernist thinking and epistemology, to the extent that it poses a challenge on whether and to what extent our appropriation of the concept may enrich or blur our object of scientific analysis. I do not undertake to fully problematize identity as a concept in this chapter. However, I suggest that it remains, in some sense, a useful analytical category in comprehending the complex demographics of African Christian communities in diaspora. This is against the background that religion is at the pivot of African immigrants' sense of individual and collective identities.

Identity formation(s) rarely exist in a social vacuum. The fluid nature of identities makes them susceptible to construction, contestation and (re)negotiation. New identities can emerge and dissolve; old identities can re-emerge and be re-invented. The invention and reconstruction of identity may be understood as ascribed or self-imposed at individual, collective and societal levels. Every immigrant lays claim to multiple identities as opposed to one. Thus, we can talk of village, town, ethnic, national, religious, Muslim, Islamic, Christian, Pentecostal, orthodox, evangelical, gendered, sex, race, colour, class, age, intergenerational and linguistic identities. In a sense, an individual might talk of one main identity in juxtaposition with other sub-identities. But even this is in itself problematic when subjected to further analysis. Every modicum of identity may be understood in terms of whether it is largely a self-ascribed, self-defined representation or a public-ascribed, reified identity representation of the 'Other'; what political, social, cultural and other factors produc such a construction and for what ends.

It is also pertinent to probe into the contextual factors, such as the politics of inclusion and exclusion, necessitating such an identity formation. This leaves us with a resounding question of whether there is indeed a fixed identity. Are there any fixed identities? Why do people strive to create one kind of identity while at the same time rejecting another form of identification? In what sense can identity formation be likened to shopping at a supermarket where one can pick and choose identities as items on a scale of preference? How helpful is it when an individual or a group of people are stamped with a kind of representation that sometimes illuminate but in other respects obscure the complex identity of that individual or group?

What comes readily to mind here is the somewhat basic, structured questions that most African immigrants claim to confront within the German public space. As an African immigrant puts it: 'As an *auslander* (foreigner) you are often slammed with the questions: *Where do you come from? What are you doing here? How long are you staying? When are you going back?*' Underlying these barrage of questions are discourses of nationality and citizenship, uncomfortable accommodation, public reception, intolerance, nostalgia, exile and return, and racial differentiation. Perhaps a more vexing question hinted by another African immigrant is when he was asked by a rather inquisitive German, '*Do you also come from Wilhelm-Busch Strasse?*' Wilhelm-Busch Strasse (Wilhelm-Busch Street) happens to be the street name on which the *Asylheim* (asylum home) is located in Bayreuth, the Bavarian town in southern Germany where my informant resided and worked as a natural scientist at the local university. Ostensibly, the question had been posed out of just assumption and an arrant ignorance that the respondent was one of the several asylum seekers or refugees often found parading the streets. As he bemoans,

> I was totally put off by the arrogance exhibited by that guy. I had expected that he would confront me with the usual question of where I come from and what I am doing here, rather than slapping me literally with an identity of a refugee or asylum seeker. I replied him angrily 'Look here you racist, do I look like one (*asylum seeker or refugee*)?' Well! I do not blame him so much, it is a mirror reflection of German public mental image about us Africans living here in Deutschland.

While his response may well be an overstatement, it sheds some light on how a reified identity discourse is being negotiated and acted out through the polar extremes of the conversation. This rhetoric may act as a further lead to investigating why, how and to what extent African immigrants engage in constructing, sustaining and (re)negotiating singular and multiple identities. In actual fact, is that 'African' identity in itself a self-construction, self-identification variable, an imposition by the host societies or a combination of both? How are African immigrants negotiating their Christian, national, ethnic and other identities in Europe and the United States?

Doing things on earth for heaven's sake: Negotiating fluid identities

Demographic variables indicate that the Africans, who make up the majority membership of African Christian communities in Europe and the United States, often come from different social, ethnic, national backgrounds, and from varied religious affiliations. Within the new cultural milieu and religious geographies, they operate on new levels of organization where doctrinal differences and ethnic exigencies do not seem to serve as the most vital reference point. Rather, what is important for the Africans in this case is simply a place to share similar sentiments, 'a place to feel at home' or 'a home away from home', thereby establishing a frame of reference for the preservation, transformation and transmission of their specific local religious traditions. The idea of 'home' in a diaspora context takes on a wider symbolic connotation representing either the original homeland in Africa that the immigrant left behind, and to which s/he hopes to return in the unforeseeable future. The new religious space may also represent a 'new' home as the immigrant straddles the intricate complexities of integration and adaptation, inclusion and exclusion, belonging and withdrawal, sameness and difference, and perceptions of 'we' versus the 'Other'. In that vein, the church vicinity as a sacred space does serve as a home against the backdrop of its social, civic and extra-religious relevance for its members particularly from the immigrant constituency. It serves as a space for socialization for members and non-members alike, an alternative social security mechanism, a place of security and a bastion of ethnic, cultural and religious identities.

As religious and ethnic/national/continental identities are intricately intertwined, they may sometimes defy any clear-cut demarcation. The complex cultural diversities and historical specificities of the African continent renders the notions of 'African identity' and 'religious identity' too simplistic to be taken unilaterally. A collective identity of being 'African' is undoubtedly not a fundamental issue among most Africans within continental shores. While residing within the continent, it is doubted whether the question 'Who are you?' would invariably provoke the response 'I am an African'. However, beyond the continent, the urge for collective representation comes to assume immense meaning and relevance thus coalescing the several, multiple identities (ethnic, national, religious, class, gender, intergenerational) into what may seem a complex whole, African identity. Similar to the issue of African identity is the

TABLE 7.1 Are you a German Citizen? If NO, state your nationality/country of origin?

Nationality	Total number of respondents
German citizen	24
Non-German citizen	126
No information	22

corollary of religious identity. The demographic structures of most African Christian communities in Europe and North America evince an interpretation of varied levels of religious identities. Members emerge from wide-ranging religious backgrounds and orientations to form a new religious diasporic identity. The statistics in the Table 7.1, based on results of questionnaire administered in two local RCCG parishes in Germany[1], underscore the complexities around figuring 'African' and 'religious' identities.

Several inferences can be drawn from Table 7.1. However, they may not be as simple as they are presented here. For instance, although Table 7.1 indicates 24 respondents as Germans and 126 as non-German citizens, almost all (except 8 respondents) were in actual fact black Germans (mostly male immigrants originally from Nigeria, Ghana and Kenya). It is puzzling that some respondents who indicated non-German citizen status hold German national passports as individual interviewing and focus-group discussion unveiled. Respondents who failed to indicate their citizenship are perhaps caught up in a quandary of where they actually belong and which nationality they should indicate. Table 7.2 indicates the nationality variable that is often times confused with the ethnic variable. Rather than viewed as a gigantic continent with immense historical and cultural diversities, Africa is often erroneously constructed as an 'ethnic box' to be ticked in some official documentation in Europe. The villagization of the continent – Africa in Western public consciousness also mirror how the complex multinational and multi-ethnic pluriformity of African Christian communities in Europe and North America is often undermined.

Table 7.2 indicates that the membership of the two RCCG parishes transcend national boundaries, a variable which can be further broken down into numerous ethnicities. The ethnic background cohort becomes a microcosm of the nationality variable, which is in fact much more complex to unravel at times in view of overlapping ethnicities as Yoruba, Igbo, Akan, Edo, Ga, Luo, Shona and so on. Besides the unidentified nationalities in Table 7.2, figures show that Nigerians and Ghanaians make up the two largest nationals in RCCG parish 1; while Kenyan and Cameroonian immigrants have numerical

TABLE 7.2 Please indicate your nationality, if you are not German?

Nationality	RCCG parish 1	RCCG parish 2
Nigeria	34	10
Ghana	15	7
Cameroon	8	13
Tanzania	3	1
Kenya	6	16
Liberia	2	3
South Africa	–	2
Zimbabwe	3	1
Britain	1	–
Poland	1	–
No information	10	12
Total number of nationalities = 10	Total number of respondents as in case example 1 = 83	Total number of respondents as in case example 2 = 65

advantage in RCCG parish 2. Nonetheless, these national identities are hardly fixed as variables may change as a result of naturalization, intermarriage or even through visa/passport racketeering processes. The membership coterie of an African-led church in diaspora, on the basis of national/ethnic considerations, is fluid depending on a number of factors. It could be due to the ethnic background of the founder, the cultural background within which the church originated, and the majority membership in both home and host contexts. It may also depend on the migration history and colonial connections of that country with the countries of the immigrants; the specific political and economic realities of the local context; the contexts of reception and the promise for immigrant's socioeconomic mobility. For instance, the RCCG founded by a Yoruba in western Nigeria is currently dominated by Yoruba people in Nigeria and the Yoruba diaspora, although the membership is now rapidly becoming multi-ethnic and multinational. While several parishes in diaspora may be dominated by the Yoruba/Nigerian diasporas, we cannot however generalize on this point as Table 7.2 above clearly shows.

Table 7.3 shows that only 44 respondents – RCCG (7) and Pentecostals (37) – out of 149 who indicated their prior religious background/church affiliation before joining either of the RCCG parishes in Germany. This means that majority of the membership in these parishes were not members of the RCCG prior to their migration to Germany. Some do not even have Christian or Pentecostal religious identification in their home countries but have come to assume this somewhat new religious identity in Germany. One level of interpretation is that while not undermining the factor of individual choice and preferences, the specific religious, political, sociocultural circumstances and climatic factors in the host contexts are quintessential factors which dictate and impact on the nature of identity – single or multiple – forged and desired by African immigrants. Religious identities are not necessarily static and fixed, but susceptible to change. People often engage in switching religious affiliation or renegotiating religious identities in time and space.

TABLE 7.3 What was your former church affiliation or religious background before you joined your present one?

Religious background/church affiliation	Number of respondents
Catholic	28
Anglican	20
Methodist	25
Presbyterian	8
Pentecostal	37
AICs	14
Evangelicals	5
Islam	2
RCCG	7
Jehovah Witness	1
Other category (Christian, EDM, Cathedral)	5
No information	23
Total number of respondents	172

At least three interlocking levels of African diaspora Christians can be distinguished: those who became Christians for the first time while residing in diaspora; members who swap religious denominational affiliations; and those who consciously maintain dual or multiple religious affiliations and identities. My findings reveal a first level of some Africans who only became Christians for the first time while residing in Germany. Such Africans either come from traditional, Islamic or other religious backgrounds, while others lay claim to a state of religious indifference, religious agnosticism or atheism. One respondent (an RCCG member) retorts:

> Back home in Nigeria, I never really gave a thumb up for religion. It was totally out of the question, not in my scheme of things ... I was actually rocking life (enjoying the niceties of life). Among my particular peer group that we see then as a modern group, you become a laughing stock when you are seen to identify strongly with any religious group. You may be nicknamed pope, pastor, imam or guru, and this has a lot of social implications and stigma for the person concerned.

Another level that can be clearly identified are members who switch or swap religious denominational affiliations. These are people who have been members in at least one church either back home (Africa) or in the diaspora before finally opting to choose their present church (RCCG). The third closely related level is that where dual or multiple religious affiliations and identities are consciously maintained. In the last category for instance, a member remains a bona fide Catholic in the home context, but takes up membership of a Pentecostal church while residing temporarily or indefinitely in the diaspora. Such a member sees no contradiction whatsoever in juxtaposing these two traditions, although occurring in different sociocultural contexts. These various levels of religious action are largely occasioned by a multiplicity of factors ranging from specific spiritual/visionary experiences, unavailability of their home church in the new context, and the spiritual quest for a panacea to existential problems. Other explanations include exigent factors, insensitivity of host historical churches, xenophobia and other prevailing socio-economic, cultural and political circumstances.

Ter Haar (1999) draws attention to the ensuing politicization of identity by addressing how relevant the issue of African identity is to African Christians in Europe. As we highlighted in Chapter 4, her observation that African Christians emphasize their religious identity over and above their ethnic identity was critiqued by Gerloff (2001) who took the other extreme, prioritizing their African identity as more important than their Christian identity. Although both scholars aptly underscore religion, in this case Christianity, as a significant identity marker in Europe, the issue of which comes first (African or Christian) may not really arise if scholars do not ask leading questions themselves. The immigrants in question are both Africans and Christians, and which identity is privileged may often depend on the given circumstances; who is being spoken to and for what purposes.

The very peculiar nature and conditions in German society, which assumes an organic definition of citizenship based on descent, may have induced the 'myth of homeland and return' among African immigrants who dominate these churches. The majority of African Christians in Germany are hoping to return home (Africa) or move elsewhere (i.e. United States, Canada) after some years when they are able to complete their education, improve their financial base or achieve other undisclosed reasons. Only a very small number indicated their plan or interest to remain in Germany permanently. One of the pioneer members at the CCOM headquarters in Hamburg remarks,

> It will be a pity for any African to live and grow old in this country (Germany). No matter how long you live here or what status you have attained, you do not have any place here. Any thought of being a 'black-German' or 'Afro-German' is simply absurd and stupendous. Your colour will always betray and disable you here. That is why again you are not welcome with open hands and heart in most German churches unlike ours (African churches). As soon as I am able to raise sufficient capital, I will go straight back home without looking back ... because your money is almost useless and does not make too much sense here.

Such remarks may sometimes appear illusory as in reality many do not return 'home' eventually but continue to maintain the myth even though in an attenuated form, while others voluntarily and involuntarily return 'home' or move to what they perceive as a more attractive and promising host contexts. Nevertheless, such attitudes represent a way of internalizing this myth that is assiduously rekindled in the German political spectrum through anti-foreigner rhetoric with the forceful insistence that Germany is not a country of immigrants. This 'homeland and return' myth plays a significant role in the religious behaviour of African immigrants in Germany, and may be reflected in their attitudes and future outlook. This may partly suggest why a migrant church like the CCOMI might look beyond Germany to the home context as well as to other host migrant societies in its expansionist policy.

The immigrant is not concerned primarily with adaptation but with survival: economic, social and psychological survival. In this context religion can be either a significant part of a 'survival-security' strategy followed by an 'adaptation' strategy, or it can reflect the suffering and the problems of the immigrants, offering them an escape route. In any case, religion is interacting with social and psychological forces: religious beliefs become altered by them but religion also affects social and psychological settings. Immigrants' actions are to be understood in terms of their own goals, goals established first in order to survive, and after that, to adapt to the new social milieu.

Although various European governments often suggest a mastery of language as the panacea to immigrants' successful integration into the host society, some immigrants pose a *widerspruch* or counter-critique to this argument and explain it off as only an excuse and a defensive mechanism for formal exclusion in paid employment and from receiving certain fringe benefits within the society. As one informant puts it:

> I have lived in Germany since 1985 and have a mastery of *Deutsch* (German language) to a reasonable extent. I schooled and worked here for sometime, but I have been without job for almost three years now. I am still heavily discriminated against when it comes to employment ... Although language is one recipe for integration; it is certainly not the only ingredient. The most important question particularly in this context is whether the German public is really willing to receive people like us on grounds of our colour. My answer is that they are not. The society is so hostile particularly towards blacks and *ausländer* (foreigners). I own a German *Pass* (German National Identity Card) for several years now but each time I am indiscriminately accosted and interrogated by the *Polizei* (German Police) on the streets, I become disgusted with their show of arrogance and ignorance. They would ask where I come from originally even though my *Pass* clearly indicates my nationality and citizenship status.

The remarks above raise the politics of citizenship and nationality. Many African immigrants who have taken up European citizenship would assert that they were driven to taking up new citizenship or dual citizenship statuses out of necessity and convenience, either in order to simplify dealing with local bureaucracy or obtain benefits. Such questions require further pondering and I shall revisit it in the next section. I shall also examine some of the ways in which African-led churches are engaged in the discourse of citizenship, and in fact, how African Christians are reconstructing citizenship as an empowerment discourse within the new diaspora.

'I am an African with a British Passport': Reconstructing citizenship

The rising tide in international migration, adoption of restrictive immigration strategies and the EU harmonization policies has partially led to renewed discourses around the enigma of citizenship, nationality, ethnicity, territoriality, race and identity. The increasing shift from autonomous nation-states to a world of blurred boundaries has helped to change the traditional notion of citizenship. Change of citizenship, the negotiation of naturalization engenders identity crises. Citizenship has become more and more contested in Europe, with new talks of 'dual citizenship' and 'dual nationality'. How and why do people undergo naturalization processes to switch their national allegiances and identities? How does the European public deal with such identity-swapping, especially in the case of African immigrants? Is attainment of new citizenship a matter of convenience or a genuine decision to switch national allegiance?

Individual African immigrants, their religious communities as well as governments negotiate flexible notions of citizenship and sovereignty as strategies for capital and power accumulation, but also as a bridge towards seeking socio-religious, economic, political empowerment and legitimacy. Before we explore how African immigrant Christian communities contribute to such public debates, what impact such discourses have on their religious communities, and how it shapes their individual and collective identities, we shall attempt a brief historicization of the concept and the politics of citizenship in the United Kingdom.

Historicizing a concept and process

The resurgence of public interest in the debate on citizenship and nationality, particularly in the last decades, points both to its complexity and to its shifting, fluid meanings, ranging from a legal status denoting formal membership of a political entity to an ideal of inclusion/exclusion and participation/non-participation applicable, in principle, to citizens of the world or global citizenship. Brubaker (1989: 4) aptly underscores how the traditional notions of citizenship themselves are 'vestigial' and 'riddled' with contradictions. The utility of citizenship as a concept representing a sacred and mutually exclusive membership in a democratic nation-state that has social and political consequences is becoming moribund. In this section I cast a critical glance at the bi-directionality of citizenship and immigration. Important in this consideration is how immigration challenges received notions of citizenship, how citizenship shapes migration and vice versa. How and to what extent does anti-immigrant public discourse and restrictive legislation by UK (EU) politicians translate and transform into effective restrictionist policy outcomes and the cosmetization of citizenship?

Public discourses on 'integration' are rife in the United Kingdom and across the European Union against the assumption that integration is the only way or process through which immigrants and their descendants can become full members of host societies, participating in a range of political, economic and social activities. This assumption has led to the invention of varied paradigms of integration such as multiculturalism, assimilation and emancipation at the expense of their real modus operandi or signification in concrete terms. Critics have pointed to the superficiality of such paradigms as evasive mechanisms to legitimize the politics of exclusion and neglect of the 'imagined Other' (immigrant, non-citizen). We need to critically interrogate what is often canvassed as ingredients of integration, such as language, epistemologies of host culture, in order to unpack them from their political abstraction and superficialities. To what extent does a grasp of language represent a yardstick of integration in real or imagined terms? Does an immigrant speaking fluent English or German make him/her a really English or German?

Stasiulis and Bakan (1997: 112–39) aptly posit a re-conceptualization of citizenship as a 'negotiated relationship' as opposed to the ideal typical, static categories. Thus,

> the view of citizenship as an ideal type associated with one type of state tends to limit our understanding of forms of inequality and modes of contestation of rights by groups which lack rights-bearing forms of membership in the territorial nation-state where they are working and residing, often for considerable lengths of time. (117)

The re-construction of citizenship rarely operates in a vacuum but is contingent upon local, contextual and global historical, social, political, economic and other strategic factors.

I contend, like Stasiulis and Bakan that the public discourse and politics of citizenship and nationality in the case of contemporary British society can be better grasped and understood against a historical backdrop. Although British public discourses on past migration policies, patterns and legislation were somewhat topical, the enactment of the British Nationality Act (BNA) 1948, however, marked a critical watershed event in the sociopolitical history of Britain and the erstwhile Empire. Hansen argues that the BNA must be understood in terms of local and global dynamics and constraints rather than as a historical accident (Hansen 1999: 69). As Hansen enthuses:

> this apparent contradiction can only be understood by examining the legislation in the context of past migration patterns and Britain's international position in 1948. The legislation was only marginally related to migration; it was rather an attempt to maintain a uniform definition of subjecthood in the face of Canada's unilateral introduction of its own citizenship, and it was an affirmation of Britain's place as head of a Commonwealth structure founded on the relationship between the UK and the Old Dominions. (67) [2]

The British stance on citizenship could be contrasted with the French universalistic and the German descent-centred notions of citizenship – citizenship linked to *jus soli* (citizenship based on soil of birth) or to *jus sanguinis* (citizenship connected to the descent of the parents) (Brubaker 1989). Nevertheless, each of these perspectives was never static; the language and meaning of citizenship have been constantly changing and undergoing transformation in the face of local and global realities.

The brief historical scenario above provides a lens through which we can understand how current public discourses of citizenship and nationality shape the ways the notion of citizenship is often perceived, constructed and reconstructed by immigrants within the new African religious diaspora. Perhaps, a glimpse of most recent government policies and political debates will help situate this negotiation process lucidly. I argue that the introduction of citizenship tests and citizenship ceremony in the United Kingdom represents a fire-fighting approach to solving the problem or perceived problem of swelling immigration. The introduction of citizenship tests undoubtedly affirms the systematic harmonization or Europeanization of migration policies and the growing fortressization of the EU geo-political space. Under new unfolding plans, immigrants who want to become British and settle permanently in the United Kingdom will need to pass more tests to 'prove their worth' to the country. The 'earned' citizenship would supplant the current system which allows people to apply for naturalization on the basis of how long they have lived in the United Kingdom. The existing citizenship requirement that a person must have lived in Britain for five years, pass a test in English and demonstrate knowledge of life in Britain would be expanded to include points awarded for civic and voluntary work. Migrants from outside the European Economic Area would be encouraged to 'move on' through a system that leads to citizenship – or choose ultimately to leave the country. The cosmetic package of measures include: raising visa fees for a special 'transitional impact' fund; more English language testing ahead of nationality; requirements to prove integration into communities; increasing how long it takes to become British (BBC News, 15 September 2008).

Earned citizenship is indeed a cosmetic citizenship package that makes mockery of concrete integration dynamics. The progressive hierarchization of immigrants in terms of active/non-active, real/imagined, first-class/second-class, good/bad, and skilled/unskilled citizens indeed have dire implications for race relations in multicultural Britain. The prerequisite for being an 'active' citizen gives away a false impression that all 'original, non-migrant' citizens are active citizens in the sense outlined above. This, in fact, runs contrary to the situation in which several thousands of British citizens are totally or partially dependent on social welfare mechanisms for survival.

Citizenship is not only about privileges, but also about allegiances; it is not only about rights but also about the responsibilities of new citizens. The dichotomization of citizenship prerequisites in terms of privileges/allegiances or rights/responsibilities is hardly any bone of contention, what is rather problematic is the politicization of citizenship in which one aspect is overemphasized against the other. The discourse is more and more skewed with policymakers across the EU political spectrum awash in their quest for new definitions of state and citizens/non-citizen relations, emphasizing responsibilities rather than rights of citizens. Perceptibly, UK governments often reify the discourse of immigrants' responsibilities and allegiances over and against rights and privileges which accrue with their new status. The imbalance in representation has a direct connect with public visualization and dual binaries of explanation of the ideal type of liberal citizenship on the one hand, and the invention of its opposite, the derogatory ideal of the dangerous, criminal, economically burdensome non-citizen. Stasiulis and Bakan (1997: 118) were quite apt in remarking that, 'New immigrants, particularly those from Third World origins, are compelled to struggle to obtain even minimal citizenship rights from reluctant host states and among populations encouraged to scapegoat those seeking permanent status and full equality.' Now we return to how some African Christians in the United Kingdom will respond to discourses of citizenship against the backdrop of its increasing politicization.

'We are citizens of heaven'! Discourses of citizenship

The extent to which the essence and rhetoric of 'citizenship' was meaningful, particularly for African immigrants in the United Kingdom is partly brought out by how they engage in discourses on citizenship, but is also expressive of how they feel about themselves and their status within the British society. Generally, citizenship is perceived as describing individuals' reciprocal relationship with society. While I do not suggest that all African immigrants understand, engage and negotiate the politics of citizenship and nationality in the same way, the following analysis based on religious ethnography in the United Kingdom is indicative of the complex diversity of understanding. Some basic models of citizenship can be observed.

First, one emerging trend by which African-led churches interrogate citizenship is by whipping up the rhetoric of citizenship as a 'universal status'. This takes a variety of ways. On the one hand, everyone is a citizen, by virtue of being a member of a community or nation, or because 'citizen' means 'person'. Here, the idea of a 'global citizen' comes into focus. This is sometimes meant as a critique of the social-contractual dimension where citizenship is understood in terms of formal rights and responsibilities. Other models of citizenship are couched in terms of constructive social and political participation, economic independence, social visibility and the right to a voice. Each of these models posit a great deal of ambivalence about the import of their nationality and in fact the meanings of 'Britishness'. The extent to which immigrants within the UK-based African churches understand and identify themselves as citizens, potential citizens or non-citizens often vary in relation to other factors, including access to waged employment and tax involvement, participation in voluntary work, voting rights, and the cultivation of a general sense of belonging. In fact, negotiating citizenship operates on a parallel level with the negotiation of cultural/national identities and integration/adaptation. African Christians in the United Kingdom who identify themselves as British, often also refer to their African, national and ethnic identities as Ghanaians (Akan, Ewe, Ga); Nigerians (Yoruba, Igbo, Edo); as Kenyans (Luo, Masai, Kikuyu); and as Zimbabweans (Shona, Tsonga, Ndebele).

The oft appropriation by African Christians of such phrases as 'We are in the United Kingdom of God', 'We are heavenly citizens or citizens of heaven', 'Global citizens' represent individual and corporate critiques of the politicization of citizenship and nationality in the United Kingdom. A further twist to the citizenship metaphor that resonates well with members is the biblical assertion that all humans are 'pilgrims', 'exiles' and 'foreigners' in this mundane world (Jeremiah 29, 1 Peter 1 and Hebrews 11). Two plains of religious interpretation are canvassed. On one level, members mirror themselves as 'foreigners', 'sojourners' or 'strangers' in both mundane and spiritual terms. They are foreigners or exiles in the physical space of Europe. Jeremiah's discourse (Jeremiah 29) is often read and interpreted as an attractive ethic of negotiating competing citizenships. Peter's description of the church as a 'holy people' is personalized as a religio-ethnic group, and Hebrews narrative of Christians as citizens of a better country, a 'heavenly homeland' with different codes of conduct. The allegiance to 'King Jesus' as opposed to any prime minister or mayor is fully endorsed. The cosmos is therefore a marketplace and they are only temporary sojourners in the journey through life. Heaven is indeed home (Adogame 2000a: 3–29).

In this wider theological sense, they would assert that all humans, whether Africans, British or Europeans, are foreigners or strangers in this world. This is one way they critique the stringent immigration policies of the European Union and the construction of a fortress Europe meant to ward off the influx of immigrants. Besides, an RCCG in Edinburgh member even critiques the rationale behind the idea of the Commonwealth of Nations in this way:

> What is common about the Commonwealth after all? In my view, Commonwealth as we are made to believe is not common … It is simply an economic, strategic gimmick which Britain has used over the years to hide their colonial shame and trickery….

This postcolonial critique does point to ways in which some immigrants or former British colonial subjects voice out what they perceive to be contradictions and visible injustices within a political-economic system.

In the prioritization of citizenship, the preference for the eschatological connotation of citizenship can be better understood against the backdrop of citizenship as a tool of inclusion and exclusion. Their common bond is their belief that their citizenship in the heavenly kingdom was far more important that their mundane citizenship in any earthly polity. The 'heavenly' citizenship is pictured as one in which there are no quotas limiting citizenship in the Kingdom. In such a scenario, citizens are not hierarchized in terms of active/non-active, real/imagined, first-class/second-class, good/bad, and skilled/unskilled. It is one in which 'all are invited to enter freely by faith in the merits of Christ alone'. Immigrants would not need to pass 'tests in order to prove their worth' to the Kingdom. However, as many African immigrants perceive their aspirations toward attaining citizenship to be increasingly gloomy and their expectations are dampened by governments' consciously imposed restrictions the rhetoric of 'heavenly citizenship', whether real or imagined, becomes an increasingly important source of consolation and inspiration.

From the foregoing, I do not suggest that the discourse on citizenship and nationality within African Christian communities follow the same trend. To do that will undermine the complex, varied notions and understandings of citizenship and nationality within these contexts. There is a sense in which such debates about citizenship becomes tools of social, economic and spiritual empowerment. It also helps to facilitate the negotiation between resilience and maintenance of ethnic, cultural, religious and national identities on the one hand; and the integrative and adaptive processes of immigrants into the host society. One African church leader admonished his congregation rhetorically:

> Do you think your living in the UK was by any accident? Far from it! God brought you here for a purpose. So long as you live here, you are a citizen of this country. You work and pay tax, so you are not a visitor any longer you are part of the system. If you exclude your self, then you do this to your own peril. Think of yourself as one who has a purpose to serve and accomplish here ... I do not care whether you have papers (valid immigration documentation or residence permits) or not, whether you are a refugee or asylum seeker. The government and the public call you those names and see you in those terms of a second-class citizen. Brother, Sister! You are perfectly and beautifully made! God created you in his own self-image as a first-class citizen, as a citizen of heaven. It is up to you to decide whose verdict is supreme.

There are certainly controversial dimensions to these statements, nevertheless it shows how the negative sides of the politics of citizenship could be rebranded and repackaged to serve as veritable tools of social-economic empowerment and mobility. The rest of the chapter will focus on a dimension of power politics. I revisit the increasing feminization of African immigrant religiosity (see Chapter 1), demonstrating with specific examples of female leadership dynamics in the 'Ladies on Fire for Jesus', the women caucus of the World Conquerors Christian Centre (WCCC), and the appropriation of empowerment rhetoric in the WCCC and the RCCG; how the polity and demography are increasingly becoming feminized. The empowerment discourse revolves around issues of marriage and the family, singles fellowship, fertility, female dignity, social and financial empowerment.

'I am married to Jesus'! Gender, identity and empowerment

I have shown elsewhere that the complex dynamism of contemporary migration within and beyond Africa is partly reflected in its increasing feminization (Adogame 2008a). Women are assuming increasing roles as resource managers, decision-makers and captains of industries. Some have become church founders, leaders and visible religious functionaries on both sides of the Atlantic. How are the dynamics of power and interpersonal relationships between husband and wife or men and women played out, altered or reconstituted in post-migration circumstances? The resurgence and public visibility of female leaders and ritual roles within African religiosity in the new diaspora and on the continent must be located in historical, sociocultural precedents.

Two field encounters in my religious ethnography starkly eulogizes an inherent contemporaneity of the discourse on how gendered negotiations of power in space-time is evanescent in academic *jaw-jaw* on religion and gender itself; but more importantly on how and ways in which the discourse does play out in the gendered forms of lived religious experiences and expressions. These field encounters also cast translocal gazes and memorializes the complex dynamism, shifting contours, permutation and specificity of women's religious lives in contradistinction to men in African geo-cultural spaces and the specific historical settings of the African diasporas. At the same time, it evokes the urgency for new narratives of identity and the sense of self; a rethinking of the gendered notions of empowerment and authority within the complex religious terrain of contemporary African societies; within transnational topography and the religious cosmos of the African diaspora.

An unpacking of some field notes flavoured with critical hermeneutics and content analysis perhaps laid the ground for a re-interrogation of the variances inherent in shifting power relationships, complex religious worldviews, and the ambivalent socio-religious encounters that spin the recentering of women in Africa and the African diaspora on the one hand but also in transnational and global geoscapes.

In the summer of 2006, I was privy as part of my ethnographic work to two religious programmes themed 'Conquerors School of Leadership' and 'Ladies on Fire for Jesus' respectively, under the auspices of the WCCC International headquarters in Edinburgh, Scotland. The first meeting was held immediately after a Sunday morning worship service while the other activity took place on the preceding Wednesday evening. My unanticipated conversation with a middle-aged, single-parent female member and participant at both events seems to evoke pertinent questions that galvanize discourses of women's resourceful appropriation of rhetoric, ideas, idioms and religious praxis. Furthermore, it suggests meanings and interpretations women themselves make of their religious lives as individuals, but also in relation to men and their immediate social and religious environments.

During our casual conversation at the end of the earlier event, I asked how her family was fairing. To this, she responded, 'My daughter and I are blessed and highly favoured', a characteristic response of WCCC members when exchanging pleasantries. The specificity of her response, referring to her daughter and herself, led me to probe further inquisitively. So I asked: 'Does your husband not attend this church?' She replied with a bit of hesitation: 'I am married to Jesus.' It took further cautious probing to unearth what this response meant in real terms. As I came to understand, this suggests at least two connotations. One, it literally expresses her religious commitment to her Christian faith, her church affiliation (the WCCC), her total reliance and dependence on Jesus Christ in the face of any predicament, adversity, disappointment and marital crisis. A more ingrained connotation was the disclosure of her status as a single parent but one that is not devoid of hopefulness and 'divine intervention' for a new spouse. Realizing how sensitive any further probing on this matter could be, I started a new topic for further conversation. Nevertheless, it took my participant observation in consequent programmes to appropriately contextualize the phrase, 'I am married to Jesus' as a symbolic rhetoric of empowerment and an idiom of rekindled hope and encouragement for a sustainable, stable marital life, one that is prone to consummation. I shall return to this dynamics in a latter discussion on the use of empowerment rhetoric within the 'Ladies on Fire for Jesus' group.

The second field encounter was at one of the RCCG parishes named 'Open Heavens', located in Edinburgh. While engaging in participant observation during Sunday worship services for several weeks, I had observed a white Scottish couple in attendance on two occasions. After a couple of weeks I began to notice their absence, being the only regular white European couple in attendance. When I inquired from one of the church leaders, she was quick to respond that the couple had stopped coming to church on grounds that they were opposed to a woman preaching in church. As she explained, the couple's position on women's role in the church was anchored on the conservative Pauline theology, which puts women on the 'back bench' in church, a somewhat passive role that denies them the opportunity to preach or play any visible leadership role. This standpoint, which was borne out of the couple's previous religious orientation, was put to test during a special Sunday service at the RCCG parish in which a woman took to the pulpit and preached the sermon. Irrespective of the truth of her message, the couple thought the mere fact of a woman preaching was an indictment of biblical principles. That was therefore also their last day of participating in the church programmes.

The ambivalence in Pauline injunctions regarding the role of women result in interpretations of a controversial nature. One strand (as expressed in I Corinthians 11: 7–9 and 14: 34–5; I Timothy 2: 11–12 and Ephesians 5: 22–4) restricts and discredits women's leadership in church and in Christian culture. The notion that a hierarchy exists in gender terms in which women are subordinate to men is rife and can be located in the history of Christianity. The biblical passages were largely recognized as normative since they form part of the Christian canon of scripture. Thus, such prohibitions ensure that sexual hierarchy becomes an essential aspect of Christian theology. This also calls into serious question the viability of a woman assuming any significant role within the power hierarchy of ecclesiastical organization. The sexual hierarchy reflected in the New Testament was criticized as being highly flavoured by Graeco-Roman cultures in the early process of generating scriptural foundations for a Christian attitude to womankind. While an elaboration of this debate goes beyond our purview here, suffice it to mention that Christians who object to prescriptions of the earlier strand often sought solace in other biblical (Pauline) injunctions that are considered less polemical. The second strand (as exemplified in Galatians 3: 26–8; I Corinthians 12: 13) was often perceived as a liberalization of gender roles, one in which the hierarchization of sex functions in ecclesiastical office and within the Christian family is non-stereotypical and less biased against women.

This second variable posits equality of opportunities that allows for the development and inclusion of both genders, as well as the democratization of gender roles with regard to leadership or preaching in and out of the church precincts. However, this multiple representation of women's roles in Pauline narrative appear to have polarized gender discourse in the various Christian traditions. The overemphasis on the first strand by missionary Christianity in Africa had the effect of eroding the ritual power and role of women in the churches they established. I contend that women exercised crucial ritual functions and occupied significant religious roles within many indigenous religious worlds prior to the introduction of missionary Christianity. Missionary Christianity seems to have hijacked these roles and stripped women of most of their ritual functions by privileging the strand of Pauline injunctions that was disadvantageous to women. Thus, the leadership and ritual role reversal witnessed in some new forms of African Christianity needs to be historically and contextually understood.

'Ladies on fire for Jesus': Women caucus of the world conquerors Christian centre

In October 2000, a Kenyan couple, Climate and Jennifer Irungu, founded the World Conquerors Christian Centre (WCCC) with international headquarters in the Leith area of Edinburgh. The WCCC foundation history is woven around Bishop Climate and Dr Jennifer – 'First Lady' as they are now affectionately known by their members. The couple claim to have been 'sent by God from London to Edinburgh to preach the Gospel of God and begin a new thing that the Lord is about to do in Edinburgh'.[3] However, this only happened following a traumatic spiritual experience which took place during Climate Irungu's incarceration in London. In what is referred to as his 'dark history', he was reported as a former 'vicious crack-dealer', a remand prisoner in a London jail, awaiting trial on criminal charges of attempted rape and possession of a firearm.[4]

During sermons, Bishop Climate sometimes make passing references to a chequered 'dark history' and recounts his 'miraculous' turn around in spiritual terms, although he cautiously spares his congregation of the gory details of his ordeal. Moreover, Climate and members of his church have consequently interpreted this experience as a 'divine intervention'. Climate Irungu's life history woven partially around his post-migration experiences in London is significant in two respects. First, it is indicative of how post-migration experiences could result in a dramatic turn in which life experiences in the new context may heighten, stultify or erode a migrant's religious commitment. Much more significantly, such narratives tend to draw scholarly attention to post-migration religious experiences and expressions, thus opening new research vistas on religion, religious and spiritual activities within prisons, the refugee camps or asylum homes.

The Ladies on Fire for Jesus International represents the women caucus of WCCC. The group was founded and led by Jennifer Irungu, the church's co-founder, fondly referred to as the 'First Lady', a title that is itself symbolizing empowerment. 'First Lady' is reminiscent of how presidents' and governors' wives in several countries carve out a public niche for themselves within their respective political apparatus. The appropriation of 'First Lady' in the WCCC was undoubtedly a re-enactment of this practice albeit in religious terms. The Founder-Leader locates the group's emergence in 2004 to a divine revelation.[5] A personalized letter from the First Lady addressed specifically to female members and women at large is rich with gender rhetoric and symbolism of empowerment. Its extensive replication here underscores the preponderance and rapidity of such rhetoric employed in the Ladies on Fire for Jesus. It reads:

Dear Powerful Lady,
The bible says that after creation, God looked and saw that everything he made was very good ... That's includes you WOMAN. As far as God is concerned, there is no ugly woman and I agree with him. The creator looked at you woman, whom he had fashioned, declared, announced, proclaimed, and introduced you as very good. I believe that anything good is beautiful. Beauty does not really depend on your shape or your physical looks ... SO BEAUTY IS ON INSIDE OF YOU. God has something special something treasure inside you. That treasure is sealed up and is waiting for the opportunity to manifest and radiate its beauty and attraction to all. As you allow yourself to be the woman God has called you to be ... we can change the whole universe. Women we are influential instrument God can use us to change men, boys, fathers, relatives, friends etc. we are women with zeal, passion, enthusiasm, and power. For generations women have been greatly abused. The women have been shattered, hated battered and rejected. BUT now we rise with one VOICE to say to the devil 'Enough Is Enough!' The battle we face is NOT with our men (husband, brothers, and fathers), the society, religion, traditions, or customs of our time. No No, No, No the battle is the DEVIL HIMSELF. Last three years God spoke in spirit to start ladies on fire for Jesus. What a powerful name, makes one explosive. I believe it's a call for all women in Scotland that we are no longer JUST ordinary but women with EXTRA.
    LADIES ON FIRE FOR JESUS' vision is to reach to all those women who want a touch from Jesus, and get inspired to acquire fire for Jesus and change the nation ... No matter how wet, soaked or soggy your life is, you can become a woman with fire for Jesus ... Woman of God you have a very expensive hidden treasure inside of you. Open your heart to God even right now as you read this article, it does not matter where you are either in your kitchen, bedroom, comfortable chair, inside your car, on sitting in the park, wherever you are, God is seeing you. God is waiting for you to break-forth those walls that hinder you to be effective to your nation, or your city,

or you neighbourhood, or your family or even your church. Women we are called to make a difference in our generation. BUT HOW? Pastor Jennifer? By willing to surrender your life to Jesus Christ and he will enable you to be free from pride, bitterness, unforgiveness, anger, envy, lust, compromise, hypocrisy, selfless ... So I challenge every lady out there CATCH THIS FIRE AND KEEP IT BURNING. AMEN.[6]

While space does not permit a detailed analysis here, suffice it to mention that the text draws upon several power genres and evokes gender discourses of a complex nature. The rhetoric centres on the dignity and vulnerability of a woman, self-worth and esteem. It focuses on the innate power of women to effect change at familial and societal levels, the history of discrimination, abuse and injustices to which women were exposed within the larger society. Quite figuratively, the malevolent forces (the devil) rather than men are held accountable for this state of affairs that confront them. The text is replete with admonitions of hope, perseverance, encouragement and empowerment in a way that captures the reader's imagination towards an imagined gender identity. As membership is open to all females, irrespective of age – married, unmarried (single), single parent, divorcee, widows, and young women – the empowerment discourse also revolves around issues of marriage and the family, singles fellowship, fertility, female dignity, social and financial empowerment. Ritual time is also structured to tackle these existential issues. For instance, the early hours (6.15–7.30 a.m.) of every Tuesday is set aside for marital and future needs 'for those believing God for the fruit of the womb or children, for an ideal partner (husband), for the broken hearted', while Thursday morning is the day for marriage and family prayer where intensive prayer rituals are enacted for 'salvation, healing, unity, love and intimacy in the family and in marriage, praying God for intervention in divorce, separation, rejection, unforgiveness'.[7] Members are encouraged to bring photographs, clothes, names of family members and other concrete objects for intensive prayer rituals to break generation-long curses. The allegorical reference to the church as 'the place where dreams become reality' explains the importance of the sacred space for family conflict resolution and a context where members seek panacea to their manifold existential problems.

If women's demography in the church was an advantage to their visibility and mobility, the church polity appears also structured in a way that favours women. Apart from the Bishop – the overall head, and the church manager who are both males, the hierarchical structure comprise over 85 per cent women who serve in various leadership capacities as pastors, lay-pastors, zone pastors, cell group leaders, choir leader, church secretary and other functions. Thus, women through various activities and functions were carving a distinctive identity for themselves. This perhaps posed a challenge to the men who later in 2006 formed a parallel men's caucus named 'Men of Power' (MOP or simply MPs as they are called). Both groups formed along women/men gender divide engage in diverse activities, sometimes jointly, in such a way that they are mutually challenging and reinforcing. In the Singles Fellowship, unmarried individuals and young people are encouraged to seek out their prospective partners for marriage. Exhortations, teachings with attractive themes such as: *'Prayer that gets results! How to Catch a man!; Winners never quit, quitters never win!'*, that address specific marital matters are transferred into audio-visual paraphernalia and circulated among members.

In one of her teachings about maintaining a happy marital life, the First Lady introduced the concept 'MAMA' which she interprets as: 'never Maximize, Advertise, Minimize but Analyse your marital problems'. The preoccupation with marital discourses is suggestive of how the group negotiates modernity. Although, the First Lady challenges the women to rediscover their self-esteem and innate potential, she nevertheless asserts a sexual hierarchy, perhaps unintentionally, in which the man 'remains the head of the home/family'. While she encourages women to keep and nurture their marital lives, she at the same time critiques illicit sexual behaviour between women and men. In practical terms, the First Lady owns and manages an employment agency that provides job opportunities for some of the women. In a sense, the quest for empowerment in the women's group moves beyond mere rhetoric to a concrete, practical sense of empowerment.

8

Globalization, media and transnationalism

Introduction

The African continent, more than ever before, has come to represent one of the major global theatres for the dramatization of religion. African Christianity, Islam and the indigenous religions continue to engage and negotiate enduring processes of renewal and revitalization. The vitality demonstrated by these religious initiatives is such that has put them and their activities within and beyond local-global spaces. As Africans migrate to Europe, North America and elsewhere, they transport aspects of their religion as 'hand baggage' in a way that helps to maintain and reinforce their identity, but also inadvertently resulting in the charting of new identities. New circumstances, contextual factors in new host cultural contexts often goad these migrants to reconstruct, organize, and identify their religion or aspects of it both for themselves and for the non-Africans around them. African Christian communities in more recent times have experienced remarkable proliferation outside the African shores where they are increasingly engaged in the task of 'self-insertion' and 'self-assertion' on the local-global religious scene. The churches are bent on implanting themselves into new local contexts, in a way that they deal with dilemmas concomitant with adapting African Christianities to new geo-cultural boundaries and non-African realities. This chapter explores the interconnectedness between new African Christian initiatives and the processes of globalization, demonstrating how they create a sensibility that attempts to assimilate notions of the global, while simultaneously maintaining their local identities. How are they engaged in translating and mediating local and global environments? One angle is the extent to which they have been able to spread their religious ideologies, taking advantage of new forms of communication technology, as well as responding to religious, economic and sociopolitical realities transnationally in Africa, Europe and North America.

Globalization has become the buzzword in academic discourses such as communication, sociology, cultural studies, political science, advertising and in history of religions. As globalization is a dynamic process, still unfolding and revealing itself in many folds of social and private life, there can therefore be no final word on the epiphany of globalization. What does the whole talk about globalization mean? What is the connecting nexus between African Christian communities in diaspora and the processes of globalization? First, let us examine globalization as a concept and process before we attempt to explore this relationship.

Globalization as a kaleidoscopic concept

Globalization is a term that has come from nowhere to occupy almost everywhere, thus becoming a household name in public-private domains, especially in the last decade. Although the focus on globalization is very diverse, what seems to run through is the view that 'the world is experienced as a single place, or even a non-place, an abstract sign space, or as subject to time-space compression' (Robertson 1992). But this one world also has its shadow world. Andre Droogers (2001: 41–61) aptly remarks that the fascination with globalization does not stem from the characteristics of the global, but from the attitude developed locally in order to survive in an era of globalization. There is often talk of a tension between the universal and the particular, the global and the local, and this has led to Roland Robertson's popularization of the term 'glocalization' (1992). The adjective *glocal* from the process noun *glocalization* relates to the nexus between the global and the local. As a portmanteau word, glocalization is a conflation of globalization and localization. The local is an integral aspect of the global rather than a discrete space, hence the term 'glocal'. It may refer to the individual, group, organization, and community with inclinations to 'think globally and act locally'.

Thus, one way of understanding globalization in a space-time continuum, is to see global and local as two faces of the same movement from one epoch. The globalization process is not static but dynamic; it is not unidirectional but multidirectional. A global space today can change to a local space and vice versa. Globalization, if it is to be of enduring analytical value, should transcend inferior and superiority boundaries. It is referring to influences at the level of elements and symbols, not entire structures but substructures. In this respect, globalization depends on where you are and what you are talking about. It is not only in terms of continents, countries or between the West and the rest of the world, or between the North and South. It could also be within a smaller entity, community or nation-state.

The glocal, an admixture of the global and the local, is a cultural, theoretical construct that is susceptible to debate. Glocalization consists of processes that lead towards global interdependence and increasing rapidity of exchange across vast distances. One challenge of a globalizing world is to think through the complex relationship between the global and the local by paying attention to how global forces influence, shape and structure local situations on the one hand, but also how local forces mediate and negotiate the global. These dialectical relationships and processes produce unique configurations for thought, praxis and action. The process is not so much in relation to the global, but much more in relation to the local translations of the global. The actual processes that lead to interdependence and exchange may not necessarily lead to homogeneity; interactions of this nature also evince heterogeneity. At the same time, such processes are often shaped by power dynamics that result in positive/negative consequences for the different local-global actors and spaces.

The take-off point of globalization, how old or new the phenomenon is, and who first coined it remain a matter of conjecture. Nonetheless, glocalization, like globalization, as a concept, slogan and as a term with a relatively short history in academic discourse has captured attention as a catchword for describing both 'the compressing of the world and the intensification of our conscious awareness of the world as a totality' (Robertson 1992: 8). Robertson used 'glocal' to describe the juncture where the global and the local meet. It could also refer to a process in which individuals, groups and organizations maintain interpersonal social networks that combine extensive local and global interactions. Glocalization involves the appropriation and dissemination of new media technologies and their resultant global impact on local economies, polities, societies, cultures and everyday life.

The etymology of glocalization

The earliest usage, history and development of the concept 'glocalization', has been traced to the Japanese society where the term was appropriated within popular business strategies. Glocalization was modelled on the Japanese word *dochakuka*, which originally meant adapting farming techniques to one's own local condition. *Dochakuka* evolved into a marketing strategy when Japanese businessmen adopted it in the 1980s to refer to global localization, indicating that products of Japanese origin should be localized – that is, they should be suited to local taste and interests – yet, the products are global in application and reach (Robertson 1985: 28). While it is unclear who first used the term or when exactly it was first employed in its original Japanese usage, Robertson was one of the pioneers who popularized this concept within Western social scientific discourse. Since the mid-1980s, Robertson has written extensively on the theory and processes of globalization. He talks about 'the crystallization of the entire world as a single place', 'the emergence of the global-human condition' and 'the consciousness of the globe as such'. Robertson did not view globalization as a recent phenomenon, nor did he see it as a consequence of modernization. This framework shows glocalization as an interdependent process. With Robertson and others popularizing the concept, sociology redefined its scope and field as the social scientific study of the global processes. This leads to the recognition that many of the social categories and practices assume a local flavour or character despite the fact that these products were invented elsewhere.

Religion and globalization

The connecting nexus between religion and globalization appear not to have been sufficiently explored theoretically and methodologically. However, some notable attempts at linking or seeing the relationship between religion and globalization or globality are evident in the extensive works of Roland Robertson (1985, 1987, 1992, 1994) and Peter Beyer (1994, 2001). On religion, Robertson based his analysis on how tensions in relations between state and religion across the globe arise from the politicization of religion, and the 'religionization of politics' resulting from the process of globalization. Beyer (1994) attempted a theoretical examination of globalization and its application to religion by combining four world-system theorists in order to show how globalization can be understood as a global economy (Wallerstein), a global culture (Robertson), a global society (Luhmann) and a global polity (Meyer). For Beyer, globalization has been a vital resource for understanding the place of religion in a modern global culture.

As Juergensmeyer (2003: 5) remarks,

> Religion therefore has always been global, in the sense that religious communities and traditions have always maintained permeable boundaries... Religion is global in that it is related to the global transportation of peoples and the transnational acceptance of religious ideas.

Prior to when the term 'globalization' gained wide currency, the expansion of Christianity has always been viewed as a transnational phenomenon with globalizing tendencies. In this sense, the Roman Catholic Church was depicted as a religious multinational. Scholars who attempted to see the link between religion and globalization have done so solely with reference to the so-called fundamentalist forms of Christianity and Islam, thus giving the impression that this is the only way that such connection can be made.

Globalization as a concept has been employed by social scientists as an appropriate category for describing and interpreting the emergence of Pentecostalism as a cultural movement. In fact, Jenkins (2002: 7–8) defined it as 'perhaps the most successful social movement of the past century'. Religious traditions have the capacity for self-reflexive critical thinking about globalization (Beckford 2003: 105). The expansion of the Pentecostal movement in the twentieth century leads to recognition of Pentecostalism as an integral part of the globalization process but also as a consequence of it.

Joel Robbins (2004) demonstrates how scholars 'use Pentecostals and Charismatics to support theories that construe globalization as a process of westernizing homogenization and those that understand it as a process of indigenizing differentiation'. Robertson's (1992: 73) innovative concept of glocalization is quite apt in exploring the interconnectedness between local and global contexts at the level of religious movements such as the Pentecostal and charismatic movements. As Droogers points out, 'this then is the somewhat gloomy globalizing world within which Pentecostal expansion occurs. In it, space and non-space intermingle, just as the global and the local – or even the fragmented ... Religion is part of the globalizing forces, as well as of the local translations. It is part both of the global impact and the local reaction' (Droogers 2001: 51). In non-Western contexts such as Africa, indigenous forms of Christianity show how people can adopt a 'global view' and at the same time remain faithful to local, indigenous 'identities'. Although the popular adagium has been, 'think globally, act locally', much of the thinking also takes place at the local level. It is within this framework that we can better understand African Christian communities in diaspora as forms of 'globalization from below'.

Are we not also global and international?

The Pentecostal and charismatic churches, like the AICs have shaped African Christianities through their increasing involvement on the wider global stage. They have taken to proselytizing in North America and Europe, viewing the regions as 'new abodes' and promising 'mission fields' (Adogame, 2005d: 504; 2007a). Hunt and Lightly (2001: 121) note that:

> The importance of the 'new' black African churches within the framework of globalization is not merely with reference to a unique expression of African Christianity. Rather, they are noteworthy in that they constitute international ministries, which have implications on a worldwide scale. As part of an increasing phenomenon of what might be termed 'reverse proselytization', these new West African churches have systematically set out to evangelize the world. In the case of the RCCG this has meant establishing churches in as far-flung places as India, the Caribbean, Hong Kong, the USA and Europe. The impact and significance of the exportation of a fiercely evangelical Nigerian church such as the RCCG, driven by a vision of winning converts, is that it offers a unique opportunity to analyse its impact at a local level, in this case the Western context.

Thus, such communities are significant within the framework of globalization, owing to the unique expression of African Christianity which they exhibit – a feature that could be described as their self-assertion and as the global preservation of their religious identity (Adogame 2003). Notions of globalization and globality are appropriated as theological and ideological constructs, and thus feature prominently in their mission statements and strategies, as well as sermon rhetoric, although these notions are used and understood differently. It is common to find churches defining themselves as 'global churches' and their mission as 'global tasks'.

From an analytical standpoint, I make a basic distinction between the global self-assertion and understanding of African Christian communities on the one hand, and actual global structures or networks they establish or are engaged with. The self-understanding of most African-led churches is revealed in the assertion that their churches transcend geographical, racial, colour and social class distinctions. This is largely exemplified by their self-identification as global; worldwide; international churches. The amplification of original appellations with such labels indicates their religiously inspired and promising access to transnationalism and the wide variety of their international linkages. The group which bore the name Christian Church Outreach Mission later took on the appendage 'International'; the Church of the Lord – Aladura rebrands as Church of the Lord – Aladura worldwide; the Mountain of Fire and Miracles Ministries became Mountain of Fire and Miracles International. Some of these churches are geographically spread across the northern hemisphere. There are even many groups consisting of a sole branch but which already call themselves global, worldwide or international. This portrays a great deal of their intent to transcend local boundaries to global ones. It was this noticeable global dispersal of these churches that perhaps inform Ter Haar's suggestion to re-christen them 'African International Churches', retaining the old initials AIC but assuming a new, contemporary meaning (1998: 24).

However, examined from the outside, these churches have yet to attract a significant percentage of non-African members. The dual strategy according to these churches was first to reach the African population in the West in order to use them as the bridge to further reach out to the wider public. Most of the non-African membership is owing to interracial couples, friendship and sometimes as a result of personal/impersonal evangelism. The membership structure may be transformed in the future as they continue to make inroads into the diasporic landscape.

The conspicuous and symbolic display of global operational frameworks through the hoisting of flags (banners) at the pulpits and within the church vicinity forms another basic characteristic of African-led churches. Thus, from at least two to several colourful flags could be counted around the pulpit or the vicinity of the altar. Each flag represents a country to which the church has branched out or where there is some form of religious affiliation, or a body/group with which they already established ecumenical relationship. This adds credibility or as an image booster to the local church. Apart from the aesthetic value that characterizes such hoisting of beautifully coloured flags, it further symbolizes their self-identification within global religious space.

Another indicator of the nexus between African Christian communities and the globalization process is in their self-definition. For instance, RCCG's self-understanding was hinted at by its General Overseer, at the Annual Holy Ghost Festival which features the public rendering of prophecies for every successive year. The increasing gaze on the global scene is shown through the 'annual prophecies'[1] vouchsafed by Adeboye to the church. The anxiety and solemnity which characterizes this festival is indicative of the significance which its members attach to it. The prophecies are usually mixed in content and scope, as some pronouncements could provoke feelings of joy and celebration while others imbue sadness, fear and excitement. Other aspects call for sober reflections or marked by intensive prayers in order to make or mar some predictions believed to have been vouchsafed in their charismatic leader.

A cursory look at the 'RCCG Annual Prophecies between 1999–2002'[2] makes evident how theological constructs may be subject to the process of globalization and, in so doing, appeal to localized communities. The prophecies are usually categorized under three or more levels. For instance, the 1999 annual prophecies[3] focused on: 'Individuals', 'Nigeria' and 'the RCCG itself' respectively. By the following year, the scope of prophecies has been enlarged to include 'the international scene'. According to Pastor Adeboye, 'the reason we are going into this area (the international scene) is because the world has become a global village'.[4]

Such a remark by the leader reveals its self-understanding within a global framework.The enlargement of the scope of prophecies does not only suggest RCCG self-understanding in relation to the globalization process, but further indicate what specific role(s) the church earmarks for itself within it. While some of the contents of these prophecies may appear speculative and imprecise to an outsider, they are usually accepted by members as sacrosanct. For instance, the prophecies disclosed by Pastor Adeboye for the year 2002 foretold that 'Floods will be on a scale that had not been seen before ... Intensify prayers against air crashes because of Hurricane and Tornadoes ...'.[5] This singular prediction was to have a lot of meaning and impact on RCCG members in Germany especially during the flood catastrophe in several parts of Germany in the same year. On this, an RCCG member at the Bonn parish remarks:

> Adeboye is really a man of God. God is really using him to make an impact in the whole world. Recent events (floods) only make clear why we need to

draw closer to God and put our trust only in Him (God). I think the Germans in our midst are even more terrified that the General Overseer predicted this late last year. This crisis has made many members to take their faith much more seriously than before. People can see that the end time is near.[6]

Although the prediction was in a local setting, that is, at the RCCG international headquarters in Nigeria, the 'flood' prediction became more real for members in Germany where the catastrophe was experienced first hand. During my field trip to some RCCG parishes in Germany at the last quarter of 2002, the 'flood issue' became a major discussion topic among members, as focal point during sermons and communal prayers. In all these cases, the 'Prophecies 2002' by Adeboye became the reference point. Such developments help to reinforce and legitimize the charisma of the leader among his followers.

Another tendency of African Christian communities towards globalization is evident in their appropriation of the new media, the deliberate effort towards making their presence known on the World Wide Web (WWW), and the use of the internet for religious communication. The media play a crucial role in establishing, maintaining and changing collective representations. Global 'mediatization' facilitates the worldwide marketing of goods, symbolic forms, and life styles. There is an interesting interconnectedness between religion and media in the practices of everyday life. The contemporary world has witnessed a rapid development, expansion and convergence of communication technologies in religious, economic, political and sociocultural spheres. One of the most prevalent forms of new technology is the use and appropriation of the computer-mediated communication technology, the internet.

Mediating religion

Communication has become an integral issue on the question of globalization because it builds bridges between the universally human, the one global place and local translations of the global (Axford 1995: 28). The dramatic increase in the use of transport and new communication facilities, suggests that we do indeed live in a 'global village' in which each fellow human being can be reached at short notice, if not instantly. People, nations, transnational corporations, and religions are all condemned to each other (Droogers 2001: 51). The conceptualization of mass media has been rendered more complex with the growth in 'new' technologies. The media landscape has been widened from established formats of print, film, radio, music and television, with the development of computer networks, digital technologies, and interactive cable television. The relationship between media and religious movements is a transaction between two complex systems, each trying to accomplish a particular goal. Today, religious movements employ the media to communicate their message to the public, while the media look to movements as one potential source of news. Religious movements usually need the mass media, especially the internet to widely publicize their activities, but also as a recruitment strategy and medium for enlarging their clientele. Appropriation of and coverage by the media may in some respects help to mobilize support, achieve validation and acquire some kind of legitimization within and around the sociocultural environment of religious organizations.

One significant asset of 'new media' in contradistinction with previous generation of mass media lies in their capability and use for interactive communication. Instantaneous communication can be carried out over long distances. New media technologies provide the populace and potential clients with the technical apparatus to do more than just receive information. They can respond to messages they receive, ask further questions or seek for clarification, select which images they want to receive, or even send out their own messages. The internet (www) provides computer links between people for either electronic conversation or the transfer of data and images. The internet is the site of many home pages for religious movements and many discussion groups that focus on religious and spiritual issues. But how and to what extent have African Christian communities exploited this to their own advantage and/or peril? In the next section I will demonstrate how new African Christianities are engaging the media, especially the Net, as conduits for the communication of their religious messages, as well as a means of developing new and sustaining old relationships and community.

Online for God: Appropriating new media technologies

The use of media is not at all a novel feature among African Christian communities. Several churches have used and still continue to use existing print and electronic media at different stages of their developmental histories. They appropriate new forms of media technologies in information processing and dissemination, in their self-insertion and self-assertion on the European and American religious scene. Intra-religious networking has been further enhanced through access to and appropriation of new forms of communication technology. This involves the creation and use of computer websites, use of fax and electronic mail systems, Facebook, Twitter, webmail, chat rooms, blogging, tele-evangelism, audio and video tapes, books, tracts, magazines, handbills and leaflets.

While openly embracing all sorts of media technologies, most African-led churches frown on and prohibit the use of cellular (mobile) phones during services within the church precincts. As they claim, the use of mobile phones disrupts and interrupts communication with God and the heavenly forces, and become a practical distraction during ritual services. Bold warning notices on billboards with such inscriptions at church entrances, 'Switch off your mobile phones! Only God's call is received here'; 'Make and receive God's calls here but not men's!' vividly illustrates one of the ways in which they negotiate modernity.

Hitherto, mediums such as print, radio and television broadcasting were used for the translation and transmission of their messages. However, what is relatively new is their recent appropriation of space on the internet; and the production of Christian home videos. The recourse to new, alternative evangelistic strategies is intricately tied to the sociocultural realities of the host societies. The appropriation of media communication technologies as an impersonal medium of communication and recruitment strategy is gaining prominence among African Christian communities in new contexts where personal mediums for which they are very familiar in their homeland have largely failed in the new contexts. The somewhat individualistic nature of Western societies renders some of the known conventional modes inept and far less productive. Thus, 'personal' modes of communication such as door to door, street to street, marketplace and bus evangelism have given way to more impersonal, neutral modes such as computer websites, electronic (web) mail, fax, Facebook, Twitter, chat rooms and blogging. The relevance and urgency which these alternative modes of communication demand in the host contexts, lends credence to why virtually all the websites of these churches have been established, developed and maintained in Europe, United States or elsewhere outside Africa. Analytically however, the new development in mission strategies with the increasing use of the new media for membership recruitment and evangelism has resulted more in a qualitative change in their religiosity rather than a quantitative change in membership. Dawson and Hennebry (1999: 26) show that the primary use of the web is clearly a way to advertise religious groups and to deliver information about them cheaply. Although the websites act as a new and relatively effective means of outreach to the larger community, most of these groups who appropriate it do so in order to also draw potential clientele or membership. Such intentions are clearly portrayed in their introductory statements.

In the RCCG[7] Internet Outreach, the introductory statement on the parish directory states:

> Over the years the RCCG has experienced an explosive growth with branches being planted all over the world. It has become pertinent to create

a directory and online database for all the RCCG parishes worldwide ... this will enable us do a complete, relational online database.... Furthermore online database will help us in our evangelism, fellowship and interaction among member parishes. It will also serve to assist travellers in their efforts to find a place of worship wherever they find themselves.

The vision and goals of the members as expressed in the RCCG 'Mission Statement', published on their site includes:

It is our goal to make heaven. It is our goal to take as many people as possible with us. In order to accomplish our goals, holiness will be our lifestyle. In order to take as many people with us as possible, *we will plant churches within five minutes walking distance in every city and town of developing countries; and within five minutes driving distance in every city and town of developed countries*. We will pursue these objectives until every nation in the world is reached for JESUS CHRIST OUR LORD.

Although, these goals may appear too ambitious and utopian to attain, yet one point of significance here is the fact that RCCG demonstrates enthusiasm towards realizing its global vision. The church is not only concerned with the local setting but what transpires beyond it, within so-called developing and developed countries.

The CCOMI boast of a website that is fairly rich in content and structure, although not professionally developed as the RCCG Internet Outreach.[8] The media section contains printed materials and audio-visual resources.[9] The CCOMI Victory Store[10] is their online resource that exhibit products such as books, DVDs, audio cassettes that are made available for sale and public consumption. In fact, the website partly embodies their history, belief system and wide-ranging activities. The opening statements of the website lends credence to the extent of their intra-religious affiliation, 'We are a member of the International Communion of Charismatic Churches, Member of the *Bund Freikirchlicher Pfingstgemeinden* (Association of German Pentecostal Churches)'. Among the common features of both sites is the presence of Discussion Forum, Question and Answer Sheet, Testimony Forum, Visitors' Form, Feedback Form, and creation of free web-based emails for branches (parishes), interested members and visitors to the sites. One of the main reasons for providing and offering free email services to interested persons is in order to establish contact and maintain transnational links through the web. By providing personal data and contact information, the group is able to keep close, intimate contact with the visitor, with the aim of recruitment. Prayer requests from interested viewers of the television programmes or visitors on their website can be sent via email, fax or simply by telephoning the 'prayer warriors' and 'counsellors' who they claim are waiting 24/7 to receive calls.

One way in which CCOMI has further appropriated the new media is in their mediatization of prayer, where prayer ritual has gone online thus transcending the *locatedness* of a ritual enactment.[11] While inviting members and the virtual public to detail their supplication and prayer requests in a customized online form, they rehash the import of their ritualized prayer:

> I urge, then, first of all, that requests, prayers, intercession and thanksgiving be made for everyone (I Timothy 2:1, NIV). Countless lives have been changed by the power of prayer. Do you need someone to agree with you in prayer? Someone who will stand in faith and believe God with you? Please fill out the form below ...!

Generally, through these mediated sources, church programmes that are publicized have local, global and transnational reach. Mediated space and new media appropriation, what Appadurai describes as Pentecostal mediascapes, therefore serves as a process of emplacement and a distinctive mark of public representation or global positioning within the religious map of the universe.

The CCC seeks to create a global network through the use of internet websites and electronic mail (Adogame 1999: 82–9).[12] In a 'web release' on 15 December 1997, announcing its (Riverdale, USA site) presence on the internet, it stated,

> Halleluyah!!! ... CCC now has a dominant presence on the World Wide Web. The main focus of this page is to present a unified and cohesive communication vehicle for Celestial Church as a whole, world-wide ... As the web site evolve, we hope to use it as a vehicle to communicate news about Celestial Church of Christ on a global basis, both information geared toward Celestians and non-Celestians alike.

The UK site complements this objective through her mission statement that states:

> To introduce CCC to the whole world ... to bring all the parishes together by obtaining free e-mail addresses for interested parishes and contribute to the free flow of information in the church ... to use the medium of the Internet as a vehicle to recruit new members.

The official website[13] of CLA was established in 1999. One introductory statement of this site is that 'the Church of the Lord – Aladura is conscious of her mission to spread the good news of our Lord Jesus Christ to every nook and corners of the world'. It describes the four tenets of the church as 'Pentecostal in Power, Biblical in Pattern, Evangelical in Ministry, and Ecumenical in Outlook'. The internet serves as a kind of status booster for the CLA as it contains a long list of local and international religious and ecumenical organizations to which it belongs or is affiliated to. This gives some kind of religious credibility to the group, especially in a society where such a group could easily be demonized and waved off as a cult or sect.

I shall now turn to exploring other mediums through which African Christian communities appropriate new technologies. Two additional points I shall examine in this section on the new media are their space appropriation in global religious TV-networks; and in the production and commodification of 'Christian home videos'. I shall use the examples of the KICC and MZFMI to illustrate these new religious developments in Africa and the African diaspora.

God Digital (The God Channel) as a global religious network

Another way through which African Christian communities have used the new technologies is through their space appropriation in global religious TV-networks. An obvious example here is the KICC in London, known for their prodigious appropriation of the new media technology. As the church asserts '... We recognise the effectiveness of using the media to communicate and draw the attention of the world to the good news. We do this by Winning Ways Programme'.[14] The Winning Ways Programme on Radio/Television is aired on TV both within and outside the United Kingdom. This is produced from the various teachings of Pastor Matthew Ashimolowo and the KICC transnational religious events. The Winning Ways Programme is categorized into TV/Radio, T.O.P 1000 Club, Video Technical, Audio Technical and Tape Production. The television programme is claimed to be transmitted across 21 European nations and has a potential viewing audience of several millions in Europe, the Caribbean as well as Africa. It lays claim to a potential television viewing and radio listening audience of over 200 million in Africa (Nigeria, Ghana, Zimbabwe, Malawi, Kenya, Southern Africa); in the Caribbean Islands (Barbados, Jamaica, Trinidad and Tobago); and in Europe on Sky Channel, the Christian Channel Europe (now God Digital) and the Inspirational Network. It is aired daily on Premier Radio London, BBC Radio Leicester and Spirit FM Amsterdam. In Nigeria and Ghana, the KICC programmes are aired and viewed on NTA 2 Channel 5, NTA Channel 10, OGTV, Channels TV, Rivers State TV, Plateau State Radio and TV Channel) and Ghana's GTV respectively.

The KICC and RCCG now have their own television channels, namely KICC TV accessible on Sky cable television network channel 594[15]; RCCG's Liveway

TV and Radio Network,[16] and Open Heavens TV (OHTV) on Sky 199 for United Kingdom, Europe and North Africa[17] that screens RCCG programmes frequently, and on Dove Vision TV Channel[18] respectively. Through these mediated sources, church programmes and other religious activities that are screened have local, global and transnational reach.

Matthew Ashimolowo is on the Board of Reference of the God Digital (Christian Channel Europe),[19] and the KICC programmes are screened from time to time on 'the God Channel' TV network. In this way, KICC targets and communicates its religious message to a wider, multi-ethnic public. The church is involved in intra-religious networks, and organizes conferences and crusades which draw local and international audiences. The annual conference tagged 'Gathering of Champions', a forum that attracts an international audience of leaders and Christians from the global Pentecostal landscape suggests a remarkable tendency towards religious internationalism and transnationalism (see the last section of this chapter on religious transnationalism).

To God be the Glory! Commodifying religious video technology

In the past couple of decades, media texts are increasingly serving as one of the significant maps through which African Christianities distinguish themselves on local-global religious landscapes (Adogame 2009: 2011). There has been an unprecedented upsurge in the production, consumption and commodification of home videos as one specific form of popular culture in Africa and the new African diaspora. Nigerian videos, a phenomenon barely two decades old, are now being produced at a phenomenal rate. Home video technology represents a basic instance of the interconnectedness of the global and the local on the level of cultural marketing, as part of the processes of African modernity. This section explores how versions of Pentecostal and charismatic Christianity increasingly engage religious video technology as conduits for the dissemination of their religious ideologies; as a means of developing new audiences, and as a channel towards negotiating old and new identities.

An enormous boom in the production of dramatic features shot on video and commodified through video cassettes, DVD and VCDs has gradually supplanted celluloid films in Nigeria since the late 1980s. Scholarly interest has been slow to focus on this new medium but that's rapidly changing (Ekwuazi 1991; Okome and Haynes 1995, 1998; Haynes 2000). Haynes provides insights and perspectives on the discourse on African cinema, focusing on Nigeria's popular video production, dubbed 'Nollywood'. He aptly remarks that Nigeria video films, a phenomenon less than a decade old, now constitutes a significant context of film practice (2000: 1).

One primary way through which African Christian communities such as the African Pentecostal and charismatic churches have used the new technologies is through the production and distribution of what has been called Christian home videos. The Mount Zion Faith Ministries International (MZFMI) provides an example of how religious video movies they produced are consumed locally and internationally. Religious videos are not only consumed by Africans in the Diaspora, they are also partly sponsored, produced and commodified by these communities as well.

The Mount Zion Faith Ministries International

The MZFMI started in Nigeria but now has branches in Europe and North America. Founded by Evangelist Mike Bamiloye in 1985 under the name Mount Zion Christian Productions, the ministry took-off with only three members who were then College of Education students in Ilesa, Nigeria. The founder became a full-time drama evangelist in 1987 and consequently changed the name of the Ministry to Mount Zion Faith Ministries.[20] It has produced at least 20 films including *Agbara Nla*, *Perilous Time*, *Ide Esu*. The first Christian video picture produced in Nigeria was probably by the MZFMI, in 1994. The relative success of MZFMI's pioneer film, *Agbala Nla*, generated enough impetus for an English-language version titled 'Ultimate Power' and other movies like 'The Blood Covenant'. These films have become very popular in sub-Saharan Africa (particularly Nigeria and Ghana) through domestic and public screening, as well as among African diaspora communities. The religious, social and economic impact of these video genres on the viewer cannot be underestimated.

A subsection within the MZFMI website is devoted to 'testimonies' and 'comments' by diverse audiences.[21] On a user's first click at this sub-page that requires no password, one is confronted instantaneously with the salutation 'Welcome to Mount Zion Faith Ministries International. This is an on-line Testimony'. The contents frame shows the titles of all articles posted to the discussion, and selecting a title calls up the corresponding article. The interactive website allows subject-specific searches and accommodates posting of new articles and personalized responses to specific posts. A careful perusal of these narratives would reveal a number of interesting characteristics and patterns (Adogame 2009).

The website commentaries provide evidence of the diversity of audiences that view Christian films, along with their motivations, meanings and interpretations. The online responses of such individuals to these media products are important objects for scholarly analysis of the economic, religious, political and social drives that accompany the production and commodification of Christian religious videos. They open up new methodologies for research. Rather than the researcher relying on his/her imagination, s/he could reconstruct the consumer's point of view as an integral basis for understanding and interpreting.

'Readers' and 'viewers' (consumers, receivers, audiences) are not passive but also active 'decoders' of 'texts' (media), who do not necessarily accept encoded meanings as offered. Depending on the religious and cultural contexts that media consumers already occupy, the author's intended interpretation may in certain instances be negotiated or even rejected. This process further shows the relevance of specific media genres for different reading or viewing publics. Pentecostal/Charismatic groups and AIC's official websites and other media products such as Christian home videos act as relatively new modes of outreach to global audiences. They provide a convenient point of access that tremendously enhances the public profile of each religious group.

In sum, although the 'mission statements' of several churches elucidate their intention and determination to appropriate the internet and Christian home videos for recruitment, there is as yet no substantial empirical evidence to suggest that they have succeeded in this regard. Recruitment seems to happen primarily through pre-existing social networks, interpersonal bonds as well as through other conventional evangelistic strategies such as revival sessions, musical concerts and jamborees, prayer and healing sessions. In this regard, the internet and the religious video technology serve more as a complementary vehicle rather than an immediate replacement for other media.

The transnational nature of several African Christian communities challenges the assumption that immigrants usually cut off ties and links with their homeland after integration into the new host context. The increasing mobility and itinerancy of religious adepts and members between the original homeland and diasporic spaces cannot be overemphasized. In the last section of this chapter I shall explore how this complex peregrination partly demonstrates an instance of religious transnationalization of new African Christian communities in diaspora.

Transnationalizing African Christian communities

The volume, scope, framework and patterns of contemporary international migration is in constant change and transformation in such a way that mirrors migration less as a single change of space and place, but rather as a complex, multidirectional movement. Earlier conceptions of immigrants and migrants as individuals uprooted from one society who then settle and become incorporated into a new land are no longer very convincing (Ebaugh and Chafetz 2002: 1). Contemporary migrant populations are largely characterized by networks, activities and life-patterns that entangle both their 'old home' and 'new home' – host societies, as well as with other host contexts. This 'simultaneous embeddedness' and multiplicity of involvements in more than one society or context produces alongside a heterogeneous set of sustained transnational activities. Smith and Guarnizo (1998) suggest a distinction between 'transnationalism from above', that is, cross-border activities initiated and conducted by powerful institutional actors, such as states and multinational corporations; and 'transnationalism from below', those that are the result of grass-roots initiatives by immigrants and their home country counterparts. Although this dichotomy dovetails into each another, our focus in this book is on transnational initiatives from below, particularly in the way such connections may help to generate, strengthen or stultify social, cultural and religious capital (see Chapter 6).

The daily lives of several immigrants and immigrant communities depend on multiple and constant interconnections across international borders and their public identities are configured in relationship to more than one nation-state. Many such immigrants are not sojourners because they settle and become incorporated in the economic and political institutions, localities and patterns of everyday life in the country in which they reside. Contemporaneously, they are engaged elsewhere in the sense that they maintain connections, build institutions, conduct transactions, and influence local and national events in the countries from which they emigrated (Glick Schiller et al. 1992: 122). Such immigrants that develop and maintain multiple relationships that span borders are often referred to as transmigrants. They have strong relationships to different places simultaneously and sometimes live neither 'here' nor 'there' but 'here' and 'there' (Goebel and Pries 2002: 37).

Transnational processes are, in themselves, not new; precedents abound in earlier trajectories of migration. However, current connections of immigrants are operating on slightly different templates, facilitated by new complex political, religious and socio-economic circumstances in a fast globalizing world. As Portes et al. (1999: 224) notes, 'Precursors of present immigrant transnationalism have existed for centuries … but they lack the elements of regularity, routine involvement, and critical mass characterizing contemporary examples of transnationalism …'. They argue that what is new is the high intensity of exchanges, the new modes of transacting business, and the multiplication of activities that require cross-border travel and contacts on a sustained basis (219). The process of transnationalism encompasses phenomena as diverse as import/export immigrant businesses, investments by migrants in the country of origin, sustained family links in both countries of origin and settlement, home-based religious and cultural organizations that set up branches in countries of new settlement and vice versa, as well as the mobilization of migrants by homeland political parties and social movements, or the diffusion of home-based conflicts to the migrant community and vice versa.

An added value of this book lies in its description and analysis of the triad relationship and multi-polarity of the transnational social field having been based on a triangular context of research in Africa (Nigeria and Ghana), Europe (Germany and United Kingdom) and North America. I explore the interconnectedness between African Christian communities on the continent and beyond; and the links, networks between them and other Christian, non-African groups and nonreligious groups as 'religious transnationalism from below'. I will draw specific examples from the EBKGC and KICC to situate African Christian communities within such global religious trends as religious transnationalism 'from below'. I will explore instances of religious transnationalization with focus on the mobility, itinerary of the leaders, some church programmes and the local-global implications of such transnational activities. These churches are no longer confined to ethnic-national boundaries, they cultivate religious internationalism.

One distinguishing feature of the recent trend as compared to previous immigration waves is the fluid processes of transnational networks, links and residencies (Adogame 2004a: 26). Most new African immigrant churches are rooted locally and in the land of origin, but also in that intra-communal web which links them with different places across the globe. These communities are connected through various ties in the realm of religion, economy, friendship, kinship, politics and increasingly so through the virtual space of telephone cells, new media such as the internet which have become a central feature of development and maintenance of diasporic identity. Scholars also need to pay more attention to the role of media in stimulating transnational religious activities. New African churches and religious organizations have appropriated new media technologies such as internet websites, TV and interactive technologies in the transmission of their religious ideologies, as a recruitment strategy for new clientele, but also as a way of maintaining links and contact with members and branches transnationally (Adogame 2000b: 404–6). The increasing itinerancy of religious leaders, freelance evangelists and members between the homeland and diasporic spaces cannot be overemphasized. While I recognize the significance of members and their groups' networks and mobility, I limit my focus here to the complex mobility of the leaders as an indication of the transnational tendencies of these new brands of African Christianities. Table 8.1 shows the itinerary of Sunday Adelaja as documented on the EBKGC website.

TABLE 8.1 Pastor Sunday Adelaja's (EBKGC) itinerary 2005, 2007 and 2008[22]

Month	2005	2007	2008
January		Jan 10–13: Kuala Lumpur, Malaysia Jan 13–19: Paradise, South Australia	Jan 28–29 Orlanda, Florida, USA Jan 29–31 Atlanta, Georgia, USA at Mount Paran Church
February	Feb 11–12 Kharkov, Ukraine Feb 22–26 SingaporeAsia Oceania Prayer Convocation 2005	Feb 9–10: Reinchenbach, Germany Feb 16–17: Donetsk, Ukraine Feb 19–23: Singapore Feb 23–Mar 1: Jakarta, Indonesia	
March	Mar. 2 Indonesia Mar. 9–12 Berea, Holland. National Leaders Conference Berea the Hague 2005 Mar. 14 Amsterdam, Holland Sunday Service	Mar. 16–17: Roskilde, Denmark	Mar. 11–14 Jerusalem, Israel
April	Apr. 5–8 Kyiv, Ukraine. Samuel's Mountain Gate Convocation April 4–10 Kyiv, Ukraine. ICCL Fellows Program Apr. 19 Billion Soul Campaign Tour, North America Apr. 20–25 - Bad Gandersheim, Germany. Men Rooted in Christ Conference	Apr. 13–14: Jamaica, New York, USA Apr. 15: Fort Myers, Florida, USA Apr. 19–21: Washington DC, USA Apr. 23–25: Rochester, New York April 26–27: Philadelphia, USA April 30–May 2: Milan, Italy	Apr. 10–14 Scotland Apr. 21–27 Soweto, South Africa

Month	2005	2007	2008
May	May 5 Orlando, Florida, USA 5 Fold Gathering May 6–8 London, England Pastors and Leadership Conference May 11, Nigeria 2005 May 25–28 Germany New Gate European Convocation With Jobst Bittner	May 11–12: Jamaica, New York, USA May 13–14: USA May 15–24: Mexico	May 5–8 Midland, Australia
June	June 10–12 Karaganda, Kazakhstan Leadership Conference June 14–17 Denver, Colorado, USA Pastoring Without Tears Conference June 17–19 Denver, Colorado, USA 2005 Convention June 21 Billion Soul Campaign Tour North America June 25–26 Berlin, Germany. Worship Service	June 7–10: Frankfurt, Germany June 17–19: Decatur, Alabama, USA June 20–21: Blountville, Tennessee, USA	June 12–15 Atlanta, USA June 24–26 Cairo, Egypt
July	July 6–9 Riga, Latvia July 10–16 Bergen, Norway Summer Festival 2005 July 17–21 Colorado, USA. Life-Giving Leadership Conference - Sunday Service	July 12–13: Houston, Texas, USA July 15–17: DFW, TX, USA July 17–19: London, England	

GLOBALIZATION, MEDIA AND TRANSNATIONALISM

Month	2005	2007	2008
August	August 11–13 Warsaw, Poland August 26–28 Helsinki, Finland	Aug. 16–20: Atlanta, Georgia Aug. 21–22: Bridgeport, Connecticut, USA Aug. 23–25: Atlanta, Georgia Aug. 26–28: Tampa, Florida, USA	August 12–14 St. Petersburg, Russia
September	Sept. 7–10 Regina, Saskatchewan, Canada Regional Apostolic Conference Sept. 11–13 Hamilton, Ontario, Canada Sept. 24–25 Kharkov, Ukraine Embassy of God: Wall Church Anniversary	Sept. 4–6: Sao Paulo, Brazil Sept. 7–9: Brazil Sept. 10–13: Solo, Indonesia Sept. 15–17: Israel, Jerusalem	Sept. 16–26 Japan
October	Oct. 4 Billion Soul Campaign Tour, N. America Oct. 11–13 Kingston, Jamaica Oct. 14–16 Sacramento, California Oct. 17–19 Altoona, Pennsylvania Oct. 20–21 New York, New York Oct. 22–30 Abuja, Nigeria. The Outpouring 2005 Oct. 30 Belaya Tserkov, Ukraine Embassy of God's 3rd Anniversary	Oct. 18–21: Lagos, Nigeria	October 23–25 Madras, India

Month	2005	2007	2008
November	Nov. 8 Billion Soul Campaign Tour, North America Nov. 12–13 Dnepropetrovsk, Ukraine. Church's 9th Anniversary Nov. 14–20 Germany. Pastors & Leaders Conference	Nov. 11–13: Oklahoma City, OK Tulsa, OK DFW, TX, USA Nov. 23–26: Gisborne, New Zealand	
December			

The travel schedule of Sunday Adelaja portrays him as a 'world class traveller' with frequent trips to virtually all continents of the world. Adelaja engages in cross-continental travel virtually every month, sometimes in multiple directions. The figures above reveal his travel schedule of 30 months out of the total 36 months between the years 2005, 2007 and 2008. The table shows the month of December is the only travel-free month across the three-year period. The most frequented is perhaps North America with several visits to a host of US states/cities and Canada. The table also shows frequent visits within European and Scandinavian countries such as Germany, United Kingdom, Poland, the Netherlands, Denmark, Finland and Norway. There were other visits to Asia (India, Singapore, Indonesia, Malaysia, Japan), Russia, Australia, New Zealand, Mexico, Brazil, Israel and to African countries such as Nigeria, South Africa and Egypt. The itineraries of leaders of the KICC, CCOMI and RCCG follow a similar rapidity and magnitude. The significance of these frequent travels does not simply lie in the number of cities or countries visited but more on the motive of the travels and the activities that took place during these travels. Space does not permit an elaborate analysis of the various events indicated in the table above, but suffice it to say that the nature of the events further eulogizes both their transnational dimension and the socio-religious, cultural, political and economic implications in local-global contexts.

Two catchwords for KICC's annual Christian conferences, the *International Gathering of Champions* (IGOC), are 'Raising Champions, Taking Territories' and 'It is not yet over until it is over'. The initiative that was started by Matthew Ashimolowo in 1991 gathers more than 180,000 Christians from over 40 nations for what is now known as Europe's premier Christian conference.[23]

Local and international evangelists and charismatic leaders participate in this ecumenical event. African-American evangelists and Pentecostal leaders who participate in this annual event include Eddie Long, Thomas Jakes, Keith Butler, Juanita Bynum and Donnie McClurkin. These are invited alongside African Pentecostal preachers and leaders such as Enoch Adeboye, David Oyedepo, Dipo Oluyomi, Mensah Otabil and Robert Kayanja.[24] Such forums often parade a mix of leaders and members from both constituencies. It is also an avenue for the commodification of sermon texts, gospel music, songs, films, anointing oil, documentaries and programmes of participating leaders and churches made into books, diaries, almanac, souvenirs and audio-visual products.[25] This singular annual event demonstrates a kind of intra-religious networking, albeit a superficial one, among and between African churches on both sides of the Atlantic and with African-American churches (Adogame 2003, 2007b: 27–8). Such a local event that brings together religious leaders and participants from various countries and continents does also have significant global and transnational implications.

Many African-led churches in the homeland are now consciously engaged in sending missionaries to evangelize Europe, the United States and other parts of the globe. Many of the African missionaries are commissioned by their home churches and provided with financial and material resources. While this 'reverse-mission' initiative cannot be claimed to be a peculiar feature of African Christian communities, they are nevertheless engaged in transmitting their religious traditions beyond their immediate geo-ethnic contexts. Ostensibly, as a critique of current immigration policies in the European Union in general and the United Kingdom in particular, one informant claims:

> Our mission here in the United Kingdom of God (UK) is a divine imperative whether the home or immigration office likes it or not, the gates of hell (borders) shall not prevail nor hinder us from spreading the gospel to an unfortunately now dead country (Britain). God owns the entire universe and we should be free to move in it, travel wherever we wish to go with the gospel. God will always make a way where there seems to be no way.[26]

Beneath this metaphorical reference and critique of stringent immigration policies lies some transnational import, the idea to move beyond and across geographical boundaries. This reverse-mission dynamics can be better analysed as an evolving dimension of the transnational process. It is to this new religious dynamic that I will now turn.

9

Reverse mission

Introduction: Europe as a prodigal continent?

The religious ethnography that took me from Germany to Nigeria in the summer of 1996 led to a striking and unprecedented finding, an advert captioned '*Europe: A Prodigal Continent!*...Europe: A Mission Field in Need of Church Attention' adorning the Missions Office notice board of RCCG' International headquarters in Lagos, Nigeria. It proclaimed: 'Why has Europe's spiritual light grown dim? A mission force of years ago, becoming another missionary field at the moment!' It is not uncommon now that Christians from the two-thirds world often employ similar narratives of representation giving the impression of a 'Christian' Europe as 'the dark continent of Europe' or 'a dead and secularized Europe'. Controversial and puzzling as such assertions may be, they cast our minds and gaze to a new, emerging global religious phenomena.

'Reverse mission' or 'reverse flow of mission' is increasingly becoming a buzz phrase in academic, mission circles, media and among Christians from the two-thirds world. The (un-) conscious missionary strategy and zeal by churches in Africa, Asia and Latin America of (re-) evangelizing the West is a relatively recent one. This enterprise, according to them, was aimed at re-christianizing Europe and North America. The rationale for reverse mission is often anchored on claims to divine commission to 'spread the gospel'; the perceived secularization of the West; the abysmal fall in church attendance and dwindling membership; desecralization of church buildings; liberalization; and on issues of moral decadence.

It is so far unclear whether 'reverse mission' is simply operating as mere rhetoric, and/or what shape, structure and dynamic will emerge through this process in the long run. It will suffice at this point to underscore public ignorance and ecclesial conspiracy that has left unnoticed this emerging mission trend, partly characterized by church proliferation in the South and its expansion from there to the Northern hemisphere and elsewhere. Nonetheless, reverse mission as 'rhetoric' or 'an evolving process' is of crucial religious, social, political, economic and missiological import for the West and world Christianity, as the non-Western world were hitherto at the receiving end of missions till the late twentieth century. The emergence of the 'global South' as the new centre of gravity of Christianity provides the watershed for the reversal and/or multidirectionality of missions.

Reverse mission: The antinomy of mission?

The moratorium discourse and its fall-outs and the very concept and process of reverse mission or reverse missionaries has been documented by scholars – scholars of religion[1], social scientists[2], historians,[3] missiologists,[4] theologians,[5] other related works[6] – and an interesting cross-section of the media, although sometimes attributing a variety of meanings and perspectives. It needs to be demonstrated further how reverse mission as a concept and process can be used as an analytical, descriptive tool. Adogame and Spickard (2010) identify reverse missions, South-South religious trade, and transnational organization theory as interrelated approaches aimed at breaking the stereotype that places the North Atlantic at the centre of the religious universe. Each of these approaches illustrates a kind of religious action that may include the West, but which does not privilege it. Adogame and Shankar (2012) have taken this argument further. They demonstrate how the comparative dynamics of religious expansion illuminates, for instance, the complex models of Christian expansion in different geo-historical epochs.

The political scientist, Timothy Byrnes (2011), in fact provided a new twist to our understanding of reverse mission. He employed the phrase 'reverse mission' to refer to 'any process through which members of religious communities speak in the US for their brothers and sisters living abroad who, though profoundly affected by US foreign policy, have no political platform in the United States from which to speak for themselves' (2). The book examines the political activities of three Catholic communities: the Society of Jesus (Jesuits), the Maryknoll Congregation, and the Benedictine Confederation, showing how they are deeply transnational in their institutional structures and in their religious missions. He argues that in all three cases, the dynamic of reverse mission resides at a fascinating intersection of two evolving strands of inquiry in the field of political science: *foreign policy interest group mobilization* from the subfield of American politics, and *transnationalism* from the subfield of international relations (13). These Jesuits, Maryknollers and Benedictines engage in reverse mission in different ways, according to their own traditions and community's practices. In all three cases 'these Catholic men and women formulate their personal and communal identities in large measure out of their participation in transnational brotherhood and sisterhood' (27).

While the three cases are instances of the same transnational dynamic, the example of Maryknoll sisters, from which the book title *Reverse Mission* is derived, stood out. This concerns Maryknollers and their reaction to US support for the counterrevolutionary insurgency against the Sandinista government in Nicaragua in the 1980s. The Maryknollers who were posted to Nicaragua employed that descriptive phrase, 'reverse mission', for the kind of transnational feedback loop within their own community, to capture the responsibility many of them felt to return from the mission field to educate US citizens about what was being done in their name to the people, the Catholic Church, and not incidentally the Maryknoll community in Nicaragua (10). Thus, the particular form that reverse mission takes in the case of the Maryknoll sisters comes directly and specifically from their experience as missioners abroad.

> The Maryknoll missioners developed a very powerful shared identity with the people with whom they lived and worked in Nicaragua. But when the time came to take political action to protect those people from the effects of US foreign policy in the region, the Maryknoll women returned home to the US for the purpose of evangelizing their fellow US citizens. (24).

But the missioners also engaged in reverse mission, because despite all the years they had spent out of the country, and despite all the solidarity they felt for the people of Nicaragua, these women remained US citizens.[7] Therefore, it was through a return to their roots in the United States that these women were best able to mobilize the resources at their disposal in favour of goals they held in common with transnational allies.

The emerging phenomenon of reverse mission has attracted media attention. For instance, *The New York Times* story captioned 'Mission from Africa' describes the mission task of the pastor of the RCCG Chapel of Restoration in the Bronx, New York and who coordinates the church's missionary activities in North America:

> Pastor Daniel Ajayi-Adeniran is coming for your soul. It doesn't matter if you are black or white, rich or poor, speak English or Spanish or Cantonese. He is on a mission to save you from eternal damnation. He realizes you may be skeptical, put off by his exotic name – he's from Nigeria – or confused by his accent, the way he stretches his vowels and trills his R's, giving his sermons a certain chain-saw rhythm. He suspects you may have some unfortunate preconceptions about Nigerians. But he is not deterred. He believes the Holy Spirit is working through him – aided by the awesome earthly power of demographics.[8]

The story continued, 'The Redeemed Church offers a case study of the crosscurrents that are drawing Christianity southward. Its leader and guiding force, Pastor Enoch Adeboye, sums up the church's history this way: "Made in heaven, assembled in Nigeria, exported to the world [...]." Today the process is reversing itself [...]'. Also, *The Chicago Tribune* with its front-page headline 'Africans now missionaries to US' signposts the RCCG as the Nigeria-based Pentecostal church that is spreading its evangelistic form of Christianity to America. It noted 'For years American missionaries brought Christianity to Africa. Now African Christians say they want to export their own brand of ecstatic worship and moral discipline to the US, a country they believe has lost its fervor'.[9] The *Christian Century*, a Christian magazine carried a story 'African missionaries to the U.S.' and reports:

> For generations, Christian missionaries from the U.S. journeyed to Africa to teach their religion. Now, however, amid a burgeoning of Christianity in Africa, churches there are sending thousands of missionaries overseas to preach the Christian message in their own unique style. And many of those missionaries are coming to the U.S. 'We have been blessed by the U.S. and now we want to give back to them through the gospel of Christ,' said Badeg Bekele, pastor of Emmanuel Ethiopian Church in Los Angeles [...] African ministries are springing up in America because 'the church in Africa is on fire, while the church in America is, for the most part, losing its zeal,' said Pastor Ivey Williams of a congregation in Tallahassee, Florida, established by the Nigerian-based Redeemed Christian Church of God. Williams is the first African-American pastor of an RCCG church.[10]

The *Herald* also captures this trend with the storyline: 'Out of Africa: now the missionaries head for Scotland'[11] and noting that:

> For centuries, the church sent missionaries to Africa to spread the word of God – now it needs them back. In a reversal of the stream of Scots who pioneered their way across the continent, one church has turned to ministers from South Africa to stem the shortage of staff at home.

In a recent development, the BBC 2 TV Series *Reverse Missionaries* epitomizes the stark reality of the enduring processes of reverse mission. In their introduction to the series, the producers note:

> Nineteenth-century Britain was a golden age for Christian missionaries, who took the word of God around the globe to countries in which that religion remains and is now thriving. In a reverse of those great missionary journeys, idealistic modern-day missionaries travel to Britain to discover

the historical roots of their faith and try to pursue their own missionary agenda in 21st-century Britain, trying to breathe new life into churches with declining attendance.

This recent documentary in March 2012 chronicled, under three episodes of one hour each, new missionaries from the two-thirds world – Jamaica, Malawi and India – to the United Kingdom.[12] The first episode focused on the Jamaican Baptist pastor, Franklin Small, who is on his way to King's Stanley, a village in the Cotswolds.[13] It is home to the oldest Baptist church in Gloucestershire, which is now threatened with closure. It was also home to Thomas Burchell, a missionary at the vanguard of the anti-slavery movement in the Caribbean. Pastor Franklin tries to bring some of his energetic Jamaican preaching style to the Cotswold community.

The second episode was set around John Chilimtsidya, a pastor of a charismatic renewal church in Blantyre, Malawi. It was 150 years ago that Dr David Livingstone left his home town Blantyre, Scotland, for Africa. He is credited with opening up Africa to Christianity. Now in a reverse mission, Pastor John is coming to Livingstone's home town where attendance at the local church is in decline. On the streets, John faces a huge culture shock – kids who know Jordan but not Jesus, and a Saturday night out in Glasgow that leaves the African pastor reeling. He seeks inspiration from Livingstone's story.[14]

In the third episode, Kshama Jayaraj's Church in Mumbai, The House of Prayer, spreads the gospel through a mixture of dance, music and prayer.[15] Belfast was home to Kshama's inspirational heroine, Victorian missionary Amy Carmichael, who spent 50 years in India helping vulnerable children. Now, in a reverse mission, Kshama arrives in a city still divided along religious lines but with some church attendances at an all-time low.

Although the three missionary figures mentioned in this documentary are hardly known within the African, Jamaican and Indian diasporic Christian communities in the United Kingdom, the trend showcased the dynamics of reverse mission.[16] It demonstrates how individuals and collective church organizations are putting reverse mission into practice. In this case, specific individuals are tracing specific missionaries back to their roots and thereby using such narratives of rediscovery as a template for religious expansion. In the examples we have discussed in this book, it was more of a rediscovery of the entire geographical context, the former heartlands of Christianity, as a new mission field.

These academic interpretations and media perceptions of the reverse mission dynamics or reverse missionaries can hardly be thought of as a historical accident or occurring as sporadic events. What circumstances have enabled the reverse mission that has dramatically shifted the centre of world Christianity to the two-thirds world?

Andrew Walls (1996, 2002) best eulogizes the complex dynamics of Christian mission by first historicizing it, and then balancing a broad, theoretical view of missions with more intensive discussions of specific missions. Walls (1996: 257) offers a panoramic view of the modern flux of the missionary movement and Christianity in general, emphasizing the recession of the Church in Europe and North America and its expansion everywhere else. Walls contends that the next phase of the missionary movement must incorporate sending and receiving. As Velho (2009: 41) highlights,

> with the secularization of Europe, the tendency has been for an enthusiastic version of Christianity to rise to the fore, [...] the *southern* Christianity of Asia, Africa, and above all Latin America. Indeed, this predominance is becoming global through migration, a diffuse influence, and in some cases even through a brand of missionization that takes the first world as its target, reversing the direction of the missionization in force from at least the sixteenth century onwards.

A historiography of reverse mission must respond to the antecedents and precedents of reverse mission process. To this I shall briefly turn.

Moratorium and reverse mission as a backlash to decolonization

The discourse on moratorium and reverse mission requires a historical backdrop especially as a backlash against decolonization. The history of the decolonization process in Africa is an intricate one that implicates all spheres of life. Kalu (2007, 2008: 271–91) best captures this complex interplay by mapping African Christianity between the World Wars and decolonization. The religious ferment in the decolonization process plays out on various levels. The character of missionary presence in the colonial enterprise shows ambivalent roles, in which the relationship of colonialists and missionaries was that of friends, partners and bedfellows on the one hand, and of foes and strange bedfellows on the other.

Kalu demonstrated how the war interregnum drastically reshaped the interior of African Christianity. The war heightened tension within African communities, because it required the services of recruits and porters and gave the local chiefs extraordinary powers to mobilize able-bodied men. Missionaries were compelled to engage themselves in these tasks; they became soldiers in the transport, supplies and medical units and performed a number of mundane tasks for the governments leaving parishes without pastoral care. Missionaries learnt to increasingly rely on indigenous resources for mission work. Indigenous people had the enviable opportunity to carry on the task. World War I severely disrupted the structure and moral economy of the missionary enterprise in Africa. As James Scherer (1964: 272) notes, 'the moratorium idea was not entirely new. During both World War I and World War II, the missionary movement had experienced the phenomenon of 'orphaned missions', or mission work disrupted by wartime conditions'.

The end of the war was fraught with ambiguities: Africans tasted a dose of responsibility in the churches and in the survival of the colonial states. Missionaries adjusted to the changing circumstances, ordained indigenous priests and waltzed with political nationalists. Besides the character of missionary presence in the colonial enterprise, the nature, process and consequences of decolonization also need to be considered. Was it planned or compelled and pursued hastily? Was it a transposition, passive revolution or a transformation? How did the missionaries respond? The post-1945 era is remarkable; the fact that Africans suffered, fought and died on the battlefield alongside their European counterparts broke the myth of European superiority. Educated elites also started to champion nationalist struggles. The post-war period witnessed planned debates, political agitation, industrial strikes and a shift from cultural to political nationalism. To a large extent, Christianity through the mission education machinery provided the impetus for African nationalism. Decolonization exposed the differing agendas of the colonial government and missionaries; differences on the goals and curricula of education and cultural policies betrayed the ideological cleavages and competing visions between missions and colonial government. Africans were sensitive to missionary unwillingness to afford them higher training, ordain an adequate number of indigenous priests, devolve power or overtly support nationalism.

Rivalry suffused the missionary enterprise as each denomination sought to imprint its own version. The main thrust of the missionary policy of indigenization was passive revolution to maintain influence using indigenous personnel and resources. People increasingly found the missionary version of indigenization to be unsatisfactory and restrictive. By the 1960s, most former European colonies in Africa underwent decolonization and became independent, although decolonization did not imply a radical change of Africa's colonial socio-economic structure. Missionaries' responses to nationalism varied according to individual whims, official or denominational policies and regional contexts. Vast changes in the political climate of the decade forced enormous changes in the religious landscape.

The impact of decolonization on church groups varied: based on the size and ecclesiastical organization; the vertical spread and social quality of adherents; the inherited pattern of colonial relationship; and the theological emphasis and international relations. Two insiders who served the home base of missionary organizations queried the motive behind the new mission strategy to maintain influence using indigenous personnel and resources. As T. A. Beetham argued:

> Are the thinking and experiment and action ... merely a fumbling attempt to retain influence, to gain some new position of authority to compensate for privileges now being rapidly lost? Or has it a significant future? (Neill 1952: 14)

As early as 1958, John V. Taylor, an Anglican missionary who later served as the General Secretary of the CMS in the 1960s, had queried how and when African Christians would begin to influence theological and ecclesiastical discourse internationally (Sundkler et al. 1969: 171–6). He reveals that decolonization caused much soul-searching about the meaning and goal of mission.

During the papal visit to Uganda in 1969, the Pope told his audience 'You must have an African Christianity ...'[17] As Kalu (2007: 331) notes,

> His challenge to the audience seems to have reversed the story of centuries of European relationship with Africa; as if he proclaimed release from a relationship that suffocated in favor of one which recognized the pluralistic context of mission ... That speech turned attention from patterns of insertion to modes of appropriation and their consequences, especially as the numbers of Christians in Africa had grown enormously.

African responses to the Pope's declaration could be traced in various liturgical initiatives and musical symbols. It meant that the story of African encounter with the gospel should privilege African initiatives and yet was told in an ecumenical and irenic manner. Vatican II which had only 61 Africans out of 2,500 Bishops was a watershed in re-designing the church's policy in mission and social service. It released African energy in the church as a number of Papal pronouncements appeared to speak to Africans in a new voice.[18]

The call for a moratorium was a more strident and different form of indigenization project. The moratorium exposed the character of Africa's relationship with the West – extraversion was in-built in the pattern of African relationship with the West as an essential ingredient to maintain 'eternal juniority'. It reflected African impatience with the nature, pace and results of mission-initiated indigenization. Africans suspected a hidden agenda to embroil them in cosmetic change while the same people retained real power (Kalu 2007). When the WCC General Assembly met in Nairobi in 1975, the choice of venue was as significant as the speech of the Pope in Kampala in 1969. The themes that emerged indicated a new mood that accepted African Christian maturity in ways hardly planned by the missionaries. Some Protestant missions took the opportunity to abandon missionary engagement.

In some cases it led to the emergence of short-term missionaries. Thus, the moratorium and African liberation struggles influenced the shifts in the strategy for decolonizing the African churches. But who is this revolutionary figure that single-handedly stirred controversy within global mission circles turning the paternalistic trend of Christian mission on its head? Where did he derive the inspiration and guts to throw such a challenging blow at an unsuspecting mission audience?

John Gatu – From colonial soldier to moratorium crusader

John G. Gatu, the man whose spark ignited the moratorium debate, has been described as 'a great leader, mediator, pastor, preacher, counselor, speaker, poet, writer and ecumenist'.[19] Born on 3 March 1925 in the Kiambu district of Kenya, where he obtained his primary and secondary education, he joined the British colonial army in 1941, following the completion of secular education. Gatu joined the Presbyterian Church of East Africa (PCEA) in Kenya after military service. Prior to ordination, Gatu studied theology at St Paul's United Theological College in Limuru (Kenya) from 1951–8. Gatu pursued additional theological training at the Divinity Faculty, New College, Edinburgh; Pittsburgh Theological College; and at Princeton Theological Seminary in 1958, 1963 and 1970 respectively. From 1960–3, he was the PCEA Deputy Secretary General and was made Secretary General in 1964. From the early 1970s, he began to serve in various senior leadership positions in his church and in several national/international ecumenical organizations including the National Council of Churches of Kenya, the Kenya Christian Churches Educational Association, the All Africa Council of Churches, the World Alliance of Reformed Churches, and the World Council of Churches.

Gatu was groomed in the heyday of colonialism and anti-colonial feelings in Kenya. Prior to Kenya's independence from the British in 1963, the country faced the full brunt of Western imperialism with the British monopolizing virtually all sectors of the economy. The Europeans took over the productive highlands from the natives, the best portions of Kenya's land, and assigned vast stretches of viable land free of charge to Europeans. It was within these stark political and socio-economic realities that Gatu was nurtured. Thus, his experiences during the decolonization era in Kenya, the mission education he received, his service in the British colonial army in the interwar years, his post-secondary education in the United Kingdom and United States, his leadership experience in ecumenical organizations, all shaped not only his theological thinking but also his drive for ecclesiastical liberation of Africa from the paternalistic apron-strings of Western mission bodies. The PCEA was under the missionary tutelage of the Church of Scotland, the Presbyterian Church in the United States, the United Church of Canada and the Reformed

Church in Hungary. One may assume that the white highlands policy and missionary control of his church could have combined to motivate Gatu to ask how and whether the African church should remain under Western control. The search for answers to these questions led him to become a revolutionary leader (Schwartz 1991: 1).

The moratorium debacle and its aftermath

Gatu initiated the call during a visit to Milwaukee, Wisconsin, USA, in February 1971. He embarrassed his ecumenical hosts by declaring that he had not come to beg for money or personnel, but to request that missionary aid in money and personnel should cease for at least five years so that African Christians can at least learn how to catch fish instead of relying on *gratis* fish from European mission boards. Earlier, he led his church to produce a document stating what they believed.[20]

The stark call by Gatu in 1971 for 'a moratorium on missions and missionaries from the West' put missions at a crossroad. As Gatu lashed out:

> Our present problems ... can only be solved if all missionaries can be withdrawn in order to allow a period of not less than five years for each side to rethink and formulate what is going to be their future relationship.... The churches of the Third World must be allowed to find their own identity, and the continuation of the present missionary movement is a hindrance to this selfhood of the church. (Anderson 1974: 43)

In fact, the Reformed Church of America, sponsors of the Milwaukee 'Mission Festival 71' meeting would probably not have invited him to speak during the event, if they had any inkling that his speech was going to be so controversial to the extent of stirring up and turning the parameters of mission praxis on its head. As Walter Buhlmann (1980: 9) remarks:

> The missions in Africa have for many years been in the crossfire of criticism. In an earlier age they were much admired, but nowadays they are attacked and accused, by radical Christians, by cold atheists and by black nationalists.

The moratorium call came under heavy criticism based on the mere fact that it emanated from the so-called Third World, a context which has been for many years the mission field. There were wide-ranging responses of mission bodies to the moratorium debate via seminars, conferences and on pages of journals. This call which took a revolutionary stance generated heated conversation, rebuttals and criticism from various quarters, particularly from the Western world. The criticisms of the moratorium were theological, ecclesiastical and logistical in nature. As Kalu (2008: 276) explained, it was argued that *theologically* a moratorium was unacceptable because of the Pauline imagery of *soma* that we are one body and one part cannot prevent the other from performing a mandatory task. *Ecclesiastically*, it was dangerous to become a national church. This threatened catholicity; the pilgrim and the indigenous principles must be held in tension. *Logistically*, it would be impossible to dismantle the mission structures which had been built up for over a century. Then, there was the *gut* reaction of those who presumed that the Africans have proved ungrateful after years of sacrifices by missionaries. Eliot Kendall, who served the same constituency as Beetham, has documented the overt and subtle pressures mounted on African church leaders (Kalu 1980: 365–74; 1975; Kendall 1978: 85).

> The moratorium debate in the early 1970s evoked consternation among the white missionary agencies who dismissed it as preposterous. Ironically, their rebuttals provided the impetus for an African Pentecostal missionary enterprise. Within a few decades, they achieved the goals that the mainline churches failed to consolidate. (Kalu 2008: 290)

Legacies of the moratorium discourse as eulogized by Gatu and his contemporaries are still fresh and resilient within world mission circles.[21] In fact, Gatu has remained very consistent, positive and vehement about the urgency for self-sufficiency and self-reliance of the church in Africa. Two and half decades later, at a consultation on self-reliance of the churches in Africa at Limuru, Kenya in May 1996, he continued to promote this goal:

> Unless African church leadership accept(s) the challenge of self-reliance in order to undo the yoke of dependence and are able to set examples in training, personal life, trusting one another regardless of the devils of ethnicity that seem to plague not only Africa but the world today, the Church in Africa will remain poor, weak and unable to engage in her missionary calling to go onto the world.[22]

Although the moratorium failed to produce a formal radical and systemic halt to the influx of Western missionaries and mission resources to Africa, it nevertheless raised a question mark that resulted in self-reflection and structural adjustment by Western missionaries and of their mission resources. It served as an eye-opener for many about the new changing dynamics of mission and religious expansion in which Africans were not only looking inward for self-reliance, but outwardly with a mission mandate to evangelize what they now refer to as 'the dark continent of Europe', 'the prodigal continent' or 'the dead West'. Several Third World Christian leaders supported this suggestion because they believed that it would break the circle of dependency on the Western churches and create room for self-development. Alongside their African counterparts, some Asian and Latin American church leaders echoed this sentiment. In actual fact, the moratorium also produced a new consciousness about dependence and strategies for self-reliance that has challenged definitions of mission but also altered the unidirectionality of missions that characterized earlier conceptions.

In 1973, his moratorium proposal took centre stage during heated debates on 'partnership in mission' by the Commission on World Mission and Evangelism of the Bangkok Assembly of the WCC. In the following year, it became a recurring topic at the All Africa Conference of Churches Third Assembly at Lusaka, Zambia.[23] This empowerment process of the Third World churches brought significant changes in mission practices as issues of cooperation and partnership were promoted as new mission strategies at the International Congress on World Evangelization, Lausanne, Switzerland in July 1974 and in subsequent congresses. Third World Christians participated in these congresses and further held continental and regional conferences, which provided global challenges and opportunities. The Lausanne Covenant gave a qualified endorsement to the moratorium call 'a reduction of foreign missionaries and money in an evangelized country may sometimes be necessary to facilitate the national church's growth in self-reliance and to release resources for unevangelized areas' (Lausanne Covenant 1975: 6). In 1975, the WCC Fifth Assembly at Nairobi continued to echo the moratorium call. The terms of the debate had moved from the discussion of a possible moratorium toward mission being seen as the joint privilege and responsibility of churches in all six continents (Scherer 1964: 273). A deal for 'mission partnership' had been brokered, this helped Western mission bodies to save face. Mission 'partners' became a leverage to deconstruct the inherent ecclesiastical paternalism that characterized the missionary enterprise.

Thus, the initiative that entailed sending African missionaries abroad came partly against the backdrop of the moratorium call to awaken 'two-third world' peoples to their responsibility, creating new goals and formulating a viable evangelism strategy towards Europe (Kalu 1980: 365–74). The Lutheran World Federation had experimented with 'reverse flow' in which African ministers were posted to German congregations where they were mostly treated with cold civility. In the early 1980s, Tanzanian Lutheran pastors were sponsored to serve in various parishes in Germany. The reverse-mission agenda is becoming a very popular feature among new African-led churches, with pastors and missionaries commissioned to head already existing branches or establish new ones in diaspora. The growth of missionary endeavours from Africa and other parts of the non-Western world has gained momentum in the 1990s, in a way that challenges Christianity in the West but also World Christianity.

By the 1990s, many churches had progressed to define their missions as witnessing communities to the Western churches and societies, which were waning numerically and spiritually. In the closing decade of the twentieth century, reverse missions became more recognized and gradually gained ascendancy due to economic decline and political conflicts, which intensified migration of Africans, Asians and Latin Americans to the West. Confronted by the secularization of the Western society and the decline of church attendance and public piety, these migrants took up a revivalist agenda. At the same time, these immigrant Christians looked at the Western churches as being in a state of apostasy, and in a spiritual wilderness that needed re-evangelization. As Ojo highlights, the founding of the Third World Missions Association (TWMA), in Portland, Oregon, USA, in May 1989 as a forum for mission-sending agencies in Africa, Asia, and Latin America to enhance their capacities to undertake extensive missionary endeavours brought in an institutional perspective and transformed non-Western world missions into a global force in world Christianity (Ojo 2007). In fact, the closure of some Arab countries to Western missionaries and the acceptance and success of African and Asian missionaries working among Arabs also proved quite significant in this process of reverse missions. Likewise, the AD 2000 and Beyond Movement, a global effort of world evangelization, directed by Third World Christian leaders provided additional involvement and networking for evangelization and cross-cultural missions.

By the mid-1990s, non-Western churches are beginning to achieve some degree of success in their missionary efforts, though they are largely using non-conventional missionaries. Many African churches have been evangelizing among whites and non-African immigrants since mid-1980s. While migration continued to provide missionary mobilization, African Christian communities were able to realize their strength within world Christianity, and perceive their missionary activities in global perspectives.

In sum, the implications of reverse mission for world Christianity are not far to seek. First, reverse mission has brought a major shift in mission understanding; provided better sensibilities to, and appreciation of the multicultural nature of Christianity in the twenty-first century. Two, new definitions of mission are emerging in which traditional 'missions fields' now form 'mission bases' of renewed efforts to re-evangelize Europe and North America. Missions changed from unilateral to multilateral, itinerant missionaries increased, short-term missions emerge, and missions moved from cultural transplantation to contextualization. Third, as churches in the West, particularly in Europe, are declining in number and in missionary significance, the impact of non-Western missions looms large in the revivification of Christianity in Europe. Fourth, this trend helps in the deconstruction and demystification of ecclesiastical paternalism that characterized global Christianity. Lastly, the proliferation of priests/missionaries from the two-thirds world may help fill a spiritual/administrative vacuum caused by the dearth of European clergy. Andrew Walls' remark: *'Europe needs immigrants but do not want them'*, sums up European attitudes towards immigrants in Europe. This reverse trend in missions now offers the 'old heartlands of Christianity' a model for renewal, and calls for a structural reform of the Church to grapple with the challenges of migration.

I will end this section with only two of the several strands of reverse mission among African Christian communities. First, I will show how a more institutional strategy for international mission and expansion developed within the RCCG. Second, I will draw upon an exceptional case of reverse mission, the Embassy of the Kingdom of God Church for all Nations (EKGCN), a church founded by an African immigrant, but which has produced an atypical case with a dominant non-African membership.

RCCG overseas mission strategies

Although individual RCCG parishes have the initiative and leverage to sponsor and establish new parishes locally and internationally, the RCCG leadership play an institutional role in international mission. While the opening of new RCCG parishes by individual local branches is not centrally controlled from the International headquarters in Lagos, the strategy towards foreign mission was however institutionalized with the appointment of the Assistant General Overseer to take charge of mission overseas. The General Overseer's wife, Folu Adeboye, led African Missions, that is, mission work within the continent. The international headquarters plays a supervisory, moderating role and intervenes where there are local problems, disputes and conflicts between different parishes. The provincial headquarters inaugurates a new parish, and the General Overseer, where possible, conducts the dedication ritual of the parish.[24] According to RCCG Provincial Pastor, Brown Oyitso,

> The church was given a micro and macro vision, with the micro driving the macro vision. God gave the micro vision to the Founder that the church will go around the world, the General Overseer (Enoch Adeboye) came in and got the macro vision. We were recruited and charged to move abroad. God gives a mission with a provision, so the first RCCG parish in London was started by Leke Sanusi. There was contemplation on several options, and the next initiative was for the US.[25]

Pastor Samuel Shorimade was officially commissioned by the RCCG leadership to return to the United States on missionary service, having studied and completed a PhD in the United States earlier and returned to Nigeria.[26] He relocated with his family to the United States and opened a parish in Boston. As Oyitso remarks,

> The General Overseer commissioned the histrionics of church development in the US. New England was a prime target, as a gateway to aristocrats and to America. Harvard University and the Massachussetts Institute of Technology became potential targets. The Shorimades were forerunners [...]. It was inaugurated, funds were generated, initial take-off grants were provided – hall rents, musical instruments and PA system. Initial support for the RCCG Boston parish was essentially from the Pen Cinema parish in Agege, Lagos (Nigeria).[27]

Occasionally, financial and material support was provided for the Boston and London parishes until they both became self-sufficient, and started to fend for themselves. Money was also sent from Nigeria to support new branches established in India, Pakistan, South Africa and elsewhere. In 2004 when I interviewed Oyitso, he disclosed that the RCCG Victory House Parish in Festac Town (Lagos) had already established six branches in Italy and committed financial and material resources to support them. Training materials, Sunday school manuals were sent from the RCCG headquarters to support mission work in all these new contexts. Besides, trainers were sent from Nigeria to conduct Ministers training workshops and conferences. In the case of international mission, pastors and church personnel were sent to head new branches. For instance, in 2002, Bosun Ajayi was sent to Bonn by the RCCG International missions department to coordinate RCCG branches in Germany.[28] In November 1994, Pastor Dr Ajibike Akinkoye moved with his family to Dallas to oversee the first parish. From this pioneer parish the Dallas metroplex played host to 14 full-fledged RCCG parishes.[29] It was this parish that later served as the RCCG North American headquarters. Akinyoye confirmed receiving financial support from the RCCG International headquarters (Lagos) towards the physical development of the over 600 hectares of land acquired for building the RCCGNA headquarters. In fact, during my research at the RCCGNA library and archives department in Dallas in 2004, I found a copy of a cheque of $500,000.00 filed in the archive, which a church official confirmed was a donation from a local RCCG parish in Nigeria to the RCCGNA headquarters. Thus, in the case of RCCG, the reverse mission process has gone beyond rhetoric in that the church consciously provides institutional support for new parishes, particularly in the diaspora. Pastor Oyitso summarizes the rationale for reverse mission (overseas) when he said:

> In those days, missionaries came and were supported from the UK and the USA. They sow seeds and are now reaping the harvest. The harvest is

churches in Africa that are now being sent and money now being ploughed back. God has turned the table. Churches are founded now to bring back the faith to revive the European and US countries.[30]

Oyitso asserts that financial and material support given to new parishes abroad has been 'a one-way thing [...] It is one way and deliberate. We do not want host governments to think that we are here (Europe, USA) to siphon money from their countries'. Nonetheless, the RCCG financial organization is structured in such a way that all parishes are required to funnel a percentage of the total tithes and offerings, through their provincial and regional offices, to the international headquarters of the church in Lagos.

I have shown that RCCG missionary pastors are now sent from its international headquarters in Nigeria to Germany, United States and other parts of the globe, with financial responsibility such as salaries or honorarium borne by the International headquarters in Lagos. Thus, while a specified proportion of income, dues and remittances are transferred from all worldwide RCCG parishes to the international headquarters, the coordinating Pastors (missionaries) sent on mission abroad are at the same time remunerated directly from the international headquarters or some local parishes in Nigeria.

Taking Kiev by surprise: Beyond the rhetoric of reverse mission

A section of the EKGCN's self-documented history captioned 'Out of Africa'[31] eulogizes the dynamic of religious expansion of new African immigrant religiosity overseas. African immigrants such as Sunday Adelaja have founded churches in Eastern Europe, and from there have spread to other host contexts including back to Africa. The example of the EKGCN, an African religiosity in the former Soviet Bloc, shows the changing dynamics of African Christian communities, and how they are contributing to the religious diversification of the diasporic context. I shall explore the contextual factors that shape its mobility in Kiev, but also how its pragmatic approach towards the existential problems faced by members and admirers has attracted a huge clientele of membership.

Sacralizing immigrant narratives: 'Go to a land that I will show you'!

In 1993, the Nigerian-born Sunday Odulaja founded the EBKGN in Kiev. It is a typical example of how African-led churches have shifted their centre of spiritual gravity from continental Europe to Eastern Europe. While most new African churches in diaspora are led and dominated by African immigrants, the Embassy is an exceptional church in Europe, and perhaps within the new African diaspora in that it boasts a majority non-African membership. More than half of the total membership is Ukrainian, or Russian (Adogame 2007b: 21). The indigenous Eastern European population that characterizes its demography turned Adelaja into a religious icon (Asamoah-Gyadu 2006:73). Adelaja is a charismatic figure, particularly among his followers in Ukraine and beyond. His mastery of the Russian language and its employment in preaching at church services and other religious programmes has endeared him to the local audience. He taps into the sensitive foreigner, racial cord to validate and legitimize his claim to a divine mission, but also uses his charisma and influence. As he affirms, 'Though I am a foreigner, God has given me the ability to go and minister beyond race, culture, and denominational barriers' (Adelaja 2003: 25).

Adelaja was raised as a Presbyterian in Nigeria. In 1986, at the age of 19, he claimed to have been 'born again' while watching Pastor William Kumuyi, leader of the Deeper Christian Life Church on local Nigerian television. Adelaja's quest for further studies and his eventual sojourn in the former Soviet bloc is an interesting dynamic of how migration narratives are often sacralized and weaved as occurrences and mobility anchored on divine design rather than by any mundane accident. Testimony genres of several African immigrants are rife with accounts of how they saw the mysterious 'hand of God' in shaping their life trajectories and migration histories. Such reconstructed tropes are also often choreographed by irregular, undocumented migrants in a way that may give meaning to the travails and excruciating ordeals that sometimes characterize decisions to travel, the harrowing experiences during the actual journey(s), zodiac boat wrecks, unanticipated deaths, and the uncertainties that hover around their sojourn in the 'new, temporary home'.

Adelaja left his home country, Nigeria in 1986 to study journalism at Belarus State University, Minsk. Later in his life he situated this initial move, 'the point of exodus', as a divine call to mission by God. He recounts a common trajectory in the narratives of many African Christians in diaspora:

> He (God) directed me to go to Russia in a way reminiscent of the call He gave to Abraham: 'Get out of your country, from your family and from your father's house, to a land that I will show you' (Gen. 12: 1). Even though I was a new believer, I had the faith to accept this as God's sovereign assignment for my future destiny. Later I realized that this was actually my missionary call; just as God called Paul on the Damascus road, so He was calling me. However, He did not reveal it to me then, because I would have had no way of even understanding what a missionary call might possibly have been.[32]

In Belarus, Adelaja joined a Christian foreign students' fellowship, became part of an underground church and embarked on active Christian ministry, which intensified with the fall of communism. As Adelaja (2004: 37–55) remarked,

> Survival during Communism's dictatorship demanded much wisdom, silent worship and many narrow escapes by the power of the Holy Spirit ... The fear of the Lord kept me focused till the year 1990, when the God-ordained reformations of Mikhail Gorbachev began to take effect. For the first time, we were able to meet with Russian believers. That turned out to be the beginning of my full-time ministry....

He survived repeated clashes with KGB officials until his official deportation from Russia opened the way for a new life and ministry in Kiev, Ukraine. In November 1993, he started a bible study group in his apartment with only 7 people. Within 3 months, the membership grew to 49. On September 12, 1994, he registered the body as a church with the Department of Religious Affairs, with the name, Word of Faith Bible Church. This name was later changed in 2002 to the Embassy of the Blessed Kingdom of God for All Nations reflecting the worldwide catchment area as his constituency for further expansion and mission.[33]

Adelaja's (2004: 37–55) original vision was first 'to establish a megachurch to win and minister to thousands of people from the Kiev area', and then

> send missionaries into the world, especially into China and the Arab countries. Just as the world used to know the former Soviet Union as an exporter of weapons of mass destruction, so now God wanted these nations to be exporters of life through the gospel of the kingdom of God.

Conflicts with Ukrainian government authorities, including several attempted deportations and numerous lawsuits aimed at closing down the church, dogged the young pastor's steps (Hanciles 2008: 105). He was perceived in several quarters 'as a foreign-financed charlatan who brainwashes and hypnotizes congregants into parting with their money' (Brown 2003: 91). The government and the Eastern Orthodox Church were critical of the new Embassy church. Opposition was also faced from pockets of anti-Westernizing political groups in Ukraine. However, the church has continued to overcome these hurdles and expand both numerically and geographically. At the end of 2000, the courts acquitted Adelaja of various charges in 22 lawsuits brought against the church by different government agencies, media and government officials.[34] In spite of the controversy that enveloped the Embassy church, it had a significant appeal to Ukrainians from various strata of society. The church claims that political leaders are members of the church and they attend programmes regularly. In fact, Leonid Chernovetskyi, the Major of Kiev is believed to be one of its members. The involvement of local influential figures in his church will have visible political, economic and strategic implications for its visibility and growing institutionalization.

With only 7 members in 1994, the church presently claims to be one of the largest congregations in Europe with over 20,000 members, with 15 satellite churches in Kiev, 15 daughter churches in Kiev District and 70 churches throughout Ukraine, Russia, Moldova, Belarus and Georgia. Branches were established in Nigeria, Germany, the Netherlands, United Arab Emirates and United States. In the United States, two branches were recently established in Sacramento and Sarasota. The church lays claim to over 300 'daughter' churches outside Ukraine.

The Embassy has grown to acquire immense property as a way of asserting and inserting herself in new geo-cultural contexts. The church acquired between 15 and 51 hectares of land in Kiev to erect a magnificent edifice for various religious purposes.[35] The Embassy is another example of an African church that has even proposed Christian banking to 'empower God's people economically, and promote the Kingdom of God'.[36] Such extra-religious activities no doubt have immense religious, social and economic import (Adogame 2004a: 35; 2005d: 509). Boasting numerous ministries, including soup kitchens and drug rehabilitation centres, radio and television programmes, and other forms of media production, the Embassy is now a significant presence in Kiev (Hanciles 2008: 105). The church seems to provide statistical evidence justifying its social relevance within the immediate society, declaring that,

> Between one to two thousand people feed daily in the church's 'Stephania Soup Kitchen' (almost two million people fed over the past 6 years); over 3,000 people set free from drug and alcohol addiction; providing homes for street and abandoned children (where over 2000 children have been restored to their families) ... unswervingly implication in the transformation of all strata of society; church members involvement in schools, factories, banks and other social groups of society; thousands of mafia members have come to the Lord through the activities of the Embassy of God, the church's hot-line has counseled over 70 thousand people, of which 1,500 are now church members.[37]

Adelaja hosts a weekly Christian TV Show and lays claim to a television ministry with coverage of over 100 million homes across Europe, Africa and Russia. He has authored numerous religious books, many of which were based on his previous sermon texts. The core of his Kiev ministry is preaching, healing and providing desperately needed services in a society that is, at best, inept at coping with rampant alcoholism, widespread poverty and several strains on families (Brown 2003: 90). The socio-economic climate of the former Soviet Union following the collapse of the Iron Curtain provided a 'breathing space' for the Embassy church and probably explains why the church has attracted a huge following from the host context. In a relative sense, poverty, acute social problems and economic uncertainty seem to assume common denominators between Africans and Ukrainians and thus provided popular appeal to new Pentecostal churches such as the Embassy. As a local pastor of the church remarks, 'Everybody who comes here has a problem. Everybody is in crisis ... Most of them are unchurched and desperate. They are searching for a way to cope with alcohol, drugs, a lack of money or spouses who stray' (Brown 2003: 90). Apparently justifying the church's raison d'etre and public relevance, Adelaja (2004: 37–55) remarks:

> Honored pastors! Beloved brothers and sisters! As long as our world moves, in which we live, anomalous things become normal. The devil will present norms of life farther and more graceless than before. Still 40 years back the whole world, specifically professional medicine, considered homosexuality and Lesbianism as a sickness, and it was seen as a lack in health, but in the 70's the same sick doctors started to accept it as a standard ideology and thinking. History shows that since that time the world began to run mad. 'First, accept us like we are and then create laws which allow unisexual marriage.' Now ideological organizations and political forces try...[38]

His pragmatic approach towards solving the varied existential problems of his members and visitors brings close the cosmological tradition within which Adelaja was born and nurtured. Frequent street processions such as the 'March for Jesus' were symbolic in ridding the society of demons, witches and evil spirits which members hold accountable for the ills and incipient social decadence in society. The chanting and rendering of songs such as '*Up, Up Jesus, Down, Down Satan*' during street processions in Kiev suggests how members have been religiously sensitized to engage in and embark on 'spiritual warfare' against malevolent spiritual powers prevalent in Ukrainian society, in this case through terrestrial processions.

Members and visitors patronize Adelaja seeking panacea to their varied existential problems. The fact that Adelaja weaves elements of indigenous African cosmology to appeal to the spiritual sensibilities of Ukrainians is significant against the backdrop of a context and people barely getting over the hangover of a Marxist-socialist Weltanschauung. The taking up of extra-religious functions and his pragmatism towards tackling these multifarious social, spiritual, economic problems, beyond the content of his message, may have been a primary stimuli and focus of attraction.

The Embassy boasts of a professionally built website that is rich in content and structure.[39] This section contains printed materials and audio-visual resources screening over 1000 sermons of the pastor and leaders of the church, over 30 books authored by the pastor, music, video coverage of programmes as well as testimonies of members.[40] Although these books were originally written in English, their translations into local Ukrainian, Russian, Dutch, German, French and other languages demonstrate their local but also global impact. The website is an embodiment of the history, belief system and wide-ranging activities of the church. It touches on virtually all aspects that an inquisitive observer might be looking out for.

Out of Africa, back to Africa

Scholarship has not paid sufficient attention to a new trend in which immigrant religious communities, specifically African-led churches, are physically retracing their roots and routes back to Africa (Adogame 2008f). The EBKGN, KICC and CCOMI represents such African-led churches in diaspora, that are establishing new 'mission-frontiers' back in Africa. The fact that several branches of these churches have now been founded in Africa is indicative of another dimension of reverse mission. In this case, it represents a kind of spiritual remittance to the continent, in that the immigrants are giving something back to the continent from which they emerged in the first instance. This is akin to the reverse mission mechanism of the Maryknollers referred to at the beginning of this chapter.

10

The politics of networking

Introduction

Religion is largely at the pivot of immigrants' sense of individual and collective identities, and immigrant communities serve as focal points for religious and social networks. In the face of contemporary religious, political and sociocultural realities, African Christian communities are increasingly engaged in charting local-global religious and extra-religious networks to further their self-insertion and self-assertion in host religious landscapes (Adogame 2003: 24–41). Their engagement in intra-religious networks far outweighs any interreligious encounters and considerations. Thus, the focus of the concluding chapter is on some of the intra-religious links they have created or are engaged with individually and collectively.

By intra-religious networks I do not suggest that these networks are essentially religious in motivation and outlook. While what I describe is mainly patterns within formal/official frameworks, there are several levels of religious networking going on within the informal strata, not to mention networks within the social, cultural, economic and political echelons. This informal and extra-religious pattern of networking are in themselves important and contribute to our general understanding of their modus operandi, although this goes beyond the purview of this chapter. These informal networks may seem to be more internal and functional, although more localized within the circles of African Christian communities. Such informal networks are significant in their own right, though they may not really be interested in ecumenical networks with host European or American churches or in fact other migrant non-African churches as much as they interact internally with other African-led churches.

Their church programmes serve as avenues for engendering new religious, socio-economic and cultural relationships as well as maintaining and sustaining old ones. These churches play a central role in providing a social space where members can meet one another and forge other networks for mutual support and assistance. Such social networks created often transcend religious boundaries into social, cultural and economic spheres in the form of social-cultural associations. These networks serve as social and cultural capital, especially for the new African immigrants (see Chapter 6). The sense of mutual obligation, the practical and emotional support given to one another, often among individuals who did not know one another prior to joining the church is akin to relationships found within families, friends and neighbourhoods in the home context.

Some of these immigrant churches from Africa are confronted with a somewhat ambivalent situation. On the one hand, many are enthusiastic about engaging in official networking as well as in seeking to attain recognition and status as full-fledged churches by the host societies – churches and the wider public. On the other hand, some of their members sometimes appear to be afraid to 'run the risk' of becoming 'too visible' or 'too open' in a context where they are obviously denied the status of a bona fide church, and where the membership is made up of undocumented immigrants. This ambivalent stance serves as another explanation for the 'politics of religious networking'. Thus, Christian communities of the African diaspora organize themselves in such a way as to reinforce and revalidate their sense of ethnic and religious identity, ensure and maintain security, seek solidarity as well as to develop survival strategies, that is, ways of negotiating a way through the hazards of Western societies.

The motivations for joining or engaging in intra-religious networks are complex and varied. It is important to explore efforts they make through such intra-religious networks to articulate and respond to varied issues. Intra-religious engagement of African Christian communities derive not so much from doctrinal affinities or leadership preferences, as from the quest for spiritual satisfaction, religious identity, and a place to feel at home and not as 'aliens, foreigners and strangers'.[1] The complexity of the motives for charting and/or participating in networks is due to religious, socio-cultural, political, economic and strategic considerations. While religious communities identify this networking as a vital strategy for global mission and evangelism, as reverse mission to a heathen Europe[2], I argue that such networks function also as conduits for negotiating, maintaining *identity* and ensuring *security*, as well as facilitating status improvement and legitimacy in Europe and North America (see Chapter 7). The public denigration (including that by some host Western churches) of African religious communities as sects, cults, exotic religions or being seen as a haven for the molestation of child witches has rekindled the fear of exclusion, ostracization, and further 'demonization' particularly within the European spiritual marketplace. Several African-led churches are partly interested in formal religious networks in the European context as a way of re-attaining and re-enacting the status and prestige they have acquired in their home countries.

The range and nature of these ties include intra-religious networks and new ecumenical affiliations that are continent-wide, such as the Council of

Christian Communities of an African Approach in Europe (CCCAAE), and nation-wide such as the Scottish Council of African Churches (SCOAC).[3] The scope of these transborder networks also include pastoral exchanges between Africa and the diaspora, or through special religious events and conferences, prayer networks, internet sites, international ministries, publications, video and tele-evangelism. African-led churches in diaspora frequently organize religious events which are local in nature but which have a global focus that links the local church with other churches globally. The rest of the chapter will focus on phases and patterns of intra-religious networking among African Christian communities in diaspora, original home contexts and between them and the new host societies.

Phases of intra-religious networking in Europe and North America

This section examines the nature and scope of intra-religious networking among African Christian communities in the earlier and later phases of their development in Europe and North America, and highlights the factors enhancing the quest for and significance of contemporary intra-religious networking. In earlier decades of African Christian movements in different parts of Europe and the United States, many were localized, with their activities resulting in part from the hostile attitude of the host society. The activities of Daniels Ekarte and the ACM in Liverpool (Chapter 4) were localized to his mission and the immediate environment. When he demonstrated a critical stance of institutional racism toward him and his work, he did so mainly through sermons from his pulpit. Lawrenson remarks:

> Rev. Ekarte conducted worship at the Mission for the very large Negro population in the area, and I for one would always go along to hear him preach. We sang Christian hymns and used Christian prayer books, but it has to be said that the sermons were political rather than Christian, outlining the perceived injustices that he received from the Liverpool City Council, rather than edifying his congregation.... I would never condone Pastor Ekarte's practice, but I can understand it, as the pulpit was the only tool he had to get over his message, which was that there were serious strained relations between him and the Council, built only upon racism.[4]

There were other African church leaders like Ekarte involved in pastoral and evangelistic ministries, who had created models of interracial and intercultural worshipping communities at the time. However, they were limited in the size of their networks and relationships. They failed to tackle the structural injustice of the societies within which they lived.

The increasing efforts directed towards charting and maintaining intra-religious networks, especially in the European Union, are linked to wide ranging religious, social, political and economic concerns. Many African Christians who come to Europe often try to identify with mainstream churches similar to their churches back home. As soon as they discover these churches, then the feeling of spiritual tepidity or the experience of being seen as undesirables confronts them. As a result, many African Christians in Europe and the United States abandon the historic churches due to the disaffection they claim to experience. They establish their own churches or turn to a number of new churches that are the products of African initiatives and under African leadership. Olu Abiola, who later founded the Aladura International Church, described his experience in this way:

> As an ordained minister of the Church Missionary Society of Nigeria (Anglican), I attended and worshipped at one of the Church of England near my home the very first Sunday after my arrival in London. But to my surprise, I was told at the end of the service by the officiating minister that I will be much at home with my own kind and he directed me to a Black Pentecostal Church. (Ludwig 1992: 136)

In the same vein, John Adegoke, the Spiritual Leader of the C&S church in Birmingham, was a member of the Anglican Church in Nigeria when he came to London in 1964. He had attended Church of England services for about a year. When the first meetings of the C&S were held, he experienced this as a breakthrough. He remarks:

> Any Nigerian will find the church here different from what he expected. The missionaries came to Nigeria, faking people to live like Christians. But here in England people do not live like Christians, many things are contrary to Christian principles. Sunday is not literally taken as the Christian Sabbath. Nobody has time for the Sunday service, whereas in Nigeria the services are long. You begin to wonder. After suffering for one year, I found people who were interested. I found myself there.[5]

One consequence of this development was a greater identity of African Christians with churches that were more likely to express their interests and sentiments. Many Africans, including ordained priests of mainstream churches, changed religious affiliation, usually from a mainstream church to an AIC or a Pentecostal church. Churches such as the AICs, and more recently the African Pentecostal/charismatic churches, have come to fill this spiritual vacuum and offer 'a home away from home' for many disenchanted African immigrants. These religious spaces also become avenues where people can go and feel important and valued. Irrespective of member's cultural backgrounds, a sense of belonging and community is rekindled in the church and a kind of religio-ethnic identity is also engendered through the process.

While we witness an increasing mobility and visibility of African Christian communities in Europe and North America, not all churches are equally enthusiastic about forming or engaging in formalized local, national and continental networks. Some relatively new religious groups may see their involvement in such networks as a means of status enhancement in Europe. There are some institutionally and financially well-established groups that exercise restraint in such networking endeavours on the grounds that 'we are already secure and well established'.

The United Evangelical Mission (UEM) programme that was coordinated by Claudia Währisch-Oblau for cooperation between German and immigrant congregations, is a case in point (Währisch-Oblau 2000: 467–83). The programme's aim is to:

> assist immigrant churches to establish a visible presence within the context of German churches and society; help German churches to understand and appreciate the movement of reverse mission that is taking place through the presence of immigrant congregations; and develop projects of common mission/intercultural evangelism. (467)

The UEM initiative has attracted the interest of several immigrant churches, including English- and French-speaking African-led churches in Germany. Although some well-established African religious groups in Germany are interested in such networks, more participation seems to have come from the less established ones. There are small groups in Germany that exist as branches of well-established churches with headquarters in Africa. Some of these groups are interested in these formal religious networks in the German context partly as a way of acquiring, in Europe, the status and prestige they enjoyed in their countries of origin. The local body of the Council of Christian Communities of an African Approach in Europe (CCCAAE) in Germany is the Council of African Christian Communities in Germany (CACCG). The RCCG and CCOMI are both members of the Council of African Pentecostal Pastors in Germany. The RCCG belongs to local ecumenical bodies such as the Pentecostal Fellowship of Nigeria and the Christian Association of Nigeria, while the CCOMI is a member of a local German Pentecostal body, *Bund Freikirchlicher Pfingstgemeinden*, as well as a more global ecumenical body, the International Communion of Charismatic Churches.

In recognition of their renewed effort towards networking within and outside Europe, Ter Haar (1998: 23) referring to AICs, noted that, 'their spread overseas has involved these churches in international networks of relations to which they did not have access until the late twentieth century'. Gerloff remarks that, 'this interconnecting has happened on three fronts: between churches; across language divisions (mainly French and English); and between African communities and the academy – such as the University of Leeds in 1997'.[6] To this description I add two points: first, that such relationships are not only intra- but also interreligious; second, that such networks have transcended religious boundaries into social, economic and political spheres. The Leeds Conference was informed, among other factors, by

> increased immigration of people of African descent into the European political and monetary union; the growing importance of issues such as human rights, religious freedom, racial equality and social justice; the deficit in partnership models between African independent groups and European religious and secular institutions; and most of all, the lack of knowledge and research in African religious communities as mainstays for their survival in indifferent or even hostile environments. (Gerloff 2000b: 281)

Among the stated objectives of the conference were:

> to facilitate dialogue between African (religious) communities and the (European) historic churches […] to help networking between scholars and African religious communities from different countries […] to help European institutions to perceive peoples' religion and spirituality as central to their survival in dignity and affirmation of life ... and to contribute to policy-making in terms of mutual support and empowerment across national borders. (281).

The 1997 Leeds conference on 'The Significance of the African Religious Diaspora in Europe' was largely the spark that ignited the zeal towards religious networking among the African Christian communities and other subsequent initiatives. One remarkable result of this was the birth of the Council of African Christian Communities in Europe.

Council of Christian Churches of an African approach in Europe

The Council of Christian Churches of an African Approach in Europe (CCCAAE), formerly known as the Council of African Christian Communities in Europe (CACCE) is an ecumenical, non-denominational organization comprising mainly African Christian communities and other African-focused para-church organizations in Europe. It represents one of the initiatives of African/African-derived Christian communities in creating new intra-religious networks at the local, national and continental levels in Europe. CCCAAE's nucleus membership was drawn largely from the United Kingdom and continental Europe. Berlin serves as its current headquarters.

The 1997 Leeds conference which brought together African and European Christians and scholars, was unique in that it provided a forum for constructing a Europe-wide African identity that was poised for dialogue with the European populations.[7] From 1997, a number of other initiatives 'African Christian Diaspora Consultations' took place in Västerâs, Sweden (1998), Glay/Doubs, France (1998), Hamburg (1998), Cambridge (1999), and Belgium/Switzerland (1999) where further attempts were made to develop mechanisms for affirming the significance and implications of this religious development particularly for contemporary Europe. The 1999 Millennial Conference 'Open Space: The African Christian Diaspora in Europe and the Quest for Human Community' which was held from 16–20 September at Westminster College, Cambridge under the auspices of the Partnership of African Christian Communities in Europe, culminated in the establishment of this network, and was born out of the desire of members and participants to facilitate such meetings, to affirm a sense of belonging, and to encourage networking in order to enhance further cooperation and build supportive relationships across the continents (Adogame 2000: 291–303).

The CACCE was formally inaugurated in December 1999. Delegates from five countries—Belgium, France, Germany, Switzerland and the United Kingdom—met at Notre Dame de Justice, Rhode Saint Genese in Belgium following the Cambridge conference that had provided the groundwork three months earlier. Their legitimacy seemed to hinge on the claim that since 'there are over three million Christians of African origin in Europe [...] it is our responsibility to network, share ideas and join in common activities for the spiritual, social, cultural and political development of these communities'. (CACCE Press Release, *Africans Unite*, July 2000). Their objectives were to: 'Create strategic partnership for spiritual and social transformation in Europe; provide a platform for Africans to share common problems and find solutions in different African countries; work for peace, social, human and economic development in Africa.' At a continental level, the council strives to represent the needs, wishes and aspirations of its members who live and operate in various European states. It also claims to be inclusive of all those who would have sympathy with its aims and raison d'être.

In a bid to widen its membership and modus operandi, the Council underwent further transition in 2001, with a name change to CCCAAE at Arzier, Switzerland. An executive body was constituted the same year at a meeting in Berlin, and the CCCAAE objectives streamlined and enlarged to include: the coordination and networking of African Christian congregations in Europe; the spiritual awakening and awareness of African Christianity in Europe; and furthering the partnership between African and European churches. Other objectives were: furthering the advancement of African theology and evangelism in Europe; developing a forum for the problems facing Africans in Europe, in particular social exclusion and discrimination; promoting research on African Christianity in Europe; promoting Christian education of African youths in Europe; and supporting projects related to economic development in Africa.

In 2003 the CCCAAE co-sponsored an interdisciplinary conference in Hirschluch (near Berlin), on 'The Berlin- Congo Conference 1884, the Partition of Africa, and Implications for Christian Mission Today', which brought together African, European and North American scholars from universities and research institutions in Africa, Europe and the United States. The conference explored the historical and sociopolitical consequences of the partition of Africa for the continent and the African Diaspora, highlighting issues such as migration, racism and sexism; and looking critically into the political role the Christian mission played in colonizing Africa, as well as, into the paradigm shift in mission locally and globally; to inquire into the significance of diverse indigenous movements emanating from the two-thirds world in their struggle for survival in dignity, as well as their interaction with religious and secular European institutions.[8] While the CCCAAE initiative operates at a continental level, there are other local networks with national scope such as the Scottish Council for African Churches. Their objectives are fairly similar to that of the CCCAAE.

Scottish Council of African Churches

In 2010, the Scottish Council of African Churches (SCOAC) was granted official registration as a public company by guarantee, a not-for-profit organization in Scotland. With the pioneering leadership of Festus Olatunde, the SCOAC aimed:

> to enhance the unity of all African-led churches and Christian Ministries in their collaboration and networking with churches and government in Scotland [...] to bring together all African churches and African Christians in Scotland [...], working closely and in partnership with the Scottish government and other key bodies like Church of Scotland, Action for Churches Together in Scotland (ACTS), Minority Ethnic Christian Together in Scotland (MECTIS), institutions, agencies, African leaders, Christian leaders, and other faith based organizations.[9]

The SCOAC mission statement 'Unity and empowerment in diversity' is very revealing of its modus operandi. As Festus Olatunde discloses,

> Following the successful collaboration of all African-led Churches in Scotland at the recent Edinburgh 2010 centenary Mission Conference and the Church of Scotland's 'Roll Away the Stone' event, we are now being taken seriously by the wider Scottish publics. The Christian community and the public is now beginning to recognize our activities, most especially with our impact on these two major events that highlight the significance of collaboration, networking and Christian witness. We believe that God is going to use this as a bridge to reenergize the Christian faith in the former heartlands of Christianity. To further strengthen this initiative, we are resolved to reach out to Christian leaders from Africa and other parts of the world to build synergies and provide spiritual guidance and support.[10]

These are examples of several institutional attempts to engineer ecumenical links and relationships, initiatives that are sometimes fraught with inherent difficulties. Forging and sustaining networking processes is often not a simple task; there are inherent problems and tensions in the nature of such relationships among African Christian communities themselves, but also in the relationship between them and other non-African Christian groups. This leads me to highlight some patterns of intra-religious networking that can be discerned among African Christian communities in diaspora and the challenges often faced in the ensuing process.

Patterns of networking

One practice becoming popular among African Christian communities in Europe and the United States is the 'switching or exchange of pulpits'. As a result of the increasing networking processes, different churches now embark on joint worship services and programmes. This initiative operates in such a way that a leader of a particular church will be invited to preach in another church. This is not restricted to African communities alone, but also between them and their host European and American churches, which in most cases provide worship space for the African congregations through rent, lease or mutual agreement. Such collaborations are not devoid of problems on both sides, given their tendency to erode members' loyalty to a particular leadership/group, or mutual suspicion leading to accusations of 'sheep-stealing', a common phrase among Christian groups referring to the switching of religious affiliation. Tensions between African and their host German churches may be illustrated by an incident that occurred during a

'Healing-Deliverance Ritual' organized by an African-led Pentecostal church in Köln. As a leader of the African church described it:

> Members of the host local German church were in attendance in their numbers. As prayers were enacted during the 'altar call', a German woman alongside some Africans fell flat on the nave of the church (were slain in the spirit). Members of the African Pentecostal congregation recognized and interpreted this phenomenon as the action and visible manifestation of the Holy Spirit. However, the visiting Germans, whose Pastor swung instantaneously and dashed to his office where he called the attention of the city ambulance service, understood this differently. All attempts to restrain him and to explain the actual situation proved abortive. Although, the emergency doctors who rushed the woman to the hospital ended their examination without any negative results, yet this singular event had strained the relationship between the African and German congregations respectively.

Thus, while various attempts have been made through language instruction and joint services at adapting African members into the new German context, the varied, religious worldviews and cultural backgrounds have perpetuated a 'stark cultural wall'. This cultural wall symbolizes, on the one hand, a reproduction of their religio-cultural identity as well as of the construction of a new migrant identity, thus creating and reinforcing a kind of locality (as opposed to globality) at the religious level. The other side of the wall encapsulates the strains and tensions experienced by Germans in the task of adjusting to these new processes and worldviews.

The initiative of African religious communities in creating and joining new ecumenical networks at the local, national, and transcontinental levels is noteworthy. Examples of such existing intra-religious networks include the African Christian Council, Hamburg, West Yorkshire African Caribbean Council of Churches, Council of African Churches in Germany, Council of African and Caribbean Churches-UK, Churches Together in Britain and Ireland, formerly the British Council of Churches, Council of African Christian Communities in Europe, and World Council of Churches. In 2000, the African Christian Council (Hamburg) had a membership of 22 churches with most of them using the premises of German congregations as temporary places of worship. The Council seeks to promote cordial relations with German churches and to work with other Christian bodies in and outside Germany. The West Yorkshire African Caribbean Council of Churches in 2000 was a collection of nineteen congregations from the inner city areas of the country, namely Leeds, Bradford, Huddersfield and Halifax, covering ten different denominations.

Also in the United Kingdom, African-led churches have essentially been worshipping communities until being drawn into areas of social and political concern. It took some time before these communities started to act on the society at a political level. Unlike the European continent, there is growing political involvement of black Christian leaders 'who share a common vision for social significance and measurable transformation' of the UK society (Gerloff 2000b: 434–83). The initiative towards mapping out strategies against racism, injustice and marginalization emerged only following the creation of umbrella religious organizations such as the Council of African and Caribbean Churches. In 1979 Olu Abiola, leader of the Aladura Church International, called together ministers from different churches to consider the necessity of creating a formal association of African churches. The outcome was the formation of the Council of African and Allied Churches, later known as the Council of African and Afro-Caribbean Churches. Its current title is the Council of African and Caribbean Churches. The council has a membership of some 40 denominations.[11] To achieve these objectives, the Council holds public meetings and seminars on wide-ranging topics, and embarks on programmes aimed at creating a more just society. As Oshun (1997) has shown,

> these bodies provided the vital links between the Black-led churches (including the Aladura churches) and the mainstream churches as represented by the British Council of Churches, on the one hand, and the British government, the British institutions and the British society on the other.

Gerloff (2001: 276–89) shows that African and Caribbean Christians organized regional and national councils such as the Council of African and Allied Churches, or the African Caribbean Evangelical Alliance. They interact with local and national authorities, and with Anglicans, Methodists, Baptists, and ecumenical bodies such as Churches Together in Britain and Ireland or the Evangelical Alliance, but do this by sustaining their particular cultural or theological traditions. As she further observes,

> bridge-building between African and Caribbean Christians leaves much to be desired; as some Caribbean Evangelicals regard the AICs as too steeped in African traditional religion. Radical black scholars utilize the African heritage in Caribbean history and theology, but seem to avoid getting involved with contemporary Africans. Dialogue between the British churches and the African Diaspora, such as promoted by the Centre for Black and White Christian Partnership (CBWCP) from 1978, has not progressed as hoped, as culturally and theologically white churches have

stayed within their domain, and black churches have begun to imitate western denominationalism.

From the 1980s, a growing number of Anglophone and Francophone African Christian communities, the majority of the African Pentecostal/charismatic type, embarked on intra-religious networks in different countries in Europe. In France they organized *La Coordination des l'Eglises Africaines* (Paris); in Belgium a Congolese Pastorate with participants from other EU countries (Brussels); and in Switzerland a Council of African Churches (Geneva). These function as supportive structures in conflict situations, partners to European churches in solidarity with the continent of Africa, and instruments for raising 'collective awareness of the missionary role of the Christian diaspora in Europe'. In the Netherlands, African Christian communities are part of at least two inter-church networks, the SKIN[12] (*Samen Kerk in Nederland*) in which over 54 Christian immigrant groups work together, and the other GATE[13] (Gift from Africa to Europe – formerly known as 'Gospel from Africa to Europe') active in the field of evangelization. In Germany, a number of regional councils have been formed, in the North (Hamburg), the West (Rhineland), the East (Berlin) and the South, in connection with German ecumenical bodies. In Scandinavia (Sweden, Denmark, Finland) gatherings with Baptist, Pietist and Pentecostal-style backgrounds are developing in the larger cities.

The social dimension is also significant for African Christian communities as measured by the wide range of activities in which they are involved. Some of the extra-religious functions they have emphasized are social welfare programmes, social work and self-help. The African Churches' Council on Immigration and Social Justice was formed in May 1990 to tackle specific issues of immigration and social justice.[14] Sharing e.V.,[15] a non-governmental organization (NGO) affiliated with the United Nations, was established by George Owusu, the overseeing pastor of the Grace Fellowship in Wuppertal, Germany. For more than a decade, Sharing e.V. claims to be actively involved in religious, humanitarian, educational, health care, immigration, communication, and cross-cultural activities in Europe and Africa.

African Christian communities in Europe and the United States are not totally inclusive in their orientation. These communities represent pivots of attraction particularly to their African membership owing to the fact that most of these churches replicate the cultural and religious sensibilities of their home context, in a way that creates a comfort zone for many African immigrants. Despite targeting both Africans and non-Africans in their membership drives, their social-ethnic composition is still dominated largely by the former, with white converts forming a negligible percentage. The religious, in addition to the social, economic and political roles that African Christian communities have come to assume in Europe and the United States help us to understand their significance for Africans within local and global ambits. The variety of physical manifestations within these communities, the 'localization of African religious cultures' includes the overwhelming display of traditional African garb during church services and in other programmes, the ebullient rendition of songs/choruses in local languages (Twi, Akan, Yoruba, Igbo, Edo) alongside English language ones, and the provision and collective sharing of meals during services.

Thus, African Christian communities comprising largely of immigrants, typically develop a set of structures and practices designed simultaneously to help their members to maintain and reproduce their cultural and religious heritage, identities on the one hand, and also assisting immigrants in the process of adapting to the new host context. In this way, the churches both ensure continuity of worldview and assume adaptive strategies of change. Through the replication of distinctive objects and worship styles, the churches formally recognize, support, reinforce and re-enact ethnic-religious identity and cultural continuity. These features are evident in such a way that they are sometimes alienating to non-Africans, who can readily opt for groups where they will not constitute an apparent 'minority of outsiders'. Some Africans who find the privileging of these features repugnant also object to being part of these religious communities. In effect, the localization of African religious cultures is both attracting and repelling to both African and non-African audiences. In the new geo-cultural setting, African-led churches face a myriad of obstacles varying from language, paucity of spaces of worship, loud services that sometimes attract the hostility of neighbours, transience of its membership, poor finances, adverse weather conditions, prohibitive practices such as alcohol and cigarette smoking. On the other hand, the long duration of their worship services deter non-Africans.

Ireke versus guilt: Tropes of 'otherness' within the African diaspora

Some assumptions can easily be made about the relationship between African Christian communities on the one hand, and the links between it and other communities like the African-Caribbean Christian communities in the United Kingdom and the African American Christian communities in the United States. In spite of any links and relationships that the ecumenical networks illustrated above show, the relationship between these religious constituencies is far from cordial. Their communities are differentiated in a variety of ways, beyond any simple reference as black people. An often neglected feature in past and current scholarship is the interrelationship between the historical and contemporary dimensions of African diaspora. What patterns of relation exist between new African immigrants and African

Americans or African Caribbeans? To what extent do new African Christian communities establish networks and maintain links with African American churches in the United States and African-Caribbean (black) churches in the United Kingdom? Do new African immigrants, African Americans and African Caribbeans operate within similar sociocultural frames of reference? I will now turn briefly to these questions by exploring the relationship between African Christian communities and African American churches in the United States.

The mission objectives of diaspora churches suggest new pathways of understanding the relationship between new African immigrants and African Americans. One characteristic of religion in North America is the ethnic dimension of 'denominationalism'. Churches, whether historical or contemporary, are mostly established along ethnic lines leading to the common description of 'ethnic-based churches' such as Korean, Irish, German and African American (black) churches. It seems as if each ethnic-based congregation is operating largely within their own group and without any significant inter-ethnic links and networks.

Two observations can be made on the relationship between African American churches and churches of new African immigrants. First, there are some levels of institutional networking and ecumenical cooperation between them especially in the planning and execution of religious programmes such as crusades, conventions, and training. The KICC's annual Christian Conference, the International Gathering of Champions (IGOC) alluded to earlier is a case in point.[16] Whether this kind of association and networking between African and African American church leaders actually extends beyond the particular event remains a larger question for further scholarly investigation.

Essentially, African American church congregations continue to be largely dominated by African Americans while the new African immigrants keep to themselves – although some intermingling does occur in a few cases. Most respondents in the new African churches indicated that they identified with African American churches upon their arrival in the United States, but later pulled out to join ranks with, or to establish, new African-led churches. Reasons adduced for this switching of religious affiliation range from perceived cultural differences and different mentalities to accusations of arrogance, mutual suspicion and lack of trust.[17]

One concern common to many new African immigrants is their experience of a cold reception from the African American community.[18] On the other hand, some African Americans confront new African immigrants with the guilt of selling their ancestors into slavery. Some African Americans thus label new African immigrants as 'primitive people', 'our primitive brothers and sisters', or as 'descendants of slave merchants or slave stealers'. They also allege that the new African immigrants consider themselves superior to their African American counterparts (a notion that arises, even among Africans, as a result of the tendency in the media and elsewhere to profile African-Americans in a derogatory way). Some new African immigrants fondly refer to their African American counterparts as *ireke/onireke* (Yoruba), *awhedeam/awhedeamni/awhedeamfoo* (Akan) both meaning literally, 'sugarcane' and 'sugar cane people'. These derogatory names suggest the plight of slaves who were rudely uprooted and forced to work on sugarcane plantations across the Americas. The tendency towards mutual suspicion and contempt characterizes one level of relationship between the new African emigrants and the African Americans. This mutual, negative perception has led to a somewhat uneasy relationship between the groups, while also polarizing the black community in a way that inhibits their ability to become a formidable force within America's sociopolitical and economic systems.

This situation is similar to the relationship between new African immigrants, African Caribbeans and the black British people in the United Kingdom. Although I am not generalizing on this point, it is however expedient to examine further the relationship patterns between the new African immigrants and African Americans on the one hand, and between them and African Caribbeans in order to establish the political, social, cultural, economic, religious and strategic factors that facilitate or inhibit such relationships on the other. Interdisciplinary approaches are needed to further explore these dynamics, as we come to appreciate the contributions made by diasporic communities to religious and civic life – both at home and abroad. The concluding section of this chapter examines issues, problems and tensions that emanate from networking processes and show implications of these for African Christian communities and their impact on the diasporic context as well as on world Christianity.

To be or not to be? Prospects and challenges of African Christian communities in diaspora

The mobility and public visibility of African Christian communities in Europe and North America is enhanced by patterns and new trends of international migration. African Christianities are carving out a niche within world Christianity in terms of demographics, their social relevance and in their profound contribution to local-global discourses. It may still be premature to fully assess their level of global impact as the religious developments are still unfolding. This is more so in the diaspora where many African Christian communities have only emerged within the last three decades. It remains to be seen how and to what extent the harmonization of immigration policies and the tightening of borders in Europe and the United States will impact on the sustainability of these religious communities or lead to their extinction. Nonetheless, the internal dynamics of African Christian communities in diaspora coupled with external social processes are integral to understanding the impact they make on the host and home societies, their successes, dilemmas, tensions, and contradictions that characterize their modes of expansion, reverse mission and networking processes.

The prevailing socio-religious and political situation in the West has heightened the prospects and rationale for reverse mission in a pluralistic mission field and to a growing multicultural population. European and American societies encourage an individualistic consumer way of life which has had an adverse impact on many shared beliefs and traditions including Christianity. In Europe, there has been an increasing distrust of historical institutions, such as the church, which hitherto exercised largely unchallenged authority. The relationship of the church to the state has shifted from Christendom to what some choose to refer to as post-secular or post-Christendom. The grip of the Christian faith upon shared morality in public life has loosened substantially. Moral decadence is seen as a common feature of modern societies. Over the last decades, Western cultures seem to have grown further apart from the culture of the church. There is a gradual desecralization of church spaces with several buildings being turned into bookshops, museums, pubs, grocery stores and other alternative uses. Church membership has continued to dwindle, and there has been an abysmal fall in church attendance.

In fact, in contemporary Western societies, a huge proportion of the adult population has never had any meaningful contact with any church tradition in their lifetime. Two-thirds of UK adults (66%) or 32.2 million people have no connection with church at present (nor with another religion).[19] This secular majority presents a major challenge to churches in that these people became a potential target for primary evangelism rather than re-evangelization. As far as African Christian communities are concerned, all these features make the task of mission in Europe and North America more compelling. As one church leader recalled, it was as if Leslie Lyall foresaw mission realities in 1963 when he said: 'It would not be surprising if Christian Africans or Asians coming to Europe or America felt that they were coming to pagan countries where Christian principles and standards had long since been abandoned'.[20] The claim that Christian principles and standards have long disappeared is highly improbable, but at least for many African Christians, Europe is increasingly becoming a 'spiritual graveyard' that must be rescued back into Christianity.[21]

Context of reception and matrix of perception

The new 'mission field' of Europe and North America is a daunting one that poses crucial challenges, beyond rhetoric, for African Christian communities. The shift in the matrix of perception, public mental images about them, attitudes towards them, and reception by host churches and publics is key. A 'strange bed-fellow' phenomenon raises mutual suspicion and ignorance between African Christian communities and several host churches in Europe and the United States. Some African Christians perceive Western churches as 'dead, spiritually bankrupt and impotent', while some Westerners see African churches as 'too African, too mixed with African culture, and not sound theologically'. Immigrant religious congregations, in spite of often acting as sites of temporary refuge, are not hermetically sealed (Stepick et al. 2009: 11). Regardless of their spiritual orientation, they of necessity interact with and react to the broader society. The context of reception provides a type of index that factors into the immigrants' likelihood of success, particularly how immigrants are treated by European and American institutions and societies, is likely to have a significant impact on their habitus, their networking patterns and consequent civic engagement. This involves government policy towards immigrants, as well as the overall economic, social and political climate that the immigrants encounter upon arrival (Portes and Rumbaut 2006).

A receptive host context makes immigrants relax in their forging of ethnic identities while a hostile environment makes for questing for national/ethnic and cultural identities. The success of African Christian communities in Europe and North America does not hinge entirely on their internal religious dynamics, the social, cultural and spiritual capital they often generate (see Chapter 6). These are of course important but far from sufficient. Also integral to their success or difficulties is how the host European and American churches and society receive and welcome African Christian communities in their midst.

While the context of reception, matrix of perception, and mode of incorporation are vitally important, a mutual change of mindset will be required for a dynamic of intentional partnership and networking. Such a partnership would need to transcend the frequent parading of African choirs or African food cultures during ecumenical programmes with host churches. Such networking processes of interaction and action is significant and must be ingrained and profound on crucial matters and discourses that positively impact and improve members' well-being in the immediate local religious communities but the wider society at large. They must demonstrate social relevance, the public face and public voice of these communities.

Repackaging narratives and ideologies

Cross-cultural mission will require a reworking of language and approach, and a tilt of their theological paradigms. The context of narrative of many African Christian communities would need to be repackaged to fit new circumstances, and made more appealing to non-African publics. African-led churches would need to negotiate between adapting or changing their religious cultures in order to more comfortably fit into their new contexts or maintaining their religious cultures and the tension that exists between it and their new contexts of Europe and North America. The fast changing nature of the religious landscape requires a new kind of inculturation of African Christian communities within the host societies. The question that needs to revolve within these communities is what African Christian communities in Europe and North America (but also host churches) can learn from the pitfalls of the European missionary enterprise in Africa and the erstwhile mission fields.

Thus, the context is very important. As Joel Edward notes, African and Caribbean Christian communities often suffer from an acute case of 'cultural dissonance', 'contextual abstinence' and 'a crisis of self-presentation'.[22] He remarks

> It is one thing to talk about black churches influencing British (western) Christian faith, but it is quite another to recognize the number of black (African and Caribbean) Christians seeking cultural refuge in white-led churches [...] African congregations replicate 'Africa' on Sunday and coexist with the culture for the rest of the week. They have a crisis of self-preservation which threatens to castrate the mission enterprise. In this sense, sometimes remaining and being African or Caribbean is the mission.

Lessons to be learnt from cross-cultural mission and evangelism will be profoundly important for second and third generation African immigrants in furthering reverse mission dynamics and networking processes in Europe and North America. The second and third generation immigrant youth might be the most versatile missionaries for the mission field of Europe and North America, if they are well harnessed and empowered.

Competition among African Christian communities for members often results in unhealthy rivalries in the spiritual marketplace. African-led groups will need to revisit to what extent a somewhat 'cloning' of churches becomes a veritable tool of church expansion. The attraction to entrepreneurialism should not simply measure success – numerical growth as icons of church growth, but also its transforming presence in reference to corresponding changes within the communities but also in the host society. A conscious shift from a market-driven church to a mission-focused church will ensure a balance between economic aspirations of African Christians in diaspora with missional intentionalities. As African Christian communities have suffered the downside of respectability, paradigms of power should seek to immunize these communities from pain and vulnerability. They should privilege models of liberation and empowerment instead of settling for debilitating paradigms of power with no real interest in justice, institutional evil and to some extent global missions. Paradigms of power aspire either to privilege positions or denigrate into egocentric doctrines of self-interest and the accumulation of personal wealth.[23] They would need to demonstrate increasing social relevance, embrace social action in addition to mission evangelism, engage in public discourses that will show their public voice. African Christian communities can be socially relevant through social and community action, in social commentary and increasingly so in political engagement in Europe and North America. Poverty alleviation is a missional tool and should remain integral to mission initiatives of African Christian communities in diaspora.

Leadership dynamics and empowerment

The question of religious leadership and role models is quintessential in examining the mobility of African Christian communities, in steering reverse mission and networking processes. Leadership also directs the tendencies towards civic engagement. Max Weber's application of 'charisma' helps our understanding of the role of leadership in African Christian communities. Weber ([1925] 1966: 241) employs the term to refer to

> a certain quality of an individual personality by virtue of which he is considered extraordinary and treated as endowed with supernatural, superhuman, or at least specifically exceptional powers or qualities. These are not to be accessible to the ordinary person, but are regarded as of divine origin or as exemplary, and not on the basis of them the individual concerned is treated as a leader.

Weber's three typologies of religious leaders: the prophet (a natural leader), the priest (an appointed leader), and the magician (an entrepreneurial diviner), although overlapping and not mutually exclusive, can be located in the complex leadership structures of African Christian communities both on the continent and in the diaspora.

African Christianities have produced leaders of various hues, different 'folks and strokes', and religious celebrities in Africa and the diaspora (Adogame 2010a). In fact, the history of church independency in Africa is replete with charismatic founders, prophets, leaders, but also sometimes perceived charlatans. The AICs produced religious icons and prophetic figures including Simon Kimbangu (Kimbaguist church) in Congo/Zaire; Jehu Appiah (Musama Disco Christo Church) in Ghana; and Samuel Oschoffa (Celestial Church of Christ) in Nigeria. Some of these earlier prophets/church leaders received hardly any Western-style education but were revered and believed by followers to be well imbued with spiritual power and charismatic gifts. Most of these churches have established branches also in Europe and North America (see Chapter 4).

The founders of several Pentecostal churches were in most cases university graduates and had worked in nonreligious professions. For instance, William Kumuyi, who founded the Deeper Life Bible Church in 1973, was a lecturer in mathematics at the University of Lagos. David Oyedepo, the founder and bishop of the Winners Chapel (1983), was originally an architect by profession. These founders have abandoned their erstwhile professions to undertake full-time church ministry. These churches are very appealing to youths, women, graduates and professionals in Africa and the African diaspora.

These religious entrepreneurs are identified by their individual peculiarities and charismatic potential. There are religious captains of industry perceived as spiritually powerful, endowed with overarching supernatural, charismatic gifts; exhibiting modest, exemplary lives, and unflamboyant lifestyles but commanding a symbolic father-figure role as 'Daddy' or 'Papa'. Enoch Adeboye (RCCG General Overseer) and David Oyedepo (General Overseer, Winners Chapel) are prominent examplars of this genre. On the global front, Peter Jasper Akinola, the former Anglican Primate of the Church of Nigeria, stands out in his mobilization of leaders of the Global South within the Anglican Communion to oppose same-sex blessings, the ordination of non-celibate homosexuals or, indeed, any homosexual practice; a development that has perceptibly shaken the very foundation and unity of global Anglicanism. African Christian communities in diaspora have also produced religious icons such as Matthew Ashimolowo (KICC), Sunday Adelaja (EBKCN), and Abraham Bediako (CCOMI).

The coterie of charismatic leaders and celebrities, religious icons, and spiritual entrepreneurs is undoubtedly robust and dynamic. Many have invented religious empires endeared to the personality of the founder/leader, sometimes leading to their being dubbed as 'family businesses' or 'private enterprises'. Nevertheless, several existing religious organizations within Christianity, mobile and institutionalized as they may be, seem awash with a visionary myopia. Many have ignored the problem of succession to leadership, the routinization of charisma and bureaucratization processes that will follow the demise of religious founders and celebrities. The lacunae created by the silence of appropriate legal provisions in constitutions, edicts, by-laws, memorandum and articles of association establishing such religious bodies often results in legal imbroglios and succession crises which challenge the post-charismatic fate and corporate existence of such religious entities. While members of African Christian communities revere their leaders as charismatic figures and role models to be emulated, this charisma is not sufficiently routinized in their members, and bureaucratization processes not fully adequate in Africa and the diaspora. Thus, the tendency of producing less charismatic leaders or even religious charlatans may become rife within these religious communities.

Weber maintains that charisma or effective religious leadership produces its greatest impact in creating and upholding congregants' worldview. 'When leaders employ a theology that is both consonant with their congregants' worldview and promotes civic engagement beyond the church doors, then charisma may be transformed into effective civic social capital' (Stepick et al. 2009: 10–11). Leadership may not necessarily be 'top-down' but 'bottom-up', emerging from a dialectical relationship between the religious leader and his/her congregation. One challenge facing African Christian communities in diaspora is that of charismatic leadership, irrespective of theological training and orientation. Thus, we need to understand the agency of members of African-led churches as well as the charismatic agency of their leaders. The dialectics of how members respond to their leaders, charismatic and less charismatic, but also when and how leaders may react to the religious communities they lead is important for understanding how they may succeed or fail in Africa and within the Africa diaspora.

African youth in Europe and North America are situated within a mixture of social differences not only because of their ethnic background and immigration circumstances but also because of their religious beliefs and activism. Youth are not only at the centre of cultural negotiations, they have a tremendous capacity for developing innovative means of intercultural dialogue. The percentage of young people among African immigrants in Europe is higher than in the population as a whole. African immigrant youth are much more likely to adhere to and practice religion than youth in the majority population.

Youth and women who dominate the membership of African Christian communities in Europe and North America therefore represent robust reservoirs of human capital that can be harnessed and empowered in the reverse mission and networking processes. African Christian communities would need to nurture and empower young people and women to pick-up the missional and transforming agenda of their communities and the society at large. Since immigrant youth and women participate more actively in religious organizations, such as African Christian communities, than their non-migrant peers, recognition of their role is essential to enhance cultural encounters, mutual understanding, and religious expansion. The role of African Christian communities in the (dis)empowerment of youth and women, and in their potential for integration and/or conflict needs to be fully documented and analysed.

Notes

Chapter 1

1 The following paragraphs were gleaned from the author's earlier article: Adogame (2008d: 129–149).

Chapter 2

1 The Andrew Syndrome refers to a paid television advertisement by the Nigerian government to stem the flow of emigration in the 1990s. It pictured a frustrated-looking 'Andrew' at the Lagos Murtala Mohammed Airport 'checking out' of the country.
2 The ECOWAS sub-region comprises countries of Ghana, Nigeria, Cote d'Ivoire, Niger, Burkina Faso, Mali, Gambia, Guinea, Benin and Togo.
3 See VFS Global website: www.ukvac-ng.com/index.aspx (accessed on 20 December 2011).
4 See Prayers Online at: www.prayersonline.net/2007/05/02/prayer-for-gods-grace-favour-and-courage-for-success-in-visa-interview/ (accessed on 07 April 2010).
5 See 'Jesus Calls: A Ministry of Love and Compassion'. Jesus Calls Prayer Tower Headquarters is located in Chennai, India. See also: 'Pray Way: Global Prayer Community' at www.prayway.com; 'Prayers Online' at www.prayersonline.net see example of visa interview prayer. 'Guardians Prayer Warrior' at www.guardiansprayerwarrior.ning.com; www.comprehensivechristian.com (accessed on 07 April 2010).
6 See: www.prayertoweronline.org/prayer/prayer.asp?reason=085 (accessed on 07 April 2010).
7 See S. Samura documentary film 'Exodus from Africa: An Immigrant's Journey': Available at: cgi.cnn.com/SPECIALS/2001/Immigration/ (accessed on 12 June 2004).
8 See full text in 'Sorious Samuras Africa', available at: www.sorioussamurasafrica.org/exodus.htm (accessed on 12 June 2004).

9. See International Dialogue on Migration 'Return Migration: Challenges and Opportunities', IOM Information Ninety-Sixth Session, 10 November 2008 available at: www.iom.int/jahia/Jahia/policy-research/international-dialogue-migration/council-sessions/return-migration-2008 (accessed on 23 March 2011).
10. See details of IOM Policies and Programmes on Return Migration at: www.iom.int/jahia/Jahia/lang/en/pid/1 and www.iom.int/jahia/webdav/shared/shared/mainsite/microsites/IDM/workshops/return_migration_challenges_120208/key_policy_principles_En.pdf (accessed on 23 March 2012).
11. Sermon text by Senior Evangelist (Dr) Stephen Adeniyi at Worship service of the CCC Parish, Dritte Welt Haus, Frankfurt am Main (13 November 1998).
12. See the special issue on World War I in the *Journal of African History*, 19 (1), 1978.
13. The figures provided here were gleaned from Tables 1–7 in K. A. Twum-Baah 'Volume and Characteristics of International Ghanaian Migration' in Takyiwaa Manuh (2005: 55–77).
14. See the special issue of *African Issues* (vol. XXX/1, 2002) devoted to the highly contentious – *brain drain-brain gain* discourse.
15. See mid-year population estimates, Statistics South Africa 2010. www.statssa.gov.za (accessed on 20 September 2011).
16. Statistics South Africa, 2010.
17. Ibid.
18. See Background Note: Zimbabwe available at: www.state.gov/r/pa/ei/bgn/5479.htm. See also: CIA. World Factbook. 'Zimbabwe.' www.cia.gov/library/publications/the-world-factbook/geos/zi.html (accessed on 12 August 2011).
19. 1964: President Kaunda takes power in Zambia, BBC News. See: news.bbc.co.uk/onthisday/hi/dates/stories/october/25/newsid_2658000/2658325.stm (accessed on 15 August 2011).
20. See 'The Levantine Community', in Robert E. Handloff (ed.) *Ivory Coast: A Country Study*. Washington: GPO for the Library of Congress, 1988.
21. See the history of Indian Diaspora in South Africa, chapter 7, Report of the High Level Committee on the Indian Diaspora, 71–88. Available online at: indiandiaspora.nic.in/diasporapdf/chapter7.pdf (accessed on 22 October 2011).
22. See staggering statistics of 'Indian Diaspora in other African countries', chapter 8, Report of the High Level Committee on the Indian Diaspora, 94.

Chapter 3

1. See details about the INA at: www.uscis.gov/portal/site/uscis/ (accessed on 15 August 2010).

NOTES

2 See *The Foreign-Born Population: 2000. Census 2000 Brief*, United States Census Bureau, December 2003. Available at: www.census.gov/prod/2003pubs/c2kbr-34.pdf (accessed on 15 August 2010).

3 Source: US Census Bureau, American Community Service 2009. 'Place of Birth of the Foreign-Born Population 2009' Issued October 2010. see: www.census.gov/prod/2010pubs/acsbr09–15.pdf (accessed on 15 August 2011).

4 Source: U.S. Census Bureau, 2009 American Community Survey, B05002, 'Place of Birth by Citizenship Status'; C05006, 'Place of Birth for the Foreign-Born Population'; and B05007, 'Place of Birth by Year of Entry by Citizenship Status for the Foreign-Born Population,' factfinder.census.gov (accessed on 10 January 2011).

5 Source: US Department of Homeland Security. 'Nonimmigrant Admissions (1–94 only) By Region and Country of Residence: Fiscal Years 2001 to 2010. www.dhs.gov/files/statistics/publications/YrBk10NI.shtm, and www.dhs.gov/xlibrary/assets/statistics/yearbook/2010/table27d.xls (accessed on 11 October 2011).

6 See Table IV: Summary of Visas Issued by Issuing Office. Fiscal Year 2010: www.travel.state.gov/pdf/FY10AnnualReport-TableIV.pdf (accessed on 11 October 2011).

7 See Table XVIII: Nonimmigrant visas issued by Nationality (Including Border Crossing Cards) Fiscal Year 2001–2010: www.travel.state.gov/pdf/FY10AnnualReport-TableXVIII.pdf (accessed on 11 October 2011).

8 See Table XV: Immigrant visas issued by Issuing Office (all categories, including replaced visas) Fiscal Year 2001–2010: www.travel.state.gov/pdf/FY10AnnualReport-TableXV.pdf (accessed on 11 October 2011).

9 See: www.uscis.gov/portal/site/uscis/. DV visas are divided among six geographic regions (Africa, Asia, Europe, North America (Bahamas), Oceania, South America, and the Caribbean). No one country can receive more than seven percent of the available diversity visas in any one year.

10 See the *Triennial Comprehensive Report on Immigration*. Available at: uscis.gov/graphics/aboutus/repsstudies/additions.html (accessed on 14 July 2011).

11 See United States Department of State Bureau of Consular Affairs Visa Bulletin for September 2011, No. 36, vol. IX, Washington, DC available at: www.travel.state.gov/visa/bulletin/bulletin_5542.html (accessed on 25 October 2011).

12 Eric M. Larson and Judith A. Droitcour, 'Estimating the Illegal Alien population in the United States: Some Methodological Considerations'. Available at: www.un.org/esa/population/publications/secoord2003/GAO_Paper17.pdf (accessed on 19 July 2011).

13 See statistical details of foreign nationals in Germany at: auslaender-statistik.de/bund/herkun_2.htm (accessed on 12 January 2001).

14 See 2010 statistical details of foreign nationals in Germany. Available at: www.auslaender-statistik.de/ (accessed on 15 October 2011).

15 See 'Area and Population: Foreign Population'. Federal Statistical Office and the Statistical Offices of the Länder. Available at: www.statistik-portal.de/Statistik-Portal/en/en_jb01_jahrtab2.asp (accessed on 15 October 2011).

16 2010 statistical details of foreign nationals in Germany. Available at: www.auslaender-statistik.de/ (accessed on 15 October 2011).

17 'Area and Population: Migration into and out of Germany'. Federal Statistical Office and the statistical Offices of the Länder: www.statistik-portal.de/Statistik-Portal/en/en_jb01_jahrtab5.asp (accessed on 17 October 2011).

18 Culled from December 1999 Statistics, Federal Statistics Office, available online at: www.auslaender-statistik.de/bund/herkun_2.htm (accessed on 12 January 2001).

19 These official figures are indeed conservative as they exclude the undocumented migrants that form a significant proportion of these immigrant communities.

20 See recent statistics (2010) available at: www.auslaender-statistik.de/ (accessed on 15 October 2011).

21 Statistical Yearbook for the Federal Republic of Germany. Statistisches Bundesamt, 2010, 52–53.

22 OPCS. 1991 Census Preliminary Report for England and Wales. HMSO, 1991; GRO(S). 1991 Census Preliminary Report for Scotland. HMSO, 1991; and 1991 Census of Population: Confidentiality and Computing (Cm 1447). HMSO, 1991.

23 'Poverty rates among ethnic groups in Great Britain', Joseph Rowntree Foundation 2007. Available online at: www.poverty.org.uk/reports/ethnicity%20findings.pdf (accessed on 12 October 2011).

24 Office for National Statistics 2004.

25 Home Office Statistical Bulletin. 'Control of Immigration: Statistics United Kingdom 2008', 14 August 2009. These estimates relate specifically to UK entries by African nationals. The figures above should take account of the fact that in 2008, only 40,395 African nationals were accepted for settlement in the United Kingdom. The majority of Africans entering the country are visitors who leave.

26 For unemployment rates statistics in the EU regions, see europa.eu.int/comm/eurostat (accessed on 23 May 2011).

27 See 'Labour, Economy and Welfare State. Five million reasons for labor market reforms', *Regierung Online* (Thursday 3 February 2005). Available at: www.bundesregierung.de/. See also figures from *Statistisches Bundesamt Deutschland 2005*. Available at: www.destatis.de/indicators/e/arb210ae.htm (accessed on 20 January 2011).

28 An unsuspecting public might misconstrue 'BBC' in this instance to mean 'British Broadcasting Corporation', an establishment that many immigrants would covet to work for. Nonetheless, a variant terminology among recent African immigrants in the United States is 'IBM', meaning in their case, 'International Bottom Management', and not to be confused with and mistaken for IBM Computers.

29 Personal Interview with James Balogun (pseudonym) in Berlin-Mitte (21 March 2001).

30 See Saskia Sassen, 'Immigration: Europe on the Move'. Head to head: Debate over Immigration. Available at: cgi.cnn.com/SPECIALS/2001/immigration/stories/dead.to.head/pros.html (accessed on 15 August 2011).

31. See Fidelia Onyuku-Opukiri, 'Report of the Council of African Christian Community in Europe (CACCE, UK) of Great Britain and Ireland' at the 3rd Interdisciplinary Conference 'African Christian Diaspora in Europe', Hirschluch-Berlin (11–15 September 2003) unpublished.
32. Fidelia Onyuku-Opukiri, 'Report of the Council of African Christian Community in Europe (CACCE, UK) of Great Britain and Ireland' (unpublished).
33. Personal Interview with James Balogun (pseudonym) in Berlin-Mitte (21 March 2001).

Chapter 4

1. There aren't several distinctive mosques or religious houses built or patronized by mainly North African Muslim immigrants. Most North African Muslims attend mosques and associate with Turkish, Iraqi, Iranian and other Muslim groups from the Middle East and elsewhere.
2. For a working typology of this religious genre in Germany, see Adogame (2005: 494–514).
3. A rudimentary list of and information about these churches have been well-documented in data bases created by the author as 'African Churches in Germany' under the auspices of the Humanities Collaborative Project (SFK/FK560) at the University of Bayreuth, available at: www.uni-bayreuth.de/sfbs/sfb-fk560/index-teilprojekte.html (accessed on 14 March 2005).
4. Ludwig (1997). The mission house was located at 122/124 Hill Street, Liverpool 8, in the heart of the town's 'coloured' community.
5. A newspaper caption for an article entitled 'GI Babies,' read: 'During the Second World War, some 100,000 black American GIs were stationed in the UK and love affairs blossomed with British girls. But many of the children born as a result were abandonedforgotten victims of war and racism.' See full-text of story by Anne Moore in *Daily Express Magazine*, 2 October 1999, at www.muskogee007.com/brown_babies.htm (accessed on 2 November 2001).
6. See stories on 'Brown Babies' by Martin Bright, *London Observer*, 10 October 1999, www.muskogee007.com/wpeA.jpg; and Peter Paterson, 'People Like Us: Solicitors (BBC2); Untold: Brown Babies (C4)' (name of newspaper and date of publication not specified) www.muskogee007.com/papers1.TIF (accessed on 2 November 2001). Also available is a documentary on Brown Babies produced by Touch Productions for Channel 4 in England. This film, which tells the story of four Brown Babies as they search to find their missing history and was screened on 11 October 1999. See www.channel4.com/untold (accessed on 2 November 2001).
7. These articles and accompanying photos located on Brian Lawrenson's website at www.muskogee007.com/acm2.JPG; www.muskogee007.com/acm4.JPG; and www.muskogee007.com/acm5.JPG (accessed on 2 November 2001), first appeared in the United States in *Ebony Magazine*

(November 1946). My thanks and gratitude go to Brian Lawrenson for the series of emails we exchanged on this issue, and particularly for granting me permission to use the newspaper extracts, stories and other invaluable information available on his website.

8 'Britain's Brown Babies: Illegitimate Tots a Tough Problem for England,' www.muskogee007.com/afrkids.jpg (accessed on 2 November 2001). This story appeared in *Ebony Magazine*, November 1946, in the United States.

9 This information was personally disclosed by Brian Lawrenson to the author through email correspondence, 8 October 2001. The children who lived at the Mission were abandoned by their English families and were supported by gifts of the church members.

10 See a short history of Lawrenson's stay at the Mission and his appreciation of Pastor Daniels Ekarte in Brian Lawrenson, 'Ancestors of Lawrenson Brian Joseph,' 16 January 2001, www.muskogee007.com/my_clan.htm; and in Brian Lawrenson, 'African Mission' at www.muskogee007.com/african_churches_mission.htm (accessed on 2 November 2001). Lawrenson stayed first at Mayfields in Leeds, Yorkshire (part of the ACM), then moved to the ACM in Liverpool where at the age of 5 he experienced the enforced move to Olive Mount Children's Hospital and then to Fazakerly Cottage Homes.

11 Brian Lawrenson, 'Childhood,' www.muskogee007.com/interest.htm (accessed on 2 November 2001).

12 Gladys Cooper was the daughter of an English girl and a white United States Army officer. Lawrenson documents that he, Gladys and other children, including Roger Rice, Peter Lawson, Adrian Gouth, James Howard and Sylvia Brown, were evicted from the mission and finally relocated in the Fazakerly Cottage Homes in the Liverpool 10 area. The matrons who looked after the children were white.

13 Ekarte continued to live in the building that once housed the Mission until the Council ordered its demolition in 1964. Sherwood (1994: 111).

14 Lawrenson, 'African Mission.'

15 Lawrenson, 'African Mission,' quotation from the *Liverpool Echo*, 23 July 1964.

16 Olu Abiola cited in Ludwig (1992: 136).

17 John Adegoke in Ludwig, 136.

18 See *CCC Bible Lessons and Parishes* 1996. The *CCC Bible Lessons and Parishes 1998* show that the number of overseas parishes had increased to 95 parishes.

19 *Evangelisches Missionswerk in Südwestdeutschland* Information titled 'The Celestial Church of Christ – A Nigerian Independent Church in Germany', Stuttgart, 21 September, 1981.

20 Personal Interview with Bona Mensah at CCC Munich Parish, Munich on 30 June 1996.

21 Personal Interview with Paul Olaniyan at CCC Overseas Diocesan Headquarters, London on 30 July 1996. He established the first CCC parish in Germany and later headed a CCC parish in United States.

22 See my publication lists from 1998–2010 in the bibliography.

23 For details about FIFMI global spread and in Europe, see their official website: www.fifmi.org/global-db and www.fifmi.org/global-db/europe (accessed on 3 July 2011). David Maxwell (2007) has chronicled a detailed history of the FIFMI.

Chapter 5

1 *'The Latter Rain' 7th Annual RCCG North American Convention Program*, Dallas, June 2003.
2 See Parish Directory for a list of parishes in North America. Available at: www.rccgna.org/login/pdirectory.asp?offset=0 and www.rccgna.org/bocus.asp (accessed on 5 September 2008).
3 See CCOMI Central and Global Assemblies at: www.ccomi.org/assemblies.php (accessed on 2 October 2005).
4 See *Eternal Sacred Order of the Cherubim and Seraphim, The Cherubim and Seraphim Memorandum and Articles of Association*, Nigeria: Ebute-Metta, 1930. Paragraph 10.
5 See Ade Bankole-Ojo, 'Deportation Order on the Illegal Immigrant', in *The Angel Voice*, 42 (6), April–June 1992, 7 and 9.
6 This text is part of 'testimony' recorded at the CCC parish, Frankfurt. Germany, 17 November 1999.
7 Dr Daniel Olukoya, 'Prayer as a Military Strategy'. Available at: www.sermoncentral.com (accessed on 3 January 2005).
8 Dr D. K. Olukoya, Sermon text 'Prayer as a military strategy', available at: www.sermoncentral.com (accessed on 3 January 2005).

Chapter 6

1 See ONS, *Social Capital: A Review of Literature*. London, 2001. Available online at: www.statistics.gov.uk/socialcapital/downloads/soccaplitreview.pdf#11 (accessed on 20 April 2006).
2 See BBC News England story 'Prince Celebrates his Birthday' indicating that the Prince of Wales has celebrated his birthday in one of London's biggest Pentecostal churches. news.bbc.co.uk/player/nol/newsid_7090000/newsid_7094600/7094698.stm?bw=bb&mp=wm&news=1&ms3=6&nol_storyid=7094698. See 'Prince Charles at RCCG London', Tuesday, 27 November 2007: rccgsing.blogspot.co.uk/2007/11/prince-charles-at-rccg-london.html (accessed on 17 December 2007).
3 See Marcia Dixon's 'Prince Charles visits black church' *The Voice Archive*, 22 November 2007, online version available at: archive.voice-online.co.uk/content.php?show=12402 (accessed on 13 March 2012). See also Dan Wooding, 'Prince Charles marks 59th birthday with tribute to black churches in the UK', *ASSIST News Service*, Thursday, 15 November 2007; and 'Prince

Charles to celebrate influence of black church in Britain, *Christian Today*, 13 November 2007.
4. Personal Interview with Pastor Festus Olatunde, Mountain of Fire and Miracles Ministries, Edinburgh (15 September 2010).
5. See KICC Ministries available at: www.kicc.org.uk/Ministries/tabid/66/Default.aspx (accessed on 21 March 2011).
6. See KICC official web site at: www.kiccdev.org.uk/igoc2004/main.asp (accessed on 21 March 2011).
7. See profiles of invited church leaders and evangelists at the IGOC 2003 and 2004 at: www.kiccdev.org.uk/igoc2003/main.asp? and www.kiccdev.org.uk/igoc2004/main.asp respectively. Other renowned American evangelists include Mike Murdock, Robb Thompson and Peter Daniels. See photo gallery: www.kicc.org.uk/Portals/0/gallery/igoc/gallery.html (accessed on 21 March 2011).
8. See IGOC 2004 Conference products at: www.kiccdev.org.uk/igoc2004/main.asp?location=products (accessed on 21 March 2011).
9. See KICC annual Winning Women Conference: www.kicc.org.uk/Conferences/WinningWomen/tabid/73/Default.aspx. See also www.kicc.org.uk/ww2011/about.aspx (accessed on 21 March 2011).
10. See 'RCCG: Past, Present and Future. The Structure, Administration and Finance of the RCCG in North America', 7th Annual RCCG North America Convention Program, June 18–20, 2003, 15 and 30.
11. The RCCG North America, Inc.: General Information and Church Planting Manual, Fall 2001 Edition.
12. Personal communication with Festus Olatunde (22 March 2008).

Chapter 7

1. Questionnaire were administered at the RCCG parish, Bonn on 15 September 2002; and RCCG parish, Hamburg on 30 September 2002. The figures shown above represent a sample of 172, being excerpts from 1200 questionnaires administered among African-led churches in Germany, United Kingdom and the United States between 2000 and 2005.
2. Hansen maintained that the impetus for the British Nationality Act originated in Canada. Although such legislation hardly appears to be the basis of a constitutional revolution, it marked the end of a centuries-old definition of British subjecthood (69).
3. Personal conversation with Bishop Climate Irungu and Pastor Dr Jennifer Irungu on 23 November 2006. For a brief history of WCCC, see also the official website of the WCCC available at: music.wccc-scotland.org/Pastor_note.htm (accessed on 12 June 2007).
4. See details of two story captions: Gitau wa Njenga, 'Former gangster ordained youngest bishop in UK' in *The Standard*, Saturday 14 May 2005. Online version available at: www.eastandard.net/archives/cl/news.php?articleid=2033#55 (accessed on 20 March 2006); and Jamie Livingstone, 'I Confess: Born-again bishop admits his blood-soaked

gangster past of guns, drug-deals and hookers', *Sunday Mail*, 22 May 2005. Online version available at: www.sundaymail.co.uk/news/tm_objectid=15543709 (accessed on 24 March 2006).

5   See full text on 'Ladies on Fire for Jesus' official website available at: www.wccc-scotland.org/ladiesoffire.html (accessed on 27 June 2007).

6   Ibid.

7   See for instance, *WCCC Sunday Bulletin*, 25 June 2006 (6–7).

Chapter 8

1   Unabridged (unedited) versions of the Annual Prophecies delivered by the General Overseer, Pastor E. A. Adeboye, are published on the RCCG website. See www.rccg.org/Church_Ministry/Annual_ Prophecies/. The prophecies are usually publicly announced at the Annual Special Holy Ghost Festival (accessed on 9 January 2010).

2   See full text of Annual Prophecies at the RCCG Internet Outreach: www.rccg.org/Church_Ministr…ual_Prophecies/prophecies_2002.htm (accessed on 20 July 2002).

3   The Annual Prophecies 1999 were released by the pastor and General Overseer of the RCCG Worldwide at the National Ministers Thanksgiving at the Redemption City, Nigeria on 4 January 1999.

4   See details at www.rccg.org/Church_Ministr..ual_Prophecies/prophecies_2000.htm.

5   See the third category of prophecies 'International' from Annual Prophecies 2002 at: www.rccg.org/Church_Ministr..ual_Prophecies/prophecies_2002.htm (accessed on 20 September 2002).

6   Personal Interview with Bosun Ajayi, RCCG Living Water Parish, Bonn on 12 August 2002.

7   See the official website of the RCCG in www.rccg.org created and maintained by the RCCG Internet Project, Houston Texas, USA. See also UK parish web sites www.jesus-house.org.uk/ and www.rccgarea4.org.uk/ (accessed on 19 February 2002).

8   See CCOMI official website available at: www.ccomi.org/; ccomi.org/ccomi/; and members.aol.com/christianmission/ (accessed on 7 March 2002).

9   See www.ccomi.org/media.php (accessed on 7 March 2002).

10 See CCOM Victory Store available at: ccomi.org/victorystore/ (accessed on 18 April 2002). The book themes vary and the DVD titles seem carefully chosen to capture members, public interest and appeal to religious sensibilities. The CCOMI Anniversary Publication '20 Years and Beyond' has a much longer list (over 60) of books and audio-visual products, essentially sermon text/messages of Bishop Abraham Bediako, his wife Pastor Vivian and other visiting evangelists. They are produced by the CCOMI Publication Ministry and sold by the bookshop.

11 See the CCOMI Prayer Request template available at: www.ccomi.org/prayerrequest.php (accessed on 23 June 2002).

12 See for instance the website addresses: www.celestialchurch.com (operated by a parish in Riverdale, USA); www.celestialchurch.mcmail.com (administered from the United Kingdom), and mageos.ifrance.com or www.ChristianismCelest.com (administered from France). Their electronic mail addresses are webmaster@celestialchurch.com, celestialchurchofchrist@mcmail, and jl_degnide@hotmail.com respectively (accessed on 10 April 2003).

13 See the official Church of the Lord (Aladura) web page at the address: www.aladura.de (accessed on 10 April 2003). It was created and managed by Dr Rufus Ositelu, who was the leader of the Langen-Frankfurt (Germany) branch and also the General Overseer of the European branches. He is currently the Primate of CLA Worldwide.

14 See details on KICC Winning Ways programme, available online at: www.kicc.org.uk/TVRadio/WinningwaysSchedule/tabid/195/Default.aspx (accessed on 21 March 2011).

15 The Online Streaming of KICC TV is available at: www.kicctv.tv/ (accessed on 21 March 2011).

16 liveway.tv/ and www.livewayradio.net/ (accessed on 21 March 2011).

17 See OHTV online website at: www.ohtv.co.uk/. There is also OHTV Africa and OHTV USA.

18 Read more about Dove Vision TV Channel at www.dovevision.tv/about/company.php; and TV Live Online Streaming of Dove Vision TV available at: www.dovevision.tv/live/tv.php (accessed on 21 March 2011).

19 God Digital (formerly known as 'the Christian Channel Europe'), the Christian Television and Radio Service of the Dream Family Network Ltd., was founded in 1995 by a South African couple, Rory and Wendy Alec in the United Kingdom. See 'The Call' and 'Mission field' at God Digital website: www.god-digital.com/rory&wendy3.htm (accessed on 21 March 2011).

20 In January 1991, the name was registered by the Federal Government of Nigeria as an Incorporated Trustee under the Land and Perpetual Act of Nigeria. See www.mzfm.com/History.htm (accessed on 21 March 2011).

21 See details of testimonies and views expressed on the Testimony Section of the MZFMI website at www.mzfm.com/Testimonies.htm and www.mzfm.org/ (accessed on 15 May 2001 and 23 January 2007).

22 I have isolated here a three-year travel schedule – 2005, 2007 and 2008 as a case in point. Culled from: www.pastorsunday.com/pages.php?id=4 and www.godembassy.org/en/pastor_/timetable.php (accessed on 24 May 2011).

23 See KICC official web site at: www.kiccdev.org.uk/igoc2004/main.asp (accessed on 24 May 2011).

24 See profiles of invited church leaders and evangelists at the IGOC 2003 and 2004 at: www.kiccdev.org.uk/igoc2003/main.asp? and www.kiccdev.org.uk/igoc2004/main.asp respectively (accessed on 24 May 2011). Other renowned American evangelists include Mike Murdock, Robb Thompson and Peter Daniels.

25 See IGOC 2004 Conference products at: www.kiccdev.org.uk/igoc2004/main.asp?location=products (accessed on 24 May 2011).

NOTES

26 Personal communication with John Bamidele, an RCCG member in London (20 August 2006).

Chapter 9

1. See Adogame (2000b: 400–9; 2005d: 494–515; 2008b: 310–36); Ojo (2007: 380–82).
2. Uka (2008); Kim (2006; 2012); Catto (2008, 2012).
3. Kalu (1980: 365–74; 2007; 2008: 271–91).
4. Walls (2002; 2004); Kendall (1978); Währsich-Oblau (2009); Makofane (2009).
5. Gatu (2006); Anderson (1974: 133–42; 1991).
6. Wagner (1975: 165–76; 1975b; Reese (2010); Rowell (2006); Scherer (1964); Schwartz (2007); Allen (1962); Bosch (1991); Howard (1997); Idowu (1965); Olofinjana (2010); Nazir-Ali (1991).
7. Chapter 2 in Byrnes (2011: 68–105) clearly exemplifies Maryknoll Sisters' experiences of this kind of reverse mission.
8. See Andrew Rice, Mission From Africa, *The New York Times*, 12 April 2009. Online version available at: www.nytimes.com/2009/04/12/magazine/12churches-t.html?pagewanted=all (accessed on 20 May 2009).
9. Julia Lieblich and Tom McCann, 'Africans now missionaries to U.S.', *Chicago Tribune*, 21 June 2002 (1).
10. See 'African Missionaries to the US' *Christian Century*, 13 August 1997.
11. See Lucy Bannermann, 'Out of Africa: now the missionaries head for Scotland', *Herald*, 28 January 2006.
12. See BBC2 Series 'Reverse Missionaries', available on BBC iPlayer at: www.bbc.co.uk/programmes/b01dmzcz/episodes/guide (accessed on 3 April 2012).
13. www.bbc.co.uk/programmes/b01dn15f. The first of a three-part BBC2 Series was aired on 16 March 2012 (9.00–10.00 p.m.).
14. www.bbc.co.uk/programmes/b01dy806. The second part was screened on 23 March 2012.
15. www.bbc.co.uk/programmes/b01f9wdq. The last version was shown on 30 March 2012.
16. See Israel Olofinjana's review of the BBC documentary, available online at: israelolofinjana.wordpress.com/2012/03/19/reverse-missionaries-a-review-of-bbc-documentary/ (accessed on 3 April 2012).
17. *Gaba Pastoral Letter*, 7 (1969) 50–51.
18. *Gaba Pastoral Letter*, 50–51; Uzoukwu (1982).
19. See Mugambi, 'Foreward' in Gatu (2006: I).
20. See 'text of address 'African Churches and Foreign Mission Board' by John Gatu, General Secretary of Presbyterian Church of East Africa, at Africa Department, D.O.M. Meeting, 17 February 1971' in Gatu (2006: 163–8).

21. See for instance the discourse on dependence and self-reliance at the World Missions Associate official website: www.wmausa.org/98600.ihtml (accessed 10 October 2007).
22. See J. Gatu, 'Rationale for Self-Reliance' at: www.wmausa.org/page.aspx?id=83845 (accessed 10 October 2007).
23. See Bangkok Assembly 1973: Minutes and Report of the Commission on World Mission and Evangelism of the WCC 31 December 1972 and 9–12 January 1973.
24. Personal interview with Brown Oyitso, RCCG Provincial Pastor, Victory House Parish, Festac Town, Lagos (6 September 2004).
25. Personal interview with Brown Oyitso (6 September 2004).
26. Personal Interview with Samuel Shorimade, RCCG Cornerstone Parish, Boston, MA. USA (16 November 2003).
27. Personal interview with Brown Oyitso (6 September 2004).
28. Personal Interview with Pastor Bosun Ajayi, RCCG Bonn, Germany (24 October 2002).
29. Personal Interview with Pastor Dr Ajibike Akinkoye at the RCCGNA Headquarters, Dallas-Texas (7 March 2004).
30. Personal interview with Brown Oyitso (6 September 2004).
31. See chapter 2 of the history of the Embassy 'Out of Africa: Go to a Land that I will Show you', available at: www.godembassy.org/en/pastor_/africa.php (accessed 18 August 2004).
32. S. Adelaja, 'Go to a land I will show you', in Wagner and Thompson (2004: 37–55). See also the Embassy of the Blessed Kingdom of God for All nations website: www.godembassy.org/en/pastor_/africa.php (accessed 10 March 2003).
33. See 'A New Name. Embassy of God' available at: www.godembassy.org/en/embassy.php (accessed 10 March 2003).
34. See details at: www.godembassy.org/en/pastor_/bigraphy.php (accessed 3 March 2005).
35. See full details at the church website available at: www.godembassy.org/eng/projnewbuild_E.shtm (accessed 3 March 2005).
36. Cf. Christian Bank Project of the Embassy, www.godembassy.org/eng/projsbank_E.shtm and the vision and plans of KICC in London at www.kicc.org.uk/ (accessed on 15 August 2005).
37. See 'Facts and Statistics Embassy of God' available at: www.godembassy.org/en/embassy.php (accessed on 27 November 2006).
38. See detailed text available at: www.godembassy.org/en/index.php (accessed on 27 November 2006).
39. See the Embassy media resources on its official website available at: media.godembassy.org/en/media/media.php?curent_sub=2 (accessed on 15 July 2007).
40. See for instance, www.godembassy.org/en/pastor_/books.php, and www.godembassy.org/en/pastor_/bigraphy.php (accessed on 19 July 2007).

Chapter 10

1. A favourite biblical passage which helps them to express this feeling is *Ephesians* 2: 19–20 'Consequently, you are no longer foreigners and aliens, but fellow citizens with God's people and members of God's household, built on the foundation of the apostles and prophets, with Christ Jesus Himself as the chief cornerstone'.
2. Communication with Rev Dr Rufus Ositelu, Primate, CLA, 15 June 2001.
3. See details on the 'Council of Christian Communities of an African Approach in Europe' available at their website: membres.lycos.fr/ccceae/; and the Scottish Council of African Churches (SCOAC) available at: www.scoac.org.uk/ (accessed on 10 January 2012). I shall come back to these two examples later in this chapter.
4. See Lawrenson, 'African Mission', for details on the Mission's involvement in political and social activities, and its relationship with other organizations; see Sherwood (1994: 83–97).
5. John Adegoke, interview by Frieder Ludwig, 18 October 1991, in Ludwig (1992: 136).
6. 'African Christian Communities in Europe: Creating an Identity,' *Newsletter of a Process*, December 1998 (1). The Leeds Conference was organized by J. Jehu-Appiah and H. Kontor (British African Community) in conjunction with R. Gerloff and K. Ward (Department of Theology and Religious Studies, University of Leeds).
7. 'African Christian Communities' (1).
8. One major achievement of the CCCAAE was in constituting a research department and co-opting this author to serve as its research coordinator. Selected papers from the Hirschluch conference are now published. See Adogame et al. (2009).
9. See SCOAC official website, available at: www.scoac.org.uk/ (accessed on 10 January 2012).
10. Personal Interview with Pastor Festus Olatunde, Executive Director, SCOAC, Head Office, Edinburgh (13 December 2010). The SCOAC established the Scotland-Africa Mass Choir that took part at the Edinburgh 2010 Mission conference's closing ceremony (see Edinburgh 2012 Mission conference closing event on Sunday 6th June at the Assembly Hall available at: www.edinburgh2010.org/en/resources/videos.html#c33174. See a letter of appreciation from the Church of Scotland (Douglas Galbraith) to the Scotland Africa Mass Choir (n.d), available at: www.scoac.org.uk/resources.htm. See also the Church of Scotland celebrated annual outdoor events such as the 'Roll Away the Stone' (22 May 2011). Programme details are available at: www.rollawaythestone.org.uk/programme/index.html and in: www.churchofscotland.org.uk/about_us/general_assembly/reports_and_information/roll_away_the_stone (accessed on 11 September 2011).
11. The CACC is a member of Churches Together in England; Churches Together in Britain and Ireland; and the Conference of European Churches.
12. An ecumenical body 'Churches Together in the Netherlands' founded in 1982 as a platform of non-Indigenous Churches in the Netherlands,

and in 1997 as SKIN. SKIN membership is only open to Christian faith communities formed by immigrants in the Netherlands. See details at SKIN official website: www.skinkerken.nl

13. See the official website of GATE, available at: gate-mission.org/about_us.html. GATE's flyer introducing its mission is available online at: gate-mission.org/GATE%20Flyer.pdf (accessed on 16 June 2011). GATE is an initiative of the Association of Evangelicals in Africa 'in fulfilment of God's plan for Europe', launched in 1995 and officially registered with Ministry of Commerce Amsterdam. Part of its activities is to network and consult among Afro-European Christian leaders, and between Afro-European and European Christian leaders. GATE's vision in Europe is summarized as 'Living and /or working in Europe for the purpose of stimulating the faith of the European Christian Community, and in partnership with them to evangelize the non-Christian European community'.

14. Oshun, 'Encountering Aladura Spirituality in Britain'.

15. Sharing e.V is a department or ministry within the Grace Fellowship, Wuppertal. The name 'Sharing' symbolizes the vision of the church not only to 'share' and disseminate the 'Word of God', but also to be actively engaged in extra-religious activities within society.

16. See profiles of invited church leaders and evangelists at the IGOC 2003 and 2004 at: www.kiccdev.org.uk/igoc2003/main.asp? and www.kiccdev.org.uk/igoc2004/main.asp respectively (accessed on 18 May 2005). Other renowned American evangelists include Mike Murdock, Robb Thompson and Peter Daniels.

17. Author's interview with Cornelius Oyelami and Pastor (Dr) Ajibike Akinyoye at the RCCGNA Headquarters, Dallas, TX, 9 March 2004. Most of my informants in Boston and Texas indicated one or more of these reasons for switching religious affiliation.

18. Author's interview with Cornelius Oyelami at the RCCGNA Headquarters, Dallas, TX, 7 March 2004. Virtually all my informants corroborated this view.

19. See Jacinta Ashworth and Ian Farthing 'Churchgoing in the UK'. A research report from TearFund on church attendance in the UK. April 2007.

20. Leslie Lyall, *Missionary Opportunity Today – A Brief World Survey*. London: Inter-Varsity Fellowship, 1963 (11).

21. Personal interview with Pastor Festus Olatunde, MFM, Edinburgh (13 April 2010).

22. Joel Edward 'Poverty Alleviation: A Missional tool for Britain's Black Majority Churches'. Mission Forum Lecture presented at the 'Missions in Britain: Prospects and Challenges' Conference, RCCG, the Hub Studios, London (10 March 2012).

23. Joel Edward 'Poverty Alleviation: A Missional tool for Britain's Black Majority Churches'.

Select bibliography

Abimbola, Wande. 'Ifa: A West African Cosmological System', in Blakely T. D. et al. (ed.) *Religion in Africa: Experience and Expression*. London: James Currey, 1994, 101–16.

Abiola, Olu. 'The History of the Aladura International Church', *An Introduction to Aladuraism*. London: O.J, n.d.

Adeboye, Enoch A. *Arresting the Arrester – Catching the Enemy in His Own Trap*. Largo, MD: Christian Living Books, 2002.

—. 'Levels of Breakthrough', *Open Heavens: A Daily Guide to Close Fellowship with God*, vol. 4.. Cape Town: Struik Christian Books Ltd, 2003.

Adelaja, Sunday. *Life and Death in the Power of the Tongue*. Kiev: Fares Publishing House, 2003.

—. 'Go to a land I will show you', in C. P. Wagner and J. Thompson (eds) *Out of Africa*. California: Regal Books, 2004, 37–55.

Adepoju, Aderanti. 'Patterns of Migration in West Africa', in Takyiwaa Manuh (ed.) *At Home in the World: International Migration and Development in Contemporary Ghana and West Africa*. Legon: Sub-Saharan Publishers, 2005, 24–54.

—. 'Rethinking the Dynamics of Migration within, from and to Africa', in A. Adepoju (ed.) *International Migration within, to and from Africa in a Globalised World*. Legon, Ghana: Sub-Saharan Publishers, 2010, 9–45.

Adogame, Afe. 'A Home Away from Home: The Proliferation of Celestial Church of Christ in Diaspora – Europe', *EXCHANGE – Journal of Missiological and Ecumenical Research*, 27 (2) 1998: 141–60.

—. Celestial Church of Christ: The Politics of Cultural Identity in a West African Prophetic-Charismatic Movement. Frankfurt am Main: Peter Lang, 1999.

—. 'Aye loja, orun nile – The Appropriation of Ritual-Spatial Time in the Cosmology of the Celestial Church of Christ', *Journal of Religion in Africa*, 30 (1) 2000a: 3–29.

—. 'The Quest for Space in the Global Religious Marketplace: African Religions in Europe', *International Review of Mission,* 89 (354) 2000b: 400–9.

—. 'Mission from Africa: The Case of the Celestial Church of Christ in Europe', *Zeitschrift für Missionswissenschaft und Religionswissenschaft*, 84 (I) 2000c: 29–44.

—. 'Partnership of African Christian Communities in Europe', *International Review of Mission,* 89 (354) July 2000d: 291–303.

—. 'Traversing Local-Global Religious Terrain: African New Religious Movements in Europe', *Zeitschrift für Religionswissenschaft*, 10 (2002a) : 33–49.

—. 'Engaged in the task of "Cleansing" the World: Aladura Churches in 20th Century Europe', in Klaus Koschorke (ed.) *Transcontinental Links in the History of Non-Western Christianity*, vol. 6. Wiesbaden: Harrassowitz, 2002b, 73–86.

—. 'Betwixt Identity and Security: African New Religious Movements and the Politics of Religious Networking in Europe', *Nova Religio: The Journal of Emergent and Alternative Religions*, 7 (2) 2003: 24–41.

—. 'Contesting the Ambivalences of Modernity in a Global Context: The Redeemed Christian Church of God, North America', *Studies in World Christianity*, 10 (1) 2004a: 25–48.

—. 'Engaging the Rhetoric of Spiritual Warfare: The Public Face of Aladura in Diaspora', *Journal of Religion in Africa*, 34 (4) 2004b: 493–522.

—. 'Conference Report' The Berlin-Congo Conference 1884: The Partition of Africa and Implications for Christian Mission Today", *Journal of Religion in Africa*, 34 (1–2) 2004c: 186–90.

—. 'To be or not to be? Politics of Belonging and African Christian Communities in Germany', in Afe Adogame and Cordula Weisskoeppel (eds) *Religion in the Context of African Migration*. Bayreuth: Bayreuth African Studies Series, No. 75, 2005a, 95–112.

—. 'A Walk for Africa: Combating the Demon of HIV/AIDs in an African Pentecostal Church – The Case of the Redeemed Christian Church of God', *Scriptura*, 89 (2005b): 396–405.

—. 'African Instituted Churches in Europe. Continuity and Transformation', in Klaus Koschorke (ed.) *African Identities and World Christianity in the Twentieth Century*. Wiesbaden: Harrassowitz Verlag, 2005c, 225–44.

—. 'African Christian Communities in Diaspora', in Ogbu Kalu (ed.) *African Christianity: An African Story*. Pretoria: University of Pretoria, 2005d, 494–514.

—.'Clearing New Paths into an Old Forest: Aladura Christianity in Europe', in Jacob K. Olupona and Terry Rey (eds) *Orisa Devotion as World Religion: The Globalization of Yoruba Religious Culture*. Madison: Wisconsin University Press, 2007a, 247–62.

—. 'Raising Champions, Taking Territories: African Churches and the Mapping of New Religious Landscapes in Diaspora', in Theodore Louis Trost (ed.) *The African Diaspora and the Study of Religion*. New York: Palgrave Macmillan, 2007b, 21–46.

—. 'Up, Up Jesus! Down, Down Satan! African Religiosity in the former Soviet Bloc – the Embassy of the Blessed Kingdom of God for All Nations', *Exchange: Journal of Missiological and Ecumenical Research*, 37 (3) 2008a: 310–36.

—. 'Globalization and African New Religious Movements in Europe', in Ogbu Kalu and Alaine Low (eds) *Interpreting Contemporary Christianity: Global Processes and Local Identities*. Grand Rapids, MI: Eerdmans, 2008b, 296–316.

—. Book Review of *African Immigrant Religions in America*. Ed. J. Olupona and R. Gemignani (2007). In *Journal of American Academy of Religion*, 76 (4) 2008c: 970–3.

—. '"I am married to Jesus!" The Feminization of New African Diasporic Religiosity', *Archives de Sciences Sociales des Religions,* 143 (2008d): 129–48.

—. '"Who do they think they are?" Mental Images and the Unfolding of an African Diaspora in Germany', in Adogame et al. (eds) *Christianity in Africa and the Africa Diaspora: The Appropriation of a Scattered Heritage.* London and New York: Continuum, 2008e, 248–64.
—. 'Claiming the Continent for Christ: The Civic Role of Christian Church Outreach Mission International in global contexts', in K. Kunter and J. Holger Schjorring (eds) *Changing Relationships between Churches in Europe and Africa: The Internationalization of Christianity and Politics in the 20th Century.* Wiesbaden: Harrassowitz, 2008f, 225–40.
—. 'Mapping Globalization with the Lens of Religion: African Migrant Churches in Germany', in Armin Geertz and Margit Warburg (eds) *New Religions and Globalization. Empirical, Theoretical and Methodological Perspectives.* Aarhus: Aarhus University Press, 2008g, 189–213.
—. 'Ranks and Robes: Art Symbolism and Identity in the Celestial Church of Christ in the European Diaspora', *Material Religion: The Journal of Objects, Art and Belief,* 5 (1) 2009a: 10–32.
—. 'To God Be the Glory! Home Videos, the Internet, and Religio-Cultural Identity in Contemporary African Christianity', *Critical Interventions: Journal of African Art History and Visual Culture,* 3 (4) 2009b: 147–59.
—. 'Pentecostal and Charismatic Movements in a Global Perspective', in Byran S. Turner (ed.) *The New Blackwell Companion to the Sociology of Religion.* Chichester: Willey-Blackwell, 2010a, 498–518.
—. 'Transnational Migration and Pentecostalism in Europe', PentecoStudies. An Interdisciplinary Journal for Research on the Pentecostal and Charismatic Movements. 9 (1) 2010b: 56–73.
—. 'From House Cells to Warehouse Churches? Christian Church Outreach Mission International in Translocal Contexts', in Hüwelmeier, Gertrud, and Kristine Krause (eds) *Traveling Spirits: Migrants, Markets and Mobilities.* New York and London: Routledge, 2010c, 165–85.
— (ed.). Who is Afraid of the Holy Ghost?: Pentecostalism and Globalization in Africa and Beyond. Trenton/Asmara/Ibadan: Africa World Press, 2011a.
—. 'Online for God: Media Negotiation and African New Religious Movements', in A. Adogame (ed.) *Who is Afraid of the Holy Ghost?.* Trenton/Asmara/Ibadan: Africa World Press, 2011b, 223–38.
Adogame, Afe and Shobana Shankar (eds). *Religions on the Move: New Dynamics of Religious Expansion in a Globalizing World.* Leiden and Boston: Brill, 2012 (in press).
Adogame, Afe and James Spickard (eds). Religion Crossing Boundaries. Transnational Religious and Social Dynamics in Africa and the New African Diaspora. Leiden and Boston: Brill, 2010.
Adogame, Afe, Roswith Gerloff and Klaus Hock (eds). *Christianity in Africa and the African Diaspora: The Appropriation of a Scattered Heritage.* London and New York: Continuum, 2008.
Adogame, Afe, Magnus Echtler and Ulf Vierke (eds). *Unpacking the New: Critical Perspectives on Cultural Syncretization in African and Beyond.* Zurich and Berlin: Lit Verlag, 2008.
Adogame, Afe and Cordula Weissköppel (eds). *Religion in the Context of African Migration.* Bayreuth: Bayreuth African Studies, 2005.
Akyeampong, Emmanuel. "Africans in the Diaspora: The Diaspora and Africa", *African Affairs,* 99 (2000): 198–200.

SELECT BIBLIOGRAPHY

Aldridge, Stephen, David Halpern and Sarah Fitzpatrick. *Social Capital: A Discussion Paper*. London, England: Performance and Innovation Unit, 2002.

Allen Hays, R. 'Habitat for Humanity: Building Social Capital Through Faith Based Service', Revised version of a paper presented at the 2001 Annual Meeting of the Urban Affairs Association, Detroit, Michigan, April 2001.

Allen, Roland. Missionary Methods: St. Paul's or Ours? Grand Rapids, MI: Eerdmans, 1962.

Anderson, G. H. 'A moratorium on missionaries?' in Anderson, G. H. and Stransky, T. F. (eds) *Mission Trends* 1. New York: Paulist Press and Grand Rapids, MI: Eerdmans, 1974, 133–42.

Appadurai, A. 'Disjuncture and Difference in the Global Cultural Economy', in M. Featherstone (ed), *Global Culture*. London: Sage, 1991, 295–310.

Arnold, James R. *Robert Mugabe's Zimbabwe*. Minneapolis: Twenty-First Century Books, 2008.

Arthur, John A. Invisible Sojourners: African Immigrant Diaspora in the United States. Westport, CT, London: Praeger, 2000.

Asamoah-Gyadu, J. K. African Charismatics. Current Developments within Independent Indigenous Pentecostalism in Ghana. Leiden: Brill, 2005a.

—. 'An African Pentecostal on Mission in Eastern Europe: The Church of the "Embassy of God" in the Ukraine', *Pneuma*, 27 (2) 2005b: 297–321.

—. 'African Initiated Christianity in Eastern Europe: Church of the "Embassy of God" in Ukraine', *International Bulletin of Missionary Research,* 30 (2) 2006: 73–6.

Awoonor, K. *Ghana: A Political History*. Accra: Woeli Pub. Services, 1990.

Axford, Barrie. *The Global System: Economics, Politics and Culture*. New York: St Martin's Press, 1995.

Bankole-Ojo, Ade. 'Deportation Order on the Illegal Immigrant', *The Angel Voice*, 42 (6) 1992: 5.

Basch, Linda, Glick-Schiller Nina and Blanc-Szanton Cristina (eds). *Nations Unbound. Transnational Projects, Postcolonial Predicaments, and Deterritorialized Nation-States*. New York: Gordon and Breach Science Publishers, 1994.

Beckford, James A. *Social Theory and Religion*. Cambridge: Cambridge University Press, 2003.

Beetham T. A. *Christianity and the New Africa*. London: Pall Mall Press, 1967.

Bierwirth, Chris. 'The Lebanese communities of Côte d'Ivoire', *African Affairs*, 98 (390) 1999: 79–99.

Bellegarde-Smith, Patrick (ed.). *Fragments of Bone: Neo-African Religions in a New World*, Chicago: University of Chicago Press, 2005.

Benneh, E. Y. 'The International Legal Regime and Migration Policies of Ghana, the ECOWAS Sub-region and Recipient Countries', in Manuh (ed.), *At Home in the World: International Migration and Development in Contemporary Ghana and West Africa*. Legon: Sub-Saharan Publishers, 2005, 78–102.

Beyer, Peter. *Religion and Globalization*. London: Sage Publications, 1994.

— (ed.). *Religion im Prozeß der Globalisierung*. Würzburg: Ergon Verlag, 2001.

Biney, Moses. From Africa to America: Religion and Adaptation among Ghanaian Immigrants in New York. New York: New York University Press, 2011.

Bosch, David. Transforming Mission: Paradigm Shifts in Theology of Mission. Maryknoll, NY: Orbis, 1991.

SELECT BIBLIOGRAPHY

Bourdieu, Pierre. 'The Field of Cultural Production or The Economic World Reversed', *Poetics*, 12 (4–5) 1983: 311–56.

— 'The Forms of Capital' in John G. Richardson (ed.), *Handbook of Theory and Research for the Sociology of Education*. New York: Greenwood, 1986, 241–58.

Bourdieu, Pierre and Jean-Claude Passeron. 'Cultural Reproduction and Social Reproduction'. In Richard K. Brown (Ed.), *Knowledge, Education and Cultural Change*. London: Tavistock, 1973, 278–302.

Bourdieu, P. and L. Wacquant. *An Invitation to Reflexive Sociology*. Chicago: University of Chicago Press, 1992.

Boyd, M. 'Family and Personal Networks in International Migration: Recent Developments and New Agendas', *International Migration Review*, 23 (3) 1989: 638–670.

Boyd, M. and E. Grieco, 'Women and migration: Incorporating gender into international migration theory', *Migration Information Source*, Washington D.C., 2003. www.migrationinformation.org/feature/print.cfm?ID=106.

Brown, F. 'Taking Kiev by Surprise', *Charisma and Christian Life*, 28 (11) 2003: 88–94.

Brubaker, William R. (ed.). *Immigration and the Politics of Citizenship in Europe and North America*. Lanham, MD: University Press of America, 1989.

Brettell, Caroline and James Hollifield (eds). *Migration Theory: Talking across Disciplines*. New York and London: Routledge, 2000.

Briggs, Xavier. 'Social Capital: Easy Beauty or Meaningful Resource?' *Journal of the American Planning Association*, 70 (2) 2004: 145–9.

Bruni, Frank. 'The Changing Church: Faith Fades Where It Once Burned Strong', *New York Times*, 13 October 2003: A1.

Buhlmann, Walter, *The Mission on Trial*. Addis Ababa: St Paul Publications, 1980.

Byrnes, Timothy A. *Reverse Mission: Transnational Religious Communities and the Making of US Foreign Policy*. Washington, DC: Georgetown University Press, 2011.

Casanova, Jose. *Public Religions in the Modern World*. Chicago: University of Chicago Press, 1994.

Castles, Stephen and Mark Miller. *The Age of Migration: International Population Movements in the Modern World* (3rd ed.). New York: The Guilford Press, 1993.

Catto, Rebecca. 'From the Rest to the West: Exploring Reversal in Christian Mission in Twenty-first Century Britain', Unpublished PhD Thesis, University of Exeter, 2008.

Celestial Church of Christ Constitution (Nigeria Diocese), revised edn. Lagos: The Board of Trustees for the Pastor-in-Council, 1980.

Chua, Edmond. 'Bishop-Missionaries Raised Largest Active Protestant Church', *The Christian Post*, Singapore Edition, 2010.

Clarke, Kamari M. Mapping Yoruba Networks: Power and Agency in the Making of Transnational Communities. Durham: Duke University Press, 2004.

Cohen, Robin. *Global Diasporas: An Introduction*. London: UCL Press, 1997.

—. (ed.). *Theories of Migration*. Cheltenham: Edward Elgar, 1996.

Cohen Robin and Zig Layton-Henry. *The Politics of Migration*. Cheltenham: Edward Elgar, 1997.

Coleman, James. 'Social Capital in the Creation of Human Capital', *American Journal of Sociology*, 94 (1988): S95–S120.

—. *Foundations of Social Theory*. Cambridge: Harvard University Press, 1990.
Collinson, Sarah. *Europe and International Migration*. London: Pinter, 1993.
Crumbley, Deidre. *Spirit, Structure, and Flesh: Gendered Experiences in African Instituted Churches among the Yoruba of Nigeria*. Madison: University of Wisconsin Press, 2008.
—. 'On both Sides of the Atlantic: Independent Church Movements in Africa and the African Diaspora', in A. Akinade (ed.) *Essays on World Christianity in Honor of Lamin Sanneh*. New York: Peter Lang, 2010, 177–208.
Daswani, Girish. 'Ghanaian Pentecostal Prophets: Travel and (Im)-Mobility', in Kristine Krause and Gertrud Huewelmeier (eds) *Travelling Spirits. Migrants, Markets, and Moralities*. New York and London: Routledge, 2010, 67–82.
Davidson, B. *Modern Africa: A Social and Political History*. London: Longman, 1989.
Dawson, L. Lorne and Jenna Hennebry. 'New Religions and the Internet: Recruiting in a New Public Space', *Journal of Contemporary Religion*, 14 (1) 1999: 17–39.
Debrunner, Hans V. *Presence and Prestige: Africans in Europe. A History of Africans in Europe before 1918*. Basel: Basler Afrika Bibliographien, 1997.
Dijk, Rijk Van. 'From Camp to Encompassment: Discourses of Transsubjectivity in the Ghanaian Pentecostal Diaspora', *Journal of Religion in Africa*, XVII (2) 1997: 135–59.
—. 'Time and Transcultural Technologies of the Self in the Ghanaian Pentecostal Diaspora', in Corten, A. and Marshall-Fratani, R. (eds) *Between Babel and Pentecost, Transnational Pentecostalism in Africa and Latin America*. Bloomington: Indiana University Press, 2001, 216–34.
Droogers, André. 'Globalization and the Pentecostal Success', in André Corten and Ruth Marshall-Fratani (eds) *Between Babel and Pentecost*. London: C. Hurst and Co., 2001, 41–61.
Dubey, Ajay. (ed.). *Indian Diaspora in Africa: A Comparative Perspective*, New Delhi: MD Publications PVT Ltd, 2010.
Ebaugh, Helen and Janet Chafetz. Religion and the New Immigrants: Continuities and Adaptations in Immigrant Congregations. Walnut Creek: Altamira, 2000.
—. (ed.). Religion across Borders: Transnational Immigrant Networks. Walnut Creek: Altamira, 2002.
Elam, Gillian and Martha Chinouya. 'Feasibility Study for Health Surveys among Black African Populations Living in the UK: Stage 2 – Diversity among Black African Communities', *Joint Health Surveys Unit, National Centre for Social Research and the Department of Epidemiology and Public Health*, London: Department of Health, University College London, 2000.
Ekué, Amélé Adamavi-Aho. '"…And how can I sing the Lord's song in a strange land?" A Reinterpretation of the Religious Experience of Women in the African Diaspora in Europe with Special Reference to Germany', in Ter Haar, Gerrie (ed.) *Strangers and Sojourners: Religious Communities in the Diaspora*. Leuven: Peeters, 1998, 221–34.
Ekwuazi, Hyginus. *Film in Nigeria*. Jos: Nigerian Film Corporation, 2nd edn, 1991.
Falola, Toyin. 'Lebanese Traders in Southern Nigeria, 1900–1960', *African Affairs*, 89 (357) 1990: 523–53.
Farwell, Scott. 'African Church Plans Christian Disneyland', *The Dallas Morning News*, 17 July 2005.

Field, J. *Social Capital*, Routledge, London, 2003.
Fikes, K. and A. Lemon. 'African Presence in Former Soviet Spaces', *Annual Review of Anthropology*, 31 (2002): 497–524.
Findlay, S. 'Compelled to Move: the Rise of Forced Migration in Sub-Saharan Africa', in M. Siddique (ed.), *International Migration into the 21st Century*. Cheltenham/ Northampton, MA: Edward Elgar, 2001, 275–8.
Fryer, Peter. Staying Power: The History of Black People in Britain. London: Pluto, 1984.
Fumanti, Mattia. 'Virtuous Citizenship, Ethnicity and Encapsulation among Akan Speaking Ghanaian Methodists in London', in special issue 'The Moral Economy of the African Diaspora: Encapsulation, Estrangement and Citizenship', *African Diaspora* (1–2) 2010: 12–41.
Garber, Marjorie B. and Rebecca L. Walkowitz. *One Nation under God: Religion and American Culture*. New York: Routledge, 1999.
Gatu, John G. *Joyfully Christian, Truly African*. Nairobi: Acton Publishers, 2006.
Gerloff, Roswith. A Plea for British Black Theologies: The Black Church Movement in Britain in Its Transatlantic Cultural and Theological Interaction with Special Reference to the Pentecostal Oneness (Apostolic) and Sabbatarian Movements. Frankfurt am Main: Peter Lang, 1992.
—. Review of Gerrie Ter Haar, Halfway to Paradise: African Christians in Europe. (1998) Journal of Religion in Africa, 30 (4) 2000a: 506–8.
—. 'The Significance of the African Christian Diaspora in Europe: A Report on Four Events in 1997/98', *International Review of Mission,* 89 (354) 2000b: 281–90.
—. 'Religion, Culture and Resistance', *Exchange,* 30 (3) 2001: 276–89.
—.'"Africa as Laboratory of the World": The African Christian Diaspora in Europe as Challenge to Mission and Ecumenical Relations', in R. Gerloff (ed.), *Mission Is Crossing Frontiers: Essays in Honour of Bongani A. Mazibuko*. Pietermaritzburg: Cluster Publications, 2003, 343–81.
Gilroy, Paul. *The Black Atlantic: Modernity and Double Consciousness*, Boston, MA: Harvard University Press, 1993.
Glick Schiller, N., L. G. Basch and C. Blanc-Szanton (eds). *Towards a Transnational Perspective on Migration*. New York: Academy of Sciences, 1992.
Goebel, Dorothea and Ludger Pries. 'Leben zwischen den Welten', *Der Überblick,* 38 (3) 2002: 37–41.
Gordon, April. 'The New Diaspora-African Immigration to the United States', *Journal of Third World Studies,* 15 (1) 1998: 79–103.
Gornik, Mark R. *Word Made Global Stories of African Christianity in New York City*. Grand Rapids, MI: Eerdmans, 2011.
Grady, Lee. 'Nigeria's Miracle: How a Sweeping Christian Revival is Transforming Africa's Most Populous Nation', *Charisma and Christian Life*, 27 (10) 2002: 38–41.
Grieco, E. M. and M. Boyd. *Women and Migration: Incorporating Gender into International Migration Theory*. Working Paper, Florida State University, 2003.
Griffith R. Marie and Barbara D. Savage (eds). *Women and Religion in the African Diaspora: Knowledge, Power and Performance*. Baltimore, MD: Johns Hopkins University Press, 2006.
Gunning, S., Hunter, T. and M. Mitchell. 'Introduction: Gender, Sexuality, and African Diasporas', *Gender and History,* 15 (3) 2003: 398.

Haddad, Smith and John Esposito (eds). Religion and Immigration: Christian, Jewish, and Muslim Experiences in the United States. Walnut Creek: Altamira, 2003.

Hagan, Jacqueline and Helen Ebaugh. 'Calling upon the Sacred: The Use of Religion in the Process of Migration', *International Migration Review*, 37 (4) 2003, 1145–62.

Haller, D. 'Transcending Locality – the Diaspora Network of Sephardic Jews in the Western Mediterranean', *Anthropological Journal on European Cultures*, 9 (1) 2001: 3–31.

Halman, L. and R. Luijkx. 'Social Capital in Contemporary Europe: Evidence from the European Social Survey', *Portuguese Journal of Social Science*, 5 (1) 2006: 65–90.

Hanciles, Jehu. *Beyond Christendom: Globalization, African Migration, and the Transformation of the West*. Maryknoll, NY: Orbis, 2008.

Handloff, Robert (ed.). *Ivory Coast: A Country Study*. Washington: GPO, 1988.

Hansen, Randall A. 'The Politics of Citizenship in 1940s Britain: The British Nationality Act', *Twentieth Century British History*, 10 (1) 1999: 67–95.

Harris, Hermione. *Yoruba in Diaspora: An African Church in London*. New York: Palgrave Macmillan, 2006.

Haynes, Jonathan. *Nigerian Video Films*. Athens: Ohio University Center for International Studies, 2000.

Healy, T. and Cote, S. *The Well-being of Nations. The Role of Human and Social Capital*. Paris: Organisation for Economic Cooperation and Development, 2001.

Howard, David. 'Incarnational Presence: Dependency and Interdependency in Overseas Partnerships', in D. Rickett and D. Welliver (eds) *Supporting Indigenous Ministries*. Wheaton, IL: Billy Graham Center, 1997, 24–35.

Hunt, Stephen. '"Neither Here nor There": The Construction of Identities and Boundary Maintenance of West African Pentecostals', *Sociology*, 36 (1) 2002: 147–69.

Hunt, Stephen and Nicola Lightly. 'The British Black Pentecostal "Revival": Identity and Belief in the "New" Nigerian Churches', *Ethnic and Racial Studies*, 24 (1) (2001): 104–24.

Hunter, B. H. Social Exclusion, Social Capital, and Indigenous Australians: Measuring the Social Costs of Unemployment. Occasional Paper No. 204, 2000.

Huysmans, Jef. 'The European Union and the Securitization of Migration', *Journal of Common Market Studies*, 38 (5) 2000: 751–77.

Ibrahim, B. and F. N. Ibrahim. 'Zuwanderer nach Deutschland: Das Beispiel der ägyptischen Kopten', in Koschyk, H., Stolz, R. (eds) *30 Jahre Zuwanderung. Eine kritische Bilanz*. Landsberg am Lech Olzog: Verlag, 1998, 129–61.

Idowu, Bolaji. *Towards an Indigenous Church*. Ibadan: Oxford University Press, 1965.

Imunde, Lawford and John Padwick. 'Advancing Legal Empowerment of the Poor: The Role and Perspective of the African Independent Churches'. OAIC Paper at the World Conference of Religions for Peace, Nairobi, Kenya. 2008.

Jach, Rejina. Migration, Religion und Raum: ghanaische Kirchen in Accra, Kumasi und Hamburg in Prozessen von Kontinuität und Kulturwandel. Münster: LIT Verlag, 2005.

Jeffries, R. 'The Political Economy of Personal Rule', in D. B. Cruise O'Brien et al. (eds) *Contemporary West African States*. Cambridge: Cambridge University Press, 1989.

SELECT BIBLIOGRAPHY

Jenkins, Philip. *The Next Christendom: The Coming of Global Christianity*. New York: Oxford University Press, 2002a.
—. 'A New Religious America', *First Things*, 125 (August/September 2002b): 25–8.
Jones, T. *Britain's Ethnic Minorities*. London: Policy Studies Institute, 1993.
Juergensmeyer, Mark. *Terror in the Mind of God: The Global Rise of Religious Violence*, Berkeley and Los Angeles, CA: University of California Press, 2003.
Kalu, Ogbu. 'Not Just New Relationship But a Renewed Body', *International Review of Missions*, 64 (1975): 143–7.
—. 'Church, Mission and Moratorium', in O. Kalu (ed.), *The History of Christianity in West Africa*. London and New York: Longman, 1980, 365–74.
—. 'The Andrew Syndrome: Models in Understanding Nigerian Diaspora', in J. Olupona and R. Gemignani (eds) *African Immigrant Religions in America*. New York and London: New York University Press, 2007, 61–85.
—. *African Pentecostalism. An Introduction*. Cambridge: Cambridge University Press, 2008.
—. (ed.). *African Christianity: An African Story*. Trenton, NJ: Africa World Press, 2007.
Katjavivi, Peter H. A History of Resistance in Namibia, London, James Currey and Paris: UNESCO, 1988.
Kendall, E. The End of an Era: Africa and the Missionary. London: SPCK, 1978.
Kerridge, Roy. The Storm is Passing Over: A Look at Black Churches in Britain. London: Thames and Hudson, 1995.
Killingray, David (ed.). *Africans in Britain*. Ilford: Frank Cass, 1994.
Killingray, David and Richard Rathbone (eds). *Africa and the Second World War*. London: Macmillan, 1986.
Kim, Rebecca Y. *God's New Whiz Kids? Korean American Evangelicals on Campus*. New York: New York University Press, 2006.
Koopmans, P. and P. Statham. 'How National Citizenship Shapes Transnationalism: A Comparative Analysis of Migrant Claims-making in Germany, Great Britain and the Netherlands'. *Transnational Communities Working Paper Series*, Oxford: ESRC/University of Oxford, 2001, 1–42.
Kritz, M. M., L. L. Lim and H. Zlotnik (ed.). *International Migration Systems: A Global Introduction*. Oxford: Clarendon, 1992.
Larm, Jackie. 'Satan, Sin and Spirit: Success at Mountain of Fire and Miracles Ministries (MFM) Edinburgh'. MSc. Essay, University of Edinburgh, 2008.
Leighton, Neil O. 'The Political Economy of a Stranger Population: the Lebanese of Sierra Leone', in William A. Shack and Elliott P. Skinner (eds) *Strangers in African Societies*. Berkeley: University of California Press, 1979: 85–103.
Levitt, Peggy. 'Local-level Global Religion: The Case of US-Dominican Migration', *Journal for the Scientific Study of Religion*, 3 (1998): 74–89.
—.*The Transnational Villagers*. Berkeley and Los Angeles: University of California Press, 2001.
Lieblich, Julia and Tom McCann. 'Africans Now Missionaries to U.S.', *Chicago Tribune*, Friday, 21 June 2002.
Lincoln, Eric C. and Lawrence H. Mamiya. *The Black Church in the African American Experience*. Durham: Duke University Press, 1990.
Ludwig, Frieder. 'Die Entdeckung der schwarzen Kirchen. Afrikanische und Afro-karibische Gemeinden in England während der Nachkriegszeit', *Archiv für Sozialgeschichte*, 32 (1992): 131–60.

—. 'Nigerian Christian Initiatives in Great Britain: The African Churches Mission in Liverpool and the Aladura Churches in London Compared'. Paper read at 'The Significance of the African Religious Diaspora in Europe' conference, University of Leeds, September 1997.

Ludwig F. and Kwabena Asamoah-Gyadu (eds). *The African Christian Presence in the West*. Trenton: African World Press, 2011.

Mabogunje, A. L. 'Systems Approach to a Theory of Rural-Urban Migration', *Geographical Analysis*, 2 (1970): 1–18.

MacGaffey, J. and R. Bazenguissa-Ganga. *Congo-Paris: Transnational Traders on the Margins of the Law*. Bloomington: Indiana University Press, 2000.

Makofane, Karabo. 'The Moratorium Debate in Christian Mission and the Evangelical Lutheran Church in Southern Africa'. Unpublished MTh thesis, UNISA, 2009.

Manuh, T. (ed.). *At Home in the World: International Migration and Development in Contemporary Ghana and West Africa*. Legon: Sub-Saharan Publishers, 2005.

Martin, Larry. The Life and Ministry of William J. Seymour and a History of the Azusa Street Revival. Joplin: Christian Life Books, 1999.

Marshall-Fratani, Ruth. 'Mediating the Global and Local in Nigerian Pentecostalism', *Journal of Religion in Africa* 28 (3) 1998: 278–315.

Masri, El and Iris Habib. *The Story of the Copts, The True Story of Christianity in Egypt*, vols I & II. Cairo: Coptic Bishopric for African Affairs, 1987.

Massey, D., Arango, J., Hugo, G., Kouaouci, A., Pellegrino, A. and Taylor, E. 'Theories of International Migration: A Review and Appraisal', *Population and Development Review*, 19 (September 1993): 431–66.

Matthews, Ojo. 'Reverse Mission', in Jonathan Bonk (ed.) *Encyclopaedia of Missions and Missionaries*. New York: Routledge, 2007, 380–82.

Maxwell, David. African Gifts of the Spirit. Pentecostalism and the Rise of a Zimbabwean Transnational Religious Movement. Athens: Ohio University Press. 2007.

McMunn, A and Brookes, M and Nazroo, J. *Feasibility Study for Health Surveys among Black African People Living in England: Stage One – The Demography and Geography of Black Africans Living in Britain*. Department of Health: London, 1999.

Meyer, Birgit. '"Praise the Lord": Popular Cinema and Pentecostalite Style in Ghana's New Public Space', *American Ethnologist* 31 (1) 2004: 92–110.

Moores, Shaun. Interpreting Audiences: The Ethnography of Media Consumption. London: Sage Publications, 1993.

Mossière, Géraldine. 'Mobility and Belonging among Transnational Congolese Pentecostal Congregations: Modernity and the Emergence of Socioeconomic Differences', in A. Adogame and J. Spickard, *Religion Crossing Boundaries. Transnational Religious and Social Dynamics in Africa and the New African Diaspora*. Leiden and Boston: Brill, 2010, 63–86.

Mottier, Damien. 'Pentecôtisme et migration: le prophétisme (manqué) de La Cité de Sion', *Archives de sciences sociales des religions*, 143 (2008):175–93.

Mugambi, N. K. 'Foreword' in John G. Gatu, *Joyfully Christian, Truly African*. Nairobi: Acton Publishers, 2006.

Nazir-Ali, Michael. From Everywhere to Everywhere: A World View of Christian Mission. London: Collins, 1991.

SELECT BIBLIOGRAPHY

Neill, Stephen. *Christian Partnership.* London: SCM Press, 1952.

Nelson, Harold (ed.). *Zimbabwe: A Country Study.* Washington, DC: US GPO, 1983.

Nwando, Achebe. 'The Road to Italy: Nigeria Sex Workers at Home and Abroad', *Journal of Women's History,* 15 (2004): 178–85.

Obadare, Ebenezer and Wale Adebanwi. 'The Visa God: Would be Migrants and the Instrumentalization of Religion', in A. Adogame and J. Spickard (eds) *Religion Crossing Boundaries, Transnational Religious and Social Dynamics in Africa and the New African Diaspora.* Leiden and Boston: Brill, 2010: 31–48.

Ojo, Matthews, 'Reverse Mission', In Jonathan Bonk (ed.), *Encyclopaedia of Missions and Missionaries.* New York, NY: Routledge, 2007: 380–2.

Okome, Mojubaolu. 'African Immigrant Churches and the New Christian Right', in J. Olupona and R. Gemignani (eds) *African Immigrant Religions in America.* New York and London: New York University Press, 2007: 279–305.

Okome, Onookome and Jonathan Haynes. *Cinema and Social Change in West Africa* (Jos: Nigerian Film Corp., 1995).

—. 'Evolving Popular Media: Nigerian Video Films', *Research in African Literatures* 29 (3) 1998: 106–28.

Olofinjana, Israel. Reverse in Ministry and Missions: Africans in the Dark Continent of Europe. Milton Keynes: Author House, 2010.

Olajubu, Oyeronke. *Women in the Yoruba Religious Sphere.* Albany: State University of New York Press, 2003.

Olupona, Jacob K. and Regina Gemignani (eds). *African Immigrant Religions in America.* New York and London: New York University Press, 2007.

Onyuku-Opukiri, Fidelia. 'The Council of African and Afro-Caribbean Churches UK', *Church and Race,* 6 (1) 1991: 2.

Oonk, Gijsbert (ed.). *Global Indian Diasporas: Exploring Trajectories of Migration and Theory.* International Institute for Asian Studies: Amsterdam University Press, 2007.

Oshun, Christopher. 'Encountering Aladura Spirituality in Britain'. Paper read at 'The Significance of African Religious Diaspora in Europe Conference', University of Leeds, 8–11 September 1997.

Ositelu, Rufus. 'Missio Africana! The Role of an African Instituted Church in the Mission Debate', *International Review of Mission,* 89 (354) 2000: 384–86.

Oyedepo, David. *Anointing for Breakthrough.* Lagos: Dominion Publishing House, 1992.

—. *Towards Mental Exploits.* Lagos: Dominion, 2000.

Pasura, Dominic. 'Religious Transnationalism: The Case of Zimbabwean Catholics in Britain', *Journal of Religion in Africa* 42 (1) 2012: 26–53.

—. 'Gendering the Diaspora: Zimbabwean Migrants in Britain', *African Diaspora: A Journal of Transnational Africa in a Global World* (1–2) 2008: 86–109.

Pinn, Anne H. and Anthony B. Pinn. *Fortress Introduction to Black Church History.* Minneapolis: Fortress Press, 2003.

Piore, M. J. *Birds of Passage: Migrant Labour and Industrial Societies.* Cambridge, Cambridge University Press, 1979.

Portes, Alejandro. 'Towards a New World – the Origins and Effects of Transnational Activities', *Ethnic and Racial Studies,* 22 (2) 1999: 463–77.

—. 'Social Capital: its Origins and Applications in Modern Sociology', *Annual Review of Sociology,* 24 (1998): 1–24.

Portes, A. and J. Böröcz. 'Contemporary Immigration: Theoretical Perspectives on Its Determinants and Modes of Incorporation', *International Migration Review*, 23 (3) 1989: 606–30.

Portes, Alejandro and G. Rubén. Rumbaut. *Immigrant America: A Portrait*. 3rd edn. Los Angeles, CA: University of California Press, 2006.

Portes, Alejandro, Luis E. Guarnizo and Patricia Landolt. 'The Study of Transnationalism: Pitfalls and Promises of an Emergent Research Field', *Ethnic and Racial Studies*, 22 (2) 1999: 217–37.

Putnam, Robert. *Making Democracy Work. Civic Traditions in Modern Italy*. Princeton, NJ: Princeton University Press, 1993.

—. *Bowling Alone: The Collapse and Revival of American Community*. New York: Simon and Schuster, 2000.

Quibria, M. G. 'The Puzzle of Social Capital. A Critical Review', *Asian Development Review*, 20 (2) 2003: 19–39.

Randall, Michael S. and Deborah J. Bell. 'Immigration, Emigration and Ageing of the Overseas-born Population in the United Kingdom'. Office for National Statistics. *Population Trends 116*, Summer 2004.

Ravenstein, E. G. 'The Laws of Migration', *Journal of the Statistical Society of London*, 48 (2) (June 1885): 167–235.

Redeemed Christian Church of God North America, Inc.: General Information and Church Planting Manual, Fall 2001 Edition.

Reese, Robert. Roots and Remedies of the Dependency Syndrome in World Missions. Pasadena, CA: William Carey, 2010.

Richardson, R. Social and Religious Capital. Literature Review. Independent Study, 2006.

Robbins, Joel. 'The Globalization of Pentecostal and Charismatic Christianity', *Annual Review of Anthropology* 33 (2004): 117–43.

Roberts, Andrew. *The Colonial Moment in Africa*. Cambridge: Cambridge University Press, 1990.

Robertson, Roland. 'The Sacred and the World System', in Philip Hammond (ed.) *The Sacred in a Secular Age: Toward Revision in the Scientific Study of Religion*. Berkeley: University of California Press, 1985.

—. 'Church-State Relations and the World-System', in Robertson, R. and Robbins, T. (eds) *Church-State Relations: Tensions and Transitions*. New Brunswick, NJ: Transaction Publishers, 1987.

—. Globalization, Social Theory and Global Culture. London: Sage Publications, 1992.

—. 'Religion and the Global Field', *Social Compass*, 41 (1) 1994: 121–35.

Rowell, John. To Give or Not to Give?: Rethinking Dependency, Restoring Generosity and Redefining Sustainability. Tyrone, GA: Authentic, 2006.

Sackey, Brigid M. New Directions in Gender and Religion: The Changing Status of Women in African Independent Churches. Lanham: Rowman & Littlefield, 2006.

Salzbrunn, Monika. 'The Occupation of Public Space through Religious and Political Events: How Senegalese Migrants Became a Part of Harlem, New York', *Journal of Religion in Africa*, 34 (4) 2004: 468–92.

Sanders, Cheryl J. Saints in Exile: The Holiness-Pentecostal Experience in African American Religion and Culture. New York: Oxford University Press, 1996.

SELECT BIBLIOGRAPHY

Sarró, Ramon and Ruy Llera Blanes. 'Prophetic Diasporas: Moving Religion across the Lusophone Atlantic', *African Diaspora,* 2 (2009): 52–72.

Sassen, S. *The Mobility of Labour and Capital.* Cambridge: Cambridge University Press, 1988.

Scherer, James. Missionary, Go Home! A Reappraisal of the Christian World Mission. Englewood Cliffs, NJ: Prentice-Hall, 1964.

Schwartz, Glenn. When Charity Destroys Dignity: Overcoming Unhealthy Dependency in the Christian Movement. Bloomington, IN: Author House, 2007.

—. *From Dependency to Fulfillment.* www.wheaton.edu/bgc/EMIS/1991/fromdepend.htm, 1991.

Sengupta, Somini and Rohter Larry. 'Where Faith Grows, Fired by Pentecostalism', *The New York Times,* Monday October 13, 2003: A5.

Sherwood, Marika. *Pastor Daniels Ekarte and the African Churches Mission.* London: The Savannah Press, 1994.

Shyllon, Folarin. 'Blacks in Britain: a Historical and Analytical Overview', in Joseph E. Harris (ed.) *Global Dimensions of the African Diaspora.* Washington, DC: Howard University Press, 1992, 172–7.

Simon, Benjamin. From Migrants to Missionaries, Christians of African Origin in Germany. Frankfurt am Main: Peter Lang, 2010.

Simon, R. and C. Brettell. 'Immigrant Women: An Introduction', in Simon and Brettell (eds), *International Migration: The Female Experience.* Totowa, NJ: Rowman and Allanheld, 1986: 3–20.

Smidt, Corwin. *Religion as Social Capital: Producing the Common Good.* Waco: Baylor University Press, 2003.

Smith, Peter and Eduardo Guarnizo (eds). *Transnationalism from Below.* New Brunswick, NJ: Transaction Publishers, 1998.

Sparks, Donald and Green December. *Namibia: The Nation After Independence.* Boulder, CO: Westview Press, 1992.

Stasiulis, Daiva and Abigail Bakan. 'Negotiating Citizenship: The Case of Foreign Domestic Workers in Canada', *Feminist Review* 57 (1997): 112–39.

Stepick, A., Rey, T., and Mahler, S. 'Religion, Immigration and Civic Engagement', in Stepick, Rey and Mahler (eds) *Churches and Charity in the Immigrant City: Religion, Immigration and Civic Engagement in Miami.* New Brunswick, NJ: Rutgers University Press, 2009.

Stoller, Paul. *Money Has No Smell. The Africanization of New York City.* Chicago and London: University of Chicago Press, 2002.

Storkey, M. 'The Demography and Geography of Africans in London', in K. Paine et al., *African Communities in London: Demography and the Epidemiology and Economics of HIV Infection.* London: King's College School of Medicine & Dentistry, 1997.

Sundkler, Bengt, Peter Beyerhaus and Carl F. Hallencreutz (eds), *The Church Crossing Frontiers: Essays on the Nature of Mission. In Honour of Bengt Sundkler.* Uppsala: Studia Missionalia Uppsaliensia, XI, 1969, 171–6.

Szreter, Simon. 'Social Capital, the Economy, and Education in Historical Perspective', in Tom Schuller (ed.), *Social Capital: Critical Perspectives.* Oxford: Oxford University Press, 2000, 56–77.

Taylor, J. V. 'Selfhood: Presence or Personae?' in B. Sundkler, P. Beyerhaus and C. Hallencreutz (eds) *The Church Crossing Frontiers: Essays on the Nature of Mission. In Honour of Bengt Sundkler.* Uppsala: Studia Missionalia Uppsaliensia, XI, 1969, 171–6.

Terborg-Penn Rosalyn and Andrea Rushing (eds). *Women in Africa and the African Diaspora – A Reader*. Washington: Howard University Press, 1996.
Ter Haar, Gerrie. *Halfway to Paradise: African Christians in Europe*. Cardiff: Cardiff Academic Press, 1998.
—. 'Imposing Identity: The Case of African Christians in the Netherlands', *DISKUS*, 5 (Web Edition) (1999).
Tettey, Wisdom. 'Transnationalism, Religion, and the African Diaspora in Canada. An Examination of Ghanaians and Ghanaian Churches', in J. Olupona and R. Gemignani (eds) *African Immigrant Religions in America*. New York and London: New York University Press, 2007, 229–58.
Thompson, Jack. 'African Independent Churches in Britain: An Introductory Survey', in Robert Towler (ed.) *New Religions and the New Europe*. Aarhus: Aarhus University Press, 1995, 224–31.
Twaddle, M. (ed.). The Expulsion of a Minority: Essays on the Ugandan Asians. London: Athlone Press, 1975.
Uka, Emele. M. Missionary Go Home? A Sociological Interpretation of an African Response to Christian Mission. Frankfurt am Main: Peter Lang, 2008.
Ugur, Etga. Lecture 'Gülen and Islam as Social Capital'. Lecture Theatre, Brunei Gallery, SOAS, London. October 2007.
U.S. Bureau of the Census, Population Division Working Paper #61, 'Evaluating Components of International Migration: The Residual Foreign Born, 1990 and 2000', 2001.
Uzoukwu, E. E. *Liturgy: Truly Christian, Truly African*. Eldoret: Gaba Publications, 1982.
van der Laan, H. Laurens. *The Lebanese Traders in Sierra Leone*. The Hague: Mouton Publishers, 1975.
Vásquez, Manuel A. and Marie F. Marquardt. *Globalizing the Sacred: Religion across the Americas*. New Brunswick, NJ: Rutgers University Press, 2003.
Velho, Otávio. "Misionization in the Postcolonial World. A View from Brazil and Elsewhere", in Csordas, Thomas J. (ed.). *Transnational Transcendence: Essays on Religion and Globalization*. University of California, 2009. 31–54
Vertovec, Steven and Robin Cohen (eds). *Migration and Transnationalism*. Aldershot: Edward Elgar, 1999.
Wagner, C. 'Colour the Moratorium Grey', *International Review of Mission*, LXIV (254) 1975a: 165–76.
—. 'Moratorium: Three views'. *World Encounter*, 12 (4), April 1975b: 10.
Währisch-Oblau, Claudia. The Missionary Self-Perception of Pentecostal/Charismatic Church Leaders from the Global South in Europe. Leiden: Brill, 2009.
—. 'From Reverse Mission to Common Mission ... We Hope: Immigrant Protestant Churches and the "Programme for Cooperation between German and Immigrant Congregations" of the United Evangelical Mission', *International Review of Mission*, 89 (354) 2000: 467–83.
Wallerstein, Immanuel. *The Modern World System, Capitalist Agriculture and the Origins of the European World Economy in the Sixteenth Century*. New York: Academic Press, 1974.
Walls, Andrew F. *The Missionary Movement in Christian History: Studies in the Transmission of Faith*. Maryknoll, NY: Orbis, 1996.
—. *The Cross-Cultural Process in Christian History. Studies in the Transmission and Appropriation of Faith*. Maryknoll, NY: Orbis, 2002.

Warner, R. Stephen and Judith W. Wittner (eds). *Gatherings in Diaspora: Religious Communities and the New Immigration.* Philadelphia: Temple University Press, 1998.

Weber, M. 'Wirtschaft und Gesellschaft'. Trans. A. M. Henderson and T. Parsons, *The Theory of Social and Economic Action.* New York: Free Press ([1925] 1966).

Westwood, S. and A. Phizacklea. *Transnationalism and the Politics of Belonging.* London: Routledge, 2000.

Woodson, Carter. *The History of the Negro Church* (2nd edn). Washington, DC: The Associated Publishers, 1921.

Woolcock, M. 'The Place of Social Capital in Understanding Social and Economic Outcomes', *ISUMA Canadian Journal of Policy Research,* 2 (1) 2001: 11–17.

Zeleza, Paul Tiyambe. 'Contemporary African Migrations in a Global Context', *African Issues,* XXX (1) 2002: 9–14.

Zolberg, A. R. 1989 'The Next Waves: Migration Theory for a Changing World', *International Migration Review* 23(3): 403–30.

Zlotnik, H. 'The Global Dimensions of Female Migration', Migration Information Source, 2003. www.migrationinformation.org/Feature/display.cfm?ID=109.

—. 'Empirical Identification of International Migration Systems,' in Mary Kritz, Lin Lean Lim and Hania Zlotnik (eds) *International Migration Systems: A Global Approach.* Oxford: Clarendon Press, 1992, 19–40.

'The Forms of Capital' in John G. Richardson (ed.), *Handbook of Theory and Research for the Sociology of Education.* New York: Greenwood, 1986, 241–58.

Index

action-orientedness 85
activities,
    extra-religious 57, 187, 226
    religious 66, 158, 162
adaptation 11, 13, 85, 93, 99, 117, 120, 125, 130, 136, 230, 232
Adeboye, Enoch 95–6, 151–2, 221, 227
Adelaja, Sunday 166, 185–8, 224, 227
Adepoju, Aderanti 11–12, 18, 31–2, 37, 40–1, 227
Adogame, Afe ii–iv, 27, 64, 70, 74–6, 81, 86–90, 92, 97, 136, 138, 149–50, 156, 158–9, 162, 170, 185, 187, 189, 197, 209, 213, 217, 225, 227, 229, 236–7
adoption 45–6, 64, 99, 131
affinities 40, 87–8
Africa ii, iv, viii–xi, 4–5, 9, 11–13, 17–18, 21, 23–4, 27–33, 35–8, 40, 42–6, 49–50, 60–2, 65, 67, 70, 72–5, 78–80, 82–3, 85, 93–4, 100, 114, 119, 121, 126, 129, 138–9, 145, 157–8, 162, 172–81, 184, 187, 192, 202, 208–10, 223, 227, 229, 230, 233, 235–7
    and Caribbean Christians 201
    migrant population of 4, 28
    northern 29
    out of 184
    triangular contexts of 102, 119
African American Church of God in Christ 60
African American Religion and Culture 238
African-American churches 167
African-American denominations 59
African-American evangelists and Pentecostal leaders 167
African-American experience 235
African Americans 5, 26, 29, 59–60, 64, 115, 204–5
African-born immigrants 52
African Caribbeans 204–5
African Charismatics 230
African Christian vii–xii, 79, 85–6, 98, 101–2, 104, 106, 108–12, 114, 116–23, 125–6, 137, 145–6, 149–54, 157, 159–60, 162, 167, 176, 181, 184, 193, 196, 199, 202, 203, 205, 210
    Communities 81, 83, 85, 87, 89, 91, 93, 95, 97, 99, 196–7, 225, 227–8
African Christian Council 200
African Christian Diaspora Consultations 197
African Christianities vii, ix–xi, 59, 69, 72, 76, 85–6, 101, 103, 105, 107–9, 111, 113, 115, 117, 119, 121, 141, 149–50, 158, 162, 174, 176, 205, 209, 228, 235
    new brands of xi, 73
African Christians 68–70, 75, 86, 112, 129, 131, 135–6, 172, 176, 178, 185, 194, 198, 206–8, 240
    in Europe 27, 69, 129, 194, 233, 240
    in Germany 130
    identity of 68, 194
African church leaders 137, 179, 193
African churches 71–2, 80, 130, 167, 177–8, 181, 187, 198, 200–2, 207, 228
African Churches Mission (ACM) 63–6, 193, 218, 236, 239

African Conference of Churches Third Assembly 180
African Council of Churches 177
African countries 4–5, 18, 28, 30, 37–8, 40–1, 44, 66, 166, 197, 214
African and European Christians 197
African and European churches 198
African and German congregations 200
African Church in London 234
African church worship services 112
African churches 71–2, 80, 130, 167, 177–8, 181, 187, 198, 200–2, 207, 228
  black 149
  in France 71
  new 149, 184, 204
African Churches' Council 202
African Churches and Foreign Mission Board 223
African Communities in London 239
African community in Germany 48
African Conference of Churches Third Assembly 180
African Council of Churches 177
African countries 4–5, 18, 28, 30, 37–8, 40–1, 44, 66, 166, 197, 214
  Anglophone West 17
African-derived churches 72
African-derived religions 59–60
African diaspora viii, 10, 18, 28, 29, 30, 59–60, 211, 229
  in Canada 240
  Christians 129
  in Europe 232
  in Germany 229
  religion 72
  religiosities 108
African Diaspora Studies 10
African Diasporas in Europe 35
African and European Christians 197
African and European churches 198
African-focused para-church organizations 196
African and German congregations 200
African immigrant Christian 99, 132
African immigrant Diaspora 230
African immigrant groups 61

African Immigrant Religions in America 234, 237, 240
African immigrant religiosity 13, 122, 138
African immigrant repertoire 24
African immigrants ii, iv, viii, x–xi, 10–13, 17, 27–9, 33, 42–4, 49, 52–5, 57, 59–61, 66–7, 69, 72, 77, 80, 82, 85, 90, 97, 101, 105, 116, 123–4, 128, 130–2, 135
  in Europe 57, 119, 211
  largest 42
  recent 216
  undocumented 15
African immigration 31, 38, 42–3
  recent 11
African Independent Churches 234, 238
African initiatives 68, 176, 194, 197
African Instituted Churches 62, 66, 237
African International Churches 150
African Islam 60
African-led AICs 75
African-led churches viii, x, xi, 54, 57, 62, 63, 67, 73–4, 80, 86, 109, 111–12, 114–15, 117–18, 127, 131, 135, 150, 154, 167, 184, 189, 191, 199
  in Europe 57, 61, 74, 109, 111, 113, 150
  in Germany 195, 220
  new 180, 204
African-led groups 208
African-led Pentecostal 61, 73, 75, 200
African Methodist Episcopal Zion Church 59
African migrants 12, 24, 26, 32, 55, 57, 77, 80, 229
  irregular 24
  regular 23
African migration vii, x, 1, 3, 5, 7–11, 13, 15, 17–19, 21, 23, 25, 27–31, 33, 35, 46, 228, 234
  to Europe 4, 30
African missionaries 167, 172, 180
African Missions 66, 182, 218, 225
African Muslims 61
African nation-states 38

INDEX

African New Religious
    Movements 228
African origin 197, 239
African pastors 61
African Pentecostal 69, 92–3, 97, 115, 159, 167, 179, 194, 202
African Pentecostal Church 228, 230
African Pentecostalism 235
African population 28, 51, 150
    black 51
African religions 60, 76, 85
African religiosities, new 78
African religious cultures 203
African religious diaspora in
    Europe 196, 236
African response 176, 240
African shores 28, 145
African societies 138, 235
African Story 176, 228, 235
African troops 29
African youth 211
African youths in Europe 198
Africanists 75
Africanness 11, 69
Africans viii, xi, 1, 4, 26–30, 32–3, 35, 38, 43, 45, 48, 51–2, 59–64, 66, 68–71, 90, 93, 124–6, 129–30, 136, 159, 175–6, 179, 181, 188, 197, 200, 202, 216, 223, 232, 237
    skilled 31
    white 33–4
Afrikaners 33–4
agency 53, 97, 101, 105, 122, 198, 211, 231
agents 7, 20, 95, 117
AICs 61, 66–73, 76, 80, 87, 92, 128, 149, 160, 194–5, 201, 209
Akyeampong, Emmanuel 29–30, 35, 38, 42, 229
Aladura 62, 67, 69, 72, 76, 87–9, 150, 156, 222, 228
Aladura Churches 67, 88, 201, 228
Aladura International Church 68, 194, 227
Alejandro, Portes 237–8
aliens, illegal 41, 45
allegiances 135–6
America 5, 27–8, 38, 59–61, 73, 75, 102, 165, 172, 183, 205–6, 230
American churches viii, 191

Americans 27, 45, 105, 204
Anglican Church 77
    in Nigeria 68, 194
Anglican Communion 77, 210
Angola 33–4, 71
anointing oil 115, 120, 167
anti-immigrant 132
applicants 20–2, 44, 52–3
army, African 29
Arthur, John 28, 42–5, 230
Asamoah-Gyadu, Kwabena 74–5, 185, 230
Asia 12, 30, 33, 38, 41, 43–5, 73, 166, 174, 181, 215
Association of German Pentecostal
    Churches 155
asylum 47–8, 52
asylum seekers 1, 12, 28, 45–6, 48, 51, 56, 80, 124, 137
Atlanta 76, 163, 165
audiences xii, 157, 159–60, 176
Australia 31, 72–3, 164, 166
authority 81–2, 95, 109, 138, 176
    local 65–6

Back-to-Africa Movement 26
Baptists 201–2
barrier 80, 107, 109
battles 94, 142
Belgium 31, 45–6, 55, 67, 70, 197, 202
belief,
    paradigms 85
    patterns 79
    structure 97
    systems 62, 85, 89, 112, 121, 155, 189
    tradition 89
beliefs 6, 85–8, 91, 100, 105–6, 112, 118, 120–1, 137, 229, 234
    religious 17, 107, 111, 130, 211
    shared 206
    spiritual 15
believer, new 185
believers 22, 112
believing 112
Berlin xii, 17, 164, 197–8, 202, 229
Beyer, Peter 148, 230
Bible 67, 82, 85, 87–8, 95, 97, 122
Biney, Moses 76–7
birth 20, 59–60, 65, 134, 196, 215
birthday 110, 219

INDEX

Bishop Climate Irungu (and Pastor) 220
black Africans 51–2
black churches 202, 208, 219–20, 233, 235, 237
Black-led churches 201
Black Majority Churches 226
black nationalists 178
Black Pentecostal Church 68, 194
black youths 56
BNA (British Nationality Act) 49–50, 133, 220
BNP (British National Party) 56
bona fide churches 110, 192
bonding 104, 107–9
Bonk, Jonathan 236–7
Bonn xii, 183, 220–1
Bonn parish 151
borders,
  continental 12
  international 161
  national 8, 18, 118, 196
Boston 183, 224, 226, 229, 233, 236–7
boundaries 5, 7, 126, 162
Bourdieu, Pierre 7, 103, 105, 231
Boyd, Monica 7, 9–12, 231, 233
branches 54, 62, 67, 73, 83–4, 120, 150, 155, 159, 162, 180, 183, 187, 189, 195, 222
  new 67, 79, 120, 183
Brazil 60, 165–6, 240
Brettell, Caroline 2, 10, 231, 239
Britain 4, 29–32, 48, 52, 64, 69–71, 77, 111, 127, 133–4, 136, 167, 172–3, 200–1, 218, 220, 225–6, 233–5, 237
  multicultural 134
British 33–4, 105, 134, 136, 177, 208, 234
  black Africans 51
  churches 201
  citizenship 49, 51
  Council of Churches 200–1
  migrants 34
  society 50, 64–5, 110, 133, 135, 201
  subjects 49
Brown Babies 64–5, 217–18
Brubaker, Rogers 132, 134, 231
Bruni, Frank 74–5, 231

C & S Church 67, 68, 71, 87–8, 194
CACCE (Council of African Christians Communities in Europe) 196–7, 200, 217
CACCG (Council of African Christian Churches in Germany) 195
Calabar 63
Cameroon 49, 83, 127
Canada 31, 70, 84, 130, 133, 165–6, 220, 239–40
capital 5, 28, 102–3, 105, 117–18, 130, 132, 231, 234, 239
  economic 102–3
  formation 57, 106, 108–9
  linking 104, 110–11
  symbolic 102–3
card, green 44
celebrities, religious 209
Castles 2–8, 10–11, 30, 32, 117
CBWCP (Centre for Black and White Christian Partnership) 201
CCC (Celestial Church of Christ) 67, 70–1, 80–2, 84, 87, 156, 209, 218, 227, 229
CCC Parish 70, 214, 219
CCOMI (Christian Church Outreach Mission International) xii, 80, 84, 130, 155–6, 166, 189, 195, 210, 221
CCCAAE (Council of Christian Communities of an African Approach in Europe) 193, 195–8, 225
census 34, 51, 215, 240
Central Africa 62
Chafetz, Janet 117, 120, 161
change xi, 13, 26, 42, 79, 85–7, 91, 93, 127–8, 132, 142, 146, 203
Changing Church 74, 231
channels, cable television network 157
charisma 152, 185, 209–11, 231, 233
charismatic 62, 75–6, 149, 210–11
  churches 61, 69, 73, 76, 80, 87, 149, 155, 159, 194–5
  gifts 209–10
  movements 73, 75, 149, 229
Charles, Prince 110–11, 219
Chicago 76, 223, 230–1, 239

INDEX

children 1, 10, 12–13, 51, 63–6, 90–1, 96–7, 114, 143, 187, 217–18
Christ Apostolic Church (CAC) 67
Christian 69, 75–6, 123, 125, 128–9, 160, 162, 172, 186, 193, 234
　African diasporic 13
Christian Channel Europe 157–8, 222
Christian Church Outreach Mission International 74, 84, 229
Christian diaspora, African religious ix
Christian home videos 121, 154, 157, 159–60
Christian leaders 198–9
Christian Mission 174, 177, 198, 231, 236, 240
Christian missionaries 172
Christian principles 68, 194, 206
Christianity ii, iv, x, 42, 59, 61, 67, 71–2, 74–6, 78, 93, 121, 129, 140, 145, 148–9, 170, 172–5, 181, 206, 210, 229–30, 235
　African new 120
Christians 68–9, 98, 115, 129–30, 136, 140, 158, 166, 169, 176, 194, 208
Church,
　affiliation 128, 139
　attendance 111, 169, 173, 181, 206, 226
　buildings 63, 82, 169
　founders 13, 138
　leaders xii, 114, 140, 206, 209, 220, 222, 226
　leadership 112, 121
　African 179
　members xii, 89, 111, 113–14, 117, 187, 218
　missions 65
　networks 117–18
　pastors 116–17
　polity 81, 143
　precincts 114, 140, 154
　programmes 111, 121, 140, 156, 158, 162, 191
　services 82, 112, 122, 185, 203
Church of England 68, 194
Church Missionary Society of Nigeria 68, 194
Church of Nigeria 77, 210
church personnel 183
Church Planting Manual 220, 238
church proliferation 169
Church of Scotland 177, 198–9, 225
Church-State relations 238
churches viii, x–xi, 17, 21, 42, 57, 62–3, 65, 67–9, 71, 73, 75–7, 80, 82–4, 86–7, 90, 96–7, 106, 110, 114–15, 117, 119, 129–30, 136, 139, 141, 143, 150, 153, 158, 162, 172, 176, 177, 182, 186, 191, 194–5, 198, 200, 203, 206, 208, 210, 217, 221, 225–6, 230, 235, 237, 239
　African indigenous 42
　based 110, 122
　charismatic renewal 173
　Christian 196
　daughter 187
　established 72
　ethnic-based 204
　foreign-led 62
　global 150
　historic 68, 194, 196
　host 77, 207–8
　independent 69
　international 150
　local 111, 151, 173, 193
　mainline xi, 179
　mainstream 68, 194, 201
　migrant 130
　mission-focused 208
　mission-related 61, 76
　national 80, 179
　new xi, 68, 194
　non-African 191
　non-Indigenous 225
　non-Western 181
cities 18, 55–6, 62, 65–7, 73, 96, 142, 155, 166, 173, 202
citizens 39, 49–51, 53, 132, 134–7
citizenship vii, x, 49, 51, 123–7, 129–35, 137, 139, 141, 143, 231, 233–4
　heavenly 137
　new 131–2
　politicization of 135–6
　politics of 51, 105, 131–3, 135, 138
　reconstructing 131
　status 131, 215
　tests 134

civic engagement 105, 108–9, 111, 114–15, 207, 209, 211, 239
civil society 102, 104, 108, 114, 116
CLA (Church of the Lord-Aladura) xii, 67, 71, 87, 156–7, 225
class 12, 54, 69, 109, 123, 125
clergy, African 62
Coleman, James 103, 231
collaboration 39, 111, 198–9
colonial 29, 35, 238
　rule 30, 33, 35, 37
colonies 49–50
　African 29
colour 92, 123, 130–1, 150
commitment, religious 139, 141
commodification 20, 121, 157–8, 160
Commonwealth 49, 50, 110, 136
Commonwealth immigrants, new 49–50
communication 104, 145, 152–4, 202, 225
communities, African 29, 52, 174, 196, 199
Communities, Christian 62, 192–3, 225
concept viii, x, 2–3, 8, 27, 97, 101–6, 108, 117–18, 123, 132, 144, 146–8, 170
conference of European churches 225
congregations, African 69, 76–7, 199
connections 22, 88, 104, 148, 161, 202, 206
construction 123, 136, 200
consulates 18, 21, 66
contemporary migration 4–5, 11, 30, 61
context,
　African 19, 229
　diasporic 13, 60, 72, 184, 205
　new 66, 72, 87, 100, 118, 129, 141, 154, 183, 208
continent, African 6, 18, 29, 33, 36, 125, 145
cosmologies,
　African 59, 188
　religious 86–7, 121
Council 65, 192–3, 195–7, 200–1, 217–18, 225
Council of African and Afro-Caribbean Churches 201, 237
Council of African and Allied Churches 201

countries, host 19, 25, 76, 120
critique 27, 98, 135–6, 167
cultural capital 7, 19, 101, 103, 105, 107, 113, 117, 192
cultural contexts 101–2, 145, 160
cultures, African 67, 207

Dallas xii, 84, 183, 219, 226
decolonization 32–3, 174–6
Deeper Christian Life Church 73, 185
Defense 95–6
demons 95–7, 188
Denmark 46, 163, 166, 202
denominations 68, 175, 200–1
departure 9, 13, 18, 48, 69, 85
Dependants 1, 10, 12, 50, 52, 54
dependence 139, 179–80, 224
Dependency 180, 234, 239
descendants 28, 33, 132, 204
Descent, African 10, 59, 196
destination 9, 13, 16, 23–5
　final 25–6, 85, 89
destiny 94, 98, 185
devil 88, 90–1, 93–6, 98, 142–3, 179, 188
diaspora churches 204
diaspora communities 205
　African viii, 28, 159
　white 34
Diaspora-Europe 70
Diaspora formations, African 61
diaspora, new 131, 138
diaspora, new African religious 59, 62, 134
Diaspora, non-African 35
Diasporic identities 33, 77, 162
　new religious 126
Dioceses 72, 82
Disciplines xii, 2, 93, 231
Discourses, public ix, 102, 132–4, 209
Diversity Immigrant Visa Program 44
documented migrants 15–16
dreams 26, 67, 86–7, 89, 93, 116, 143
Droogers, André 149, 152, 232
dynamic process 1, 3, 146
dynamics 6, 9–11, 16, 45, 57, 70, 108, 139, 205
　internal religious 85, 207

East Africa 29, 36, 83
Eastern Africa 62, 73, 82
Eastern African 34, 73
Eastern Europe 5, 53, 74, 184
Ebaugh, Rose Helen 117, 120, 161, 232
EC (European Community) 45–6, 226
Economic Community of West African States (ECOWAS) 18
economic development 40, 104, 197–8
economic problems 38–40, 189
economies, political 4, 7, 17, 37–8, 235
ECY (Evangelical Church of Yahweh) 67
Edinburgh xii, 74, 139, 141, 177, 220, 225–6, 235
EEA (European economic area) 30, 134
EEC (European Economic Community) 45, 51
Egypt 26, 61, 72, 76, 164
Ekarte, Daniels, 63–6, 193, 218
EKGCN 182, 184
eldorado 23, 36
embassies 18, 20–2
Embassy 74, 182, 185–9, 224, 228
Embassy church 186, 188
emergence 28, 69, 85–6, 147–8, 170, 177
Emigrants 31–3
  new African 205
emigration iv, 2, 16–17, 28, 33–4, 40–1
  African 3
  flow of 17, 213
  wave of 41
Employment 16–17, 19–20, 44, 50, 131, 185
empowerment 13, 26, 82, 99–100, 115, 138–9, 142–4, 196, 199, 208–9, 211
  rhetoric 13, 138–9
England 3, 51, 56, 64, 164, 194, 216–17, 225, 230
English 70, 133–4, 171, 189, 196, 238
EU 27, 42, 45, 52, 53, 132, 134–5
  countries 47, 50, 53, 202

immigration laws 47, 51
immigration policies 42
Europe,
  Christian 169
  continental ix, 47, 67, 69, 184, 197
  the dark continent of 169, 179
  a dead and secularized 169
  fortress 24, 27, 136
  heathen 192
  re-christianizing 169
  re-evangelize 1181
Europe and North America viii–xii, 9, 18, 30, 32, 38, 42, 59, 61–2, 67, 77, 82, 85, 102, 119, 126, 145, 159, 174, 192–3, 195, 205–9, 211
European,
  branches 222
  citizenship 131
  clergy 182
  context 192
  continent 201
  countries 4, 28, 47, 53, 55
  descent 34
  diasporas in Africa 33, 35
  minorities 34
  missionaries 75
  nations 157
  society 57
European and American churches xi, 112, 199, 202, 207, 225
European Union 5, 24, 45–6, 105, 132, 136, 167, 194, 234
Ethnic groups 17, 216
ethnic minorities 50, 52, 235
ethnicities 105, 107, 126, 131, 179, 233
  African 110
ethnography 16–17
evangelism 74, 111–12, 120, 154, 180, 192, 208, 224
Evangelists 220–2, 226
evil 19, 55, 87, 92, 95
exclusion 101, 107, 124–5, 132–3, 137, 192
exiles 16, 26–7, 124, 136, 238
exodus 32, 41, 97, 213
expansion 67, 69, 85, 148–9, 152, 169, 174, 182, 186, 206
experiences, post-migration 141

factors 5, 11, 13, 16, 19, 22, 25–6, 114, 127–8, 136, 193, 196, 207
faith xii, 42, 95, 104, 106, 114, 137, 152, 156, 173, 184–5, 198, 226, 230, 240
Faith Bible Church 74, 186
Faith communities 104, 108, 114
Faith, religious 106
faith-based groups 106
faith-based groups, African 108
Fazakerly Cottage Homes 218
fellowship, singles 138, 143–4
female migrants 12–13
female migration 9, 241
females 12, 55, 67, 84, 143
field, religious diaspora 76
FIFMI 73, 219
Finland 76, 165–6, 202
First Lady 141–2, 144
flags 150
flesh 95, 232
foreign nationals 47, 49
  statistical details of 215–16
foreigners 27, 30, 47–9, 53, 55, 124, 131, 136, 185, 192, 225
Forms, religious 60
founders 60, 94, 127, 159, 182, 210
Framework 101, 104–5, 109, 148–9, 160
France 4, 29–31, 45–6, 48, 53, 67, 70–1, 73, 105, 197, 202, 222
functions viii, 143, 202
  extra-religious 188, 202

Gatu, John 177–9, 223–4, 233
gender 9–11, 13, 41, 69, 72, 84, 109, 125, 138, 140, 144, 233, 238
gender roles 13, 140
General Overseer 70, 83–4, 119, 121, 151–2, 182, 210, 221–2
General Secretary of Presbyterian Church of East Africa 223
generation immigrant youth 208
geo-cultural contexts, new viii, 60, 86, 92, 187
Georgia 163, 165, 187
Gerloff, Roswith 69, 129, 196, 201, 225, 233
German churches 61, 195, 199–200
German congregations 180, 200

German context 71, 195
German language 90, 131
German society 130
Germans 34, 53, 70–1, 84, 105, 124, 126–7, 133, 152, 189, 195, 200
Germany ix, xii, 26, 29–31, 35, 45–9, 52–4, 61–2, 67, 70–4, 76–7, 80, 84, 90, 126, 128–30, 151, 166, 183, 187, 197, 200, 215–18, 222, 224, 228–9
Ghana xii, 5, 12, 18, 31, 35–6, 38–41, 44–5, 49, 51, 61–2, 69, 73, 77, 84, 126–7, 157, 209, 213, 230
Ghanaian immigrants 30
Ghanaian migration history 41
Ghanaian origin 30
Ghanaian Pentecostal Diaspora 232
Ghanaians 5, 17, 30, 40–1, 43–4, 49, 51, 71, 76, 84, 86, 126, 136, 230, 240
Global citizens 135–6
Global context 149, 228–9, 241
globalization iv, vii, x, 54, 145–53, 155, 157, 159, 161, 163, 165, 167, 229–30, 232, 234, 238, 240
  context of viii, 8
  framework of 149–50
  process 146, 148–9, 151
  processes of 145–7
globe 147–8, 162, 167, 172, 184
Glocal 146–7
glocalization 146–9
God 22, 26–7, 57, 60, 65, 80, 86, 88–95, 97–8, 112–13, 118, 122, 137, 141–2, 151–4, 156, 158, 164, 182, 184–5
God Digital 157–8, 222
God, immigrant 85
Gordon, April 30–1, 45, 230, 233
Gospel 95, 167, 172–3, 176, 186
governments 41, 53, 56, 65, 83, 96, 114, 116, 132, 137, 174, 186, 198
  African 35
  colonial 175
  national 8
  various European 131
graduates ix, xi, 32, 93, 210
Great Britain iv, xii, 46, 62, 76, 110, 216, 235–6
Griffith, Ruth Marie 10, 233

INDEX

Group membership 105, 107
groups xi, 4, 7, 60, 62, 67–8, 79–80, 88, 103–5, 124, 133, 139, 141, 146–7, 150–1, 153–5, 157, 162, 186, 195
   African 62, 77
   anti-immigrant 53
   non-African 162
   nonreligious 162
   religio-ethnic 136
   social 108, 187

Habitus 105, 207
Hamburg xii, 62, 74, 77, 80, 84, 197, 200, 202, 220, 234
Hanciles, Jehu 186–7, 234
Hansen, Randall 49–50, 133, 220, 234
Haynes, Jonathan 158, 234
headquarters 60, 62, 74, 79–80, 83, 195, 197
healing 94, 97, 143, 187
   rituals 94–5
health 56, 88, 102, 188, 232, 236
Heaven 27, 88–9, 113, 136–7, 155, 172
Hierarchical structure 83–4, 143
Hierarchies 9, 80–1, 84, 140
   lower 81–2
   sexual 140, 144
HIPC (Highly Indebted Poor Countries) 39
historiography viii–ix, 1, 59, 174
Historiography of new African Christianities vii, 59
History,
   Christian 240
   church's 172
   religious 15, 69
Holy Ghost 94, 98, 229
Holy Spirit 87, 89, 116, 171, 186, 200
home churches 67, 129, 167
home communities 119, 122
home contexts 100, 118, 120, 129–30, 192–3, 202
home countries 25, 31, 38, 73, 109, 114, 120, 128, 185, 192
Home Fellowships 83
home, new 2, 13, 24–5, 33, 38, 55, 99, 112, 161

Home Office date 51
Homeland 2, 16, 26, 54, 67, 125, 154, 160, 162, 167
homosexuality 96, 122, 188
host societies viii, 1–2, 7, 9, 13, 61, 117, 119, 124, 131–2, 137, 154, 161, 192–3, 208
human capital 3, 102, 211, 231
Hunter 107, 233–4
husbands 1, 11–13, 90, 114, 138–9, 142–3

Ibadan 229
identities vii, xi, 8, 11, 32, 33, 61, 69, 77, 85, 86, 92, 100, 104, 107, 109, 117, 118, 123–9, 132, 136, 137, 145, 149, 158, 161, 170, 191, 203, 207, 228, 234
identities,
   African 228
   ethnic 136, 203, 207
   multiple 123–5
   national 127, 136–7
   new 69, 86, 123, 145, 158
   religio-cultural 86, 109
   socio-religious 100
Identity formation 70, 123–4
ideologies, religious 86, 145, 158, 162
idioms 139
IEB (International Executive Board) 84
Ifa priests 60
IGOC (International Gathering of Champions) 115, 166, 204, 220, 222, 226
Illnesses 87
Immigrant Christianity 16
immigrant Christians viii, 99, 181
   new African viii
immigrant churches 16, 76, 162, 192, 195, 237
Immigrant churches, African 76, 162, 237
immigrant communities 26, 54, 61, 75, 122, 161, 191, 216
   African 61, 75
   new African 75
immigrant condition 16
immigrant congregations 120, 195, 232, 240

immigrant countries, traditional 47
Immigrant population, African 45
immigrant settlement 15
immigrant visas 43, 44, 215
Immigrant youth, African 211
immigrant's journey 24, 213
immigrants viii, x, xi, 1, 7, 8, 10,
    15–17, 22–3, 25, 27, 29–34, 40,
    42–9, 50–7, 61, 62, 66–7, 69,
    70, 72–3, 75–6, 80, 85–6, 90,
    98–9, 100, 105, 116–18, 122,
    124–8, 130–2, 134–7, 160–1,
    181–2, 184–5, 189, 191–2, 194,
    202–5, 207–8, 211, 216–17, 226,
    230, 232
  criminalization of 51, 55
  female 10
  illegal 90, 219, 230
  irregular 23
  legal 48, 90
  long-term 67
  non-African 181
  racialization of, the 32
  receiving 31
  skilled 53
  undocumented 118, 192
  white European 34
immigration 2, 3, 5, 7, 11, 15, 16, 18,
    20, 22–5, 27, 29, 31–3, 35, 38,
    40, 42–9, 50–3, 55, 71, 99, 114,
    116–17, 131–2, 134, 136–7, 162,
    167, 196, 202, 205, 211, 213,
    215–16, 231, 233–4, 238–9, 243
  controls 45, 52
  feminization of African 9, 11–13,
    138, 228
  laws 42, 46, 47, 51, 53, 99
  lawyers 20
  personnel 23
  policies 24, 25, 27, 31, 42, 45,
    47–8, 51, 99, 116, 136, 167, 205
  politicization of 46, 51
  processes vii
  status 114, 116
  stories 116, 216
Immigration Act 43, 44, 50
Immigration and Nationality Act
  (INA) 43
Immigration and Naturalization Service
  (INS) 43
Immigration Reform and Control Act
  (IRCA) 43
inclusion 101–2, 106–7, 124–5, 132,
  137, 140
Independence 13, 18, 30, 33–4, 37–9,
  41, 66, 136, 177, 239
independence, African 30
Indian Diaspora 35, 36, 214, 232,
  237
indigenes 53, 60
indigenization 175–6
indigenous 20, 28, 34, 42, 59, 60–1,
  67, 75–6, 86–7, 89, 91–3, 99,
  100, 121, 141, 145, 149, 174–6,
  179, 185, 188, 198, 225, 230,
  234
  personnel 175–6
  religions 76, 145
Indonesia 163, 165–6
infrastructure 18, 39, 40, 108, 120
initiative, religious ix, 8, 67, 145
institutions, religious 108, 116, 118,
  120
Integration 13, 25, 46, 48, 85–6, 99,
  117, 125, 131–4, 136, 160, 211
intention 6, 15, 18, 19, 26, 36, 67, 69,
  71, 79, 144, 154, 160, 207, 208
International Central Gospel
  Church 73
International Communion of
  Charismatic Churches 155, 195
international headquarters 73, 74, 80,
  82, 83, 84, 119, 121, 139, 141,
  152, 169, 182, 183, 184
international migrants 4, 12, 28, 30,
  32
International migration ix, 1–6, 8–9,
  11, 17–19, 25, 30, 32–3, 37,
  42, 45, 75, 131, 160, 205, 227,
  230–6, 238–9, 240–1
Internet 22, 23, 60, 121, 152–7, 160,
  162, 193, 221, 229, 232
internet prayer sources 22, 23
intra-religious networking 153, 167,
  193, 199
intra-religious networks 74, 153, 158,
  167, 191–2, 193, 197, 199, 200,
  202
Investments 25, 106, 161
Ireland 31, 46, 200, 201, 217, 225

INDEX

Islam 59, 60–1, 74–6, 123, 128–9, 145, 148, 240
Israel 72, 76, 83, 163, 165–6, 223, 237
itinerary 162–3

Jesus 22, 71, 88–9, 95, 98, 110, 136, 138–9, 141–3, 155–6, 170, 173, 188, 213, 221, 225, 228
journey 13, 15–16, 18, 20, 22–7, 36, 44, 85, 89, 136, 172, 185, 213

Kalu, Ogbu xii, 16, 26–7, 31, 77, 174, 176, 179, 180, 223, 228, 235
Kenya 34, 36, 49, 62, 74, 86, 126, 127, 136, 141, 157, 177, 179, 234
KICC (Kingsway International Christian Centre) 75, 115, 157, 158, 162, 166, 189, 210, 220, 222, 224, 226
Kiev 74, 184, 186, 187, 188, 231
Killingray 29, 235
Kimbanguist Church 71

Lagos xii, 17, 22, 70, 80, 82, 83, 93, 97, 119, 160, 165, 182, 183, 184, 210, 213, 224, 231, 237
language 51, 70, 90, 107, 109–17, 131, 133, 134, 159, 185, 189, 196, 200, 203, 207
Latin America 5, 12, 28, 43, 160, 174, 180, 181, 232
Lausanne Covenant 180
Laws 3, 7, 42, 43, 46, 47, 51, 53, 99, 186, 188, 210, 218, 238
Leaders xii, 13, 26, 33, 39, 66, 68, 72, 81, 83, 88, 109–17, 138–43, 158, 162–7, 177, 179, 180, 181, 182, 187, 189, 192, 193, 194, 198, 199, 201, 204, 209, 210, 211, 222, 226, 240
  charismatic 211
Leadership 13, 33, 39, 66, 68, 72, 81, 83, 88, 109, 112, 115, 131, 138, 139, 140, 141, 143, 164, 177, 179, 182, 192, 194, 198, 199, 209, 210, 211
leadership role 140
Lebanese 33, 35, 230, 232, 235, 240
Lebanese diaspora in West Africa 35

Leeds conference 196, 197, 225
Legislation 49, 50, 51, 132, 133, 220
Leiden 229, 230, 236, 237, 240
Lieblich 75, 223, 235
lifeworlds 61, 85, 86
Lighthouse Gospel Church 73
Lisbon 71
Liverpool 51, 63–6, 183, 217, 218, 236
Living Faith Tabernacle 92
locus x, 26, 55, 80, 121
London ix, 17, 49, 51, 56, 67, 70–4, 75, 77, 78, 110, 115, 141, 157, 164, 182, 183, 194, 217, 218, 219, 223–6, 229–41
Ludwig, Frieder 235

Mabogunje, Akin 6, 236
Mahler, Sarah 239
Malawi 34, 157, 173
malevolent 86
Marriage 19, 20, 22, 32, 48, 64, 87, 93, 110, 112, 122, 127, 138, 143, 144, 188
Maryknoll Sisters 171, 223
Maryknollers 170, 171, 189
material resources 4, 119, 167, 183
Media vii, ix, x, xi, 4, 7, 11, 18, 19, 20, 23, 26, 41, 56, 63, 72, 75, 84, 86, 88, 90, 92, 101, 114, 118, 139, 145–77, 186, 187, 193, 205, 207, 221, 224, 229, 236, 237
media, mass 152, 153
media technologies xi, 84, 141, 153, 154, 164
mediums 121, 154, 157
megachurch 186
meso-structures 7, 9, 101
MFM xii, 92, 97, 98, 114, 121, 226, 235
micro-structures 6, 7
migrant communities 26, 54, 61, 75, 76, 79, 122, 161, 191, 216
migrants, irregular 23, 25, 44
migration 33–75, 85, 99, 114, 116–18, 127–41, 160–7, 174, 181, 182, 185, 196, 198, 202, 205, 211
  chain 6, 19, 44, 47
  commercial 12, 37, 40

complex forms of 32, 61
histories 185
industry 7, 18, 20
international patterns of 5, 73
involuntary 17, 28
narratives 185
networks 6, 7, 117
patterns 11, 133
policies 6, 24–31, 42–51, 99, 116, 133, 134, 136, 167, 205, 230
processes 2, 10, 13, 15, 99
systems 6, 7, 235, 241
theory 2, 4, 6, 231, 233, 241
Militant prayer 97, 98
military strategy 97, 98, 219
Miller 2–8, 10–11, 30, 32, 117
ministers 68, 77, 82–4, 115, 172, 180, 183, 201, 221
African 180
ministries, African 172
missiological 71, 75, 169, 227, 228
mission x, xi, 19, 43–184, 209–39
churches 62
cross cultural 181, 207, 208
religious 170
resources 179
statements 150, 160
Missionaries 1, 68, 74, 77, 111, 167, 170–86, 194, 208, 223, 230, 231, 235, 236, 237, 239
Missionary Christianity 141
missionary enterprise 175, 179, 180, 208
missionary movement 174–8, 240
missioners 171
missionization 174
mobility 12, 13, 18, 23, 31, 32, 33, 45, 57, 73, 75, 76, 82, 90, 98, 99, 100, 105, 107, 127, 138, 143, 160, 162, 184, 185, 195, 205, 209, 232, 236, 239
modernity, African 158
moratorium 77, 78, 170–80, 230, 235, 236, 240
call 77, 178, 180
debate 177–9, 236
mosques 21, 217
motivations 5, 15, 37, 150, 192
motives 11, 18, 19, 192
movements, religious 19, 75, 149, 152, 153, 227–9

MST (migration systems theory) 6, 8, 12, 17, 19, 26, 28, 40, 52, 57, 64, 69, 85–7, 101, 111, 114, 128–30, 138, 145, 157, 161, 163, 173, 175, 207, 211, 226, 237
Munich 70, 71, 218
Muslim immigrants 61, 217
Myth 26, 130, 175
MZFMI (Mount Zion Faith Ministries International) 157, 159, 222

Nairobi 176, 180, 233–4, 236
Namibia 34–5, 235, 239
Narratives of African migration, vii, x, 15
nationalism, African 175
nationality 43–4, 49, 51, 124, 126–7, 131–7, 215, 220, 234
nationals, African 30, 49, 216
Neoclassical 3–4, 6
Netherlands 31, 45–6, 55, 67, 69–70, 166, 187, 202, 225–6, 235, 240
networking process 68, 199, 205–9, 211
Networks viii, xi, 6–8, 18, 23, 35, 74, 77, 84, 101, 103–9, 112, 116–19, 122, 147, 150, 152, 157–8, 160–2, 191–8, 200, 202–4, 231, 232
extra-religious 191
inter-church 202
Nigeria ix, xii, 5, 12, 16–18, 21–2, 31, 35–45, 49, 51, 54, 61–3, 67–8, 70–7, 82–3, 86, 90, 97, 115, 120–1, 126–7, 129, 136, 149, 151–2, 157–9, 162, 164–6, 169, 171–2, 182–5, 187, 194–5, 209–10, 213, 218–19, 221–2, 231–7
Nigerian churches 72, 234
Nigerian diasporas 127
Nigerian government 41, 213
Nigerian students 67, 70
Nodes 2, 9, 118
non-African membership 74, 150, 182, 185
non-citizen 53, 133, 135–6
non-governmental organization (NGOs) 7, 20, 106, 202
norms, religious 120
North Africans 29, 51

INDEX

North America viii, ix, x–xii, 9, 11, 18, 26, 28, 30, 32, 38, 40–2, 45, 54, 59, 61–2, 67, 72–4, 77, 82–5, 102, 117, 119, 126, 145, 149, 159, 162–4, 166, 169, 171, 174, 181, 183, 192–3, 195, 198, 204–9, 211, 215, 219, 220, 228, 231, 238

OECD countries 31
offerings 113–14, 119, 184
Ojo, Matthews 181, 236–7
Okome, Mojubaolu 72, 237
Okome, Onookome 158, 237
Olupona, Jacob xii, 75–6, 228, 235, 237, 240
Online 22, 121, 153, 155, 156, 159, 213–14, 216, 219, 220–3, 226, 229
Organizations, religious 108, 153, 162, 201, 210–11
orientations 2, 62, 87, 93, 126
origin, countries of xi, 9, 19, 25, 161, 195
origin, home of 1, 13, 17–18, 25, 85, 99
Orisa 60, 89, 228
Oxford ix, 235, 238–9, 241
Oyedepo, David 94, 115, 167, 210, 237
Oyitso, Brown xii, 182–4, 224

para-churches 74
paraphernalia, religious 120–2
Paris 55, 71, 235–6
parishes 62, 70–1, 82–4, 119–21, 126–8, 139, 152, 155–6, 174, 180, 182–4, 218–19
participant observation 77, 93, 139
Partnership 21, 180, 196–8, 201, 207, 226–7, 234, 237
Pastor Enoch Adeboye 95–6, 115, 121, 151–2, 167, 172, 182, 210, 221, 227
Pastor Festus Olatunde xii, 198–9, 220, 225–6
Pastor-Founder 70, 81
PCEA (Presbyterian Church of East Africa) 177
Pentecostal 16, 42, 59–62, 68–9, 71, 73–6, 80, 87, 92–3, 96–7, 115, 123, 128–9, 148–9, 155–60, 167, 172, 179, 188, 194–5, 200, 202, 210, 219, 228–30, 232–6, 238–40
Pentecostal Movement 59–60, 93, 149
Pentecostalism 74, 93, 96, 148–9, 229–30, 232, 235–6, 239
phases 16–17, 28, 61, 86, 193
Phenomenology vii, x, 79
Police 16, 20, 23, 55–6, 63–4, 90, 116, 131
political independence 33, 38, 66
population, foreign born 43, 215
Population, total 30, 34, 47–9
Portes 6, 8, 101, 106–7, 161, 207, 237–8
Portugal 31, 46, 47, 53, 71, 73
Portuguese ix, 33–4, 234
Poverty 11, 52, 55, 87, 93, 96, 114, 188, 209, 216, 226
poverty alleviation 114, 209, 226
power vii, x, 5, 8, 11, 13, 20, 26–7, 31, 33, 38, 42, 72, 82, 86–7, 89–90, 95–7, 99, 100–2, 104–5, 108–10, 114–15, 123, 131–2, 137–44, 147, 156–7, 159, 161, 171, 174–6, 180, 186–8, 196, 199, 208–11, 214, 227, 231, 233–4
  paradigms of 208–9
prayer rituals, intensive 143
prayers 16, 22, 67, 82, 97, 151–2, 156, 200, 213
Prayers Online 22, 213
priests, African 77
privileges 135, 176
processes,
  bureaucratization 210
  decision-making 21
  negotiation 84
prodigal continent 169, 179
products 38, 68, 115, 147–8, 155, 159–60, 167, 194, 220–2
professionals 24, 31–2, 41, 210
proliferation vii, ix, 27, 38, 53, 55, 60, 74–5, 101, 145, 169, 182, 227
prophecies 116, 151–2, 221
  annual 151, 221
prophets 20, 97, 116, 209, 225, 232
prosperity gospel 96

publics, non-African 207
pulpit 140, 150, 192, 199
Putnam, Robert 103–4, 108, 238

racism, institutional 56, 90, 193
ranks 48, 55, 81, 204, 229
RCCG North America (RCCGNA) xii, 83–4, 119, 183, 219–20, 224, 226
RCCG parishes 83, 121, 126, 128, 139, 152, 155, 182–4
receiving countries 7, 9
reception, context of 206–7
recession, economic 46
reciprocity 104–5, 108–9, 113–17, 122
recruitment strategy 153–4, 162
Redeemed Christian Church of God (RCCG) xii, 73, 75–6, 80, 83–4, 92, 95–6, 110–11, 119–22, 126–9, 136, 138–40, 149, 151–2, 154–5, 157–8, 166, 169, 171–2, 182–4, 195, 210, 219–21, 223–4, 226, 228
religion vii, xii, 10–1, 15–17, 19, 26, 28, 42, 59–61, 63, 72, 75–6, 85–6, 88, 96, 99, 101–2, 106–8, 111–13, 116, 123, 129–31, 138, 141–2, 145–6, 148–9, 152, 162, 170, 172, 192, 196, 201, 204, 206, 211, 227–40
  scholars of 75, 170
religiosity,
  African 138, 184, 228
  church-oriented 74
religious,
  action 129, 170
  backgrounds 126, 129
  capital 101–2, 106–8, 112, 161, 238
  cultures 59, 203, 208
  cultures, localization of African 203
  entrepreneurs 110, 210
  ethnography viii, 70, 135, 138, 169
  expansion 27, 170, 172, 179, 184, 211, 229
  experience 10, 72, 138, 141, 232
  ferment viii, 62, 174
  functionaries 13, 138
  geographies 59, 63, 125
  icons 209–10
  identities 100, 118, 125–6, 128
  internationalism 158, 162
  landscapes viii, 59, 62, 158, 191
  leadership 209, 211
  networking 68, 115, 153, 167, 191–3, 196, 199, 228
  networks xi, 74, 77, 118–19, 122, 158, 191–2, 194–5, 197, 200, 202
  relations, social 8, 103, 105, 108
  repertoires 13, 62
  rituals 16, 57
  specialists 20–1
  traditions, African 60
  transnationalization 160, 162
  TV-networks, global 157
  videos 159, 160
  worldviews 79, 85–6, 99, 139, 200
remittances 54, 99, 114, 117–19, 122, 184
resources xii, 4, 7, 15–17, 21–3, 38, 72, 101, 103–4, 108, 114, 116, 118–19, 121–2, 155, 167, 171, 174–6, 179, 180, 183, 189, 224–5
  religious 16, 72
return migration 13, 22, 24–7, 85, 214
reverse mission vii, x, xi, 19, 78, 167, 169–74, 180–4, 189, 192, 195, 206, 208–9, 211, 223, 231, 236–7, 240
reverse mission dynamics xi, 167, 173, 208
rhetoric 10, 13, 24, 26, 55, 92, 95, 97, 120, 124, 130, 135, 137–9, 142–4, 150, 169, 183–4, 206, 228
  anti-immigrant 55
ritual enactments 86–7
ritual functions 82, 141
rituals 16, 21, 23, 57, 82, 86, 87–90, 93–5, 97–8, 100, 122, 143
Robbins, Joel 149, 238
Robertson, Roland 146–9, 238
role, extra-religious 64
role models 209–10
role, women's 140
Roman Catholic Church xi, 148
rural-urban migration 6, 236
Russia 74, 165–6, 185–7, 189

INDEX

salvation 87–8, 94, 143
Santeria 60
Sassen, Saskia 4–5, 55, 216, 239
Satan 88, 90–1, 94–5, 98, 188, 228, 235
scholars, African 31
SCOAC (Scottish Council of African Churches) 193, 198–9, 225
Scotland 139, 142, 163, 172–3, 177, 198, 199, 216, 220–1, 223, 225
self-reliance 179–80, 224
sending 1–2, 6–7, 9, 29, 31, 77, 117–18, 120, 167, 172, 174, 180–1
sermons 26, 71, 82, 96, 117–18, 121, 141, 152, 171, 189, 193
settlers 33–4, 67, 79
Sherwood, Marika 63–4, 218, 225, 239
sickness 87, 93–4, 96, 188
Sierra Leone 5, 35, 51, 235, 240
Simon, Benjamin 71, 239
social capital x, 7, 102–5, 107–9, 111–12, 114–19, 121–2, 211, 219, 230–1, 233–4, 237–9, 240–1
  bridging 104, 108
  downside of 107–8
  formation 112, 117
  religious 111
social inclusion 101–2, 107
social justice 116, 196, 202
social networks 7–8, 35, 103–7, 116–17, 147, 160, 191
social reproduction 105, 231
social sciences 2, 3, 104
socialization 57, 80, 108–9, 118, 121, 125
sojourn viii, 13, 15, 18, 26–7, 33, 90, 136, 161, 185, 230, 232
Somalians 30, 51
songs 115, 167, 188, 203
South Africa 5, 33–6, 83, 127, 163, 166, 172, 183, 214, 222
Southern Africa 42, 73, 157, 236
Soviet Bloc 184–5, 228
Spain 24, 31, 46–7, 53, 55, 67
Spickard, James 75, 170, 229, 236–7
spiritual attack 87, 91–2
spiritual capital vii, xi, 101–2, 106, 108–9, 111, 118, 207
spiritual terrorism 92–3

spiritual warfare 86, 93, 95–7, 188, 228
Stasiulis, Daiva 133, 135, 239
Stepick, Alex 108, 114, 207, 211, 239
structures,
  normative 119–22
  organizational x, 79, 80, 84
sub-Saharan Africa 24, 29–31, 33, 159, 233
success 16, 21–3, 35, 39, 50, 56, 66, 74, 81, 90–1, 93, 115, 120, 131, 148, 151, 159, 181, 199, 206–8, 210, 213, 232, 235
Sudan 5, 45, 61, 72, 76
Sundkler 176, 239
support, spiritual 117
survival 11, 16, 32, 42, 53, 66, 98–9, 130, 134, 175, 186, 192, 196, 198
Switzerland 70, 180, 197, 202
syndrome, Andrew 16, 213, 235
systems vii, ix, 3–7, 13, 35, 47, 50, 52, 55, 62, 84–5, 89, 90–1, 98, 105–7, 109, 112, 116, 121, 134, 137, 148–9, 152–3, 155, 179, 183, 189, 205, 227, 230, 235–6, 238, 240–1

Tanzania 34, 36, 49, 77, 127, 180
technology,
  new 152
  religious video 158–60
Ter Haar, Gerrie xii, 69–70, 129, 150, 195, 232–3, 240
terror 56, 92–7, 235
theologies 79, 85–6, 98, 233
theories, migration systems (MST) 6, 8, 12
theory, world systems 5
Third World 5, 77, 135, 178–81, 233
Third World Missions Association 181
tithes 113–14, 119, 184
tithing 113–14
Togo 40, 49, 62, 71, 82, 213
Tokoism 71
transients 23, 26, 44
transmigrants 8, 161
Transnational, trasnationalism vii, viii, x, xi, 6–12, 15–16, 18, 22–3, 28, 44, 55, 75–7, 79, 84, 102,

INDEX

117–19, 122, 138–9, 145, 148, 150, 152, 155–8, 160–2, 166–7, 170–1, 229–41
transnational communities 7, 231, 235
transnational theory 6–7
transnationalism, religious xi, 9, 77, 158, 162, 237
trust 19, 27, 56, 65, 78, 82, 103–5, 108–9, 111, 114–17, 152, 179, 204, 206, 222, 231
trustworthiness 103–4, 108, 115–16
Turkey 46–8

Uganda 30, 36, 51, 176, 240
Ukraine 163, 165–6, 185–7, 230
Ukrainians 186, 188
undocumented migrants 15–17, 48, 185, 216
unemployment 41, 52–3, 55, 57, 64, 87, 90, 93, 112, 116, 216, 234
United Evangelical Mission (UEM) 195, 240
United Kingdom ix, xii, 12, 17, 21, 23, 30, 47, 49, 50–3, 56, 67, 70, 73, 76, 97, 102, 110, 114, 132, 134–6, 157–8, 162, 166–7, 173, 177, 197, 201, 203–5, 216, 220, 222, 238
United States ix, x, xi, xii, 5, 12, 17, 24, 26–7, 29–31, 35, 42–5, 47, 54, 57, 60–2, 67, 70–9, 83, 101–2, 104, 107–12, 114, 118–20, 122, 125, 130, 154, 167, 170–1, 177, 182–4, 187, 193–4, 198–9, 202–5, 207, 215–18, 220, 230, 233–4

values 77, 101, 103–5, 107–8, 112, 116, 120–1
vendors 21, 54, 110
vigils 94–5, 111
visas 16, 20–1, 43–4, 49, 52, 87, 89, 99, 100, 215
  non-immigrant 43–4
volunteering 111, 115
volunteerism 111–12

Wales 3, 110, 216, 219

Warfare,
  motif 95
  rhetoric 97
wars 12, 29, 37–8, 64, 174
Washington 65, 76, 163, 214–15, 231, 234, 237, 239–41
waves 2, 28, 40, 42, 50, 162, 241
WCCC (World Conquerors Christian Centre) 138–9, 141–2, 220–1
Weber 209, 211, 241
Website 60, 84, 120, 153–6, 159–60, 162, 189, 213, 217–22, 224–6
  computer 153–4
Weisskoeppel, Cordula 75, 228
welfare 1, 4, 46, 55, 66, 86, 90, 107, 114, 116, 134, 202, 216
West Africa 5, 11, 17–18, 29, 33, 35, 37, 40, 49, 51, 54, 60, 63, 72–3, 82, 149, 227, 230, 234–7
West Yorkshire African Caribbean Council of Churches 200
Western Africa 62, 72
Western churches 180–1, 192, 207
Western Europe 30, 32, 45–6, 55
Winners Chapel 73, 92–4, 210
Winning Ways Programme 157, 222
Witches 19, 20, 89, 92, 100, 188, 192
Woman 11, 12, 65, 140, 142–3, 200
Women 1, 10–13, 30, 53, 56, 63–6, 71–2, 82, 109, 114–15, 138–44, 170–1, 210–11, 220, 231–3, 237–40
  African 11, 72
Word of Faith Bible Church 74, 188
World Christianity ix, xii, 170, 173, 180–1, 205, 228, 232
World Council of Churches 177, 200
world, developing 74–5
world evangelization 180–1
World Wars 37, 174
worldviews x, 61, 80, 85–6, 99, 102, 113, 118, 120–2, 139, 200
worship 67–8, 72, 75, 80, 89–90, 104, 106, 108–12, 118–19, 122, 139–40, 155, 164, 172, 186, 193–4, 199–201, 203, 214
  spaces of 109–10, 203

Yoruba 17, 60, 88, 92, 110, 126–7, 136, 203, 205, 228, 231–2, 234, 237
youths 17, 32, 53, 56, 72, 109, 111, 114–15, 198, 208, 210–11
 black African 56

Zambia 34, 180, 214
ZAOGA 73
Zeleza, Paul 4, 28, 30, 32, 45, 241
Zimbabwe 5, 32–4, 62, 73, 77, 127, 136, 157, 214, 230, 236–7
Zolberg, Aristides 3–4, 8, 241